CLAIMS

ADVENTURES IN THE GOLD TRADE

CLAIMS

ADVENTURES IN THE GOLD TRADE

KEN LEFOLII

KEY PORTER·BOOKS

Canadian Cataloguing in Publication Data

Lefolii, Ken
   Claims: adventures in the gold trade

Includes index.
ISBN 1-55013-000-5

1. Gold.   2. Gold mines and mining — Ontario — Hemlo.
3. Speculation.   4. Lefolii, Ken.   5. Lac Minerals
Limited — Trials, litigation, etc.   6. International
Corona Resources — Trials, litigation, etc.
I. Title.

HD9536.A2L43   1987   338.2′741   C87-094237-9

Key Porter Books Limited
70 The Esplanade
Toronto, Ontario
Canada   M5E 1R2

Typesetting: Compeer Typographical Services Ltd.
Printing: John Deyell Company

Printed and bound in Canada

87 88 89 90 6 5 4 3 2 1

C O N T E N T S

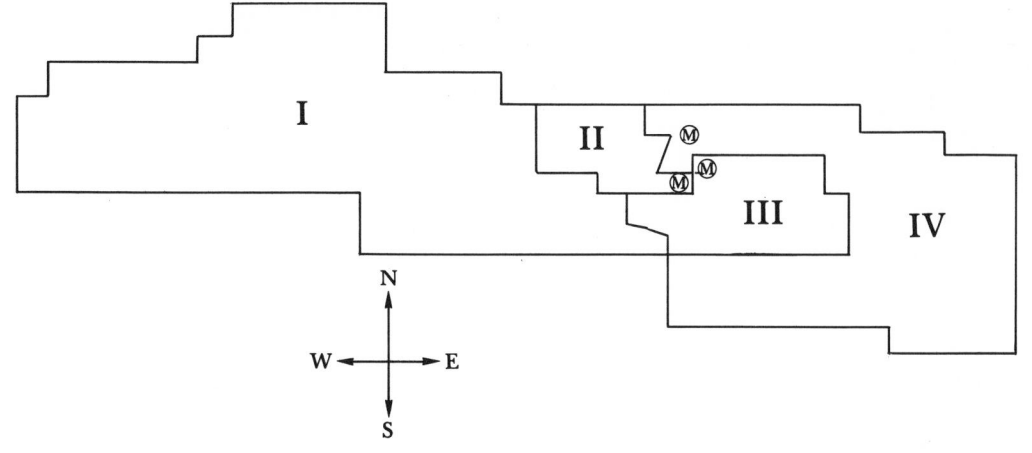

Hemlo Gold Deposits

BLOCK I *Walter Baker saw gold in the sands*
McKinnon staked
Hughes-Lang acquired, sold to
Noranda, which sold to
Hemlo Gold Mines, Inc., in 1987

BLOCK II *Dr. J.K. Williams staked*
Lac acquired from Williams Estate, found gold mine
Ontario Supreme Court awarded to Corona in 1986

BLOCK III *Trevor Page staked and drilled, 1930s–40s*
Lake Superior mines drilled
McKinnon-Larche staked
Corona acquired, found gold mine
Corona owned in 1987

BLOCK IV *McKinnon-Larche staked*
Hughes-Lang acquired, found gold mine, sold to
Noranda, which sold to
Hemlo Gold Mines, Inc., in 1987

Ⓜ *Gold Mines*

THE OLD WORD MAGIC

Certainly goldmaking, as also chemical research in general, was of great concern to alchemy. But a still greater, more impassioned concern appears to have been — one cannot very well say the investigation — but rather the experience of the unconscious. . . .

They [the alchemical symbols] represent collective contents that stand in painful contrast to our highest convictions and values. They give the strange answers of the natural psyche to the ultimate questions which reason has left untouched.

—C.G. Jung, *Alchemical Studies*

THE GREAT ANNUAL GOLD FAIR at New Orleans opens with a cocktail party in a vast hotel ballroom where two thousand people gather each autumn to reconfirm the tie that binds them, which is a shared belief in gold. Edging through this throng one November, I pressed the flesh of many fairly rich people, among them some of the celebrities of the international gold circuit. One of these, Ian McAvity, the publisher of a gold newsletter called *Deliberations*, asked whether I was buying gold. I said no.

"That's a relief," McAvity said, parting his moustache from his wisp of beard with a small smile. "I meet people here — you know, they're almost praying for an international crisis so their gold holdings will go up."

On the morning after the cocktail party, McAvity was a member of a panel chaired by Louis Rukeyser, the host of "Wall Street Week", a Public Broadcasting Service television program that is mainly about money.

"We have a news bulletin," Rukeyser said, flashing a white grin in a pocked face, a combination that has made him unmistakable on camera, particularly in close-up. "Chrysler has announced a merger with DeLorean." An appreciative murmur went through the convention hall; everybody there knew that John DeLorean, a bankrupt car maker, had been convicted of drug trading and was on his way to jail.

"Chrysler will make the cars," Rukeyser said. "DeLorean will make the licence plates."

Laughter rocked the hall; for this crowd, this was evidently the right joke. When McAvity's turn to speak came he foretold a rise in the price of gold to three thousand dollars an ounce before 1986. Like the other experts who that morning had predicted exhilarating advances in the price of gold, he had to pause after the word "thousand" to let the applause die down. Unlike any other expert who spoke that week, though, McAvity went on to say that if he was right about the price of gold reaching the thousands, it would be because inflation had gutted the international money supply, the global economy was in crisis, and governments would soon be imposing emergency controls. When he sat down a few people rustled their papers together and left, but that was the only sound in the hall.

There was a hostile edge to the silence that was hard to account for until I remembered McAvity's remark the night before about the people he met who were hoping for a crisis to drive up the price of their gold. They had not come all the way to New Orleans, these people, to have McAvity or anybody else tell them that if they were to get richer by owning gold, a lot of other people would have to be beggared first. They just wanted the crisis to get started so their gold would go up and they could feel good about being right while nearly everybody else was wrong. They had laughed too loud at Rukeyser's meagre joke for much the same reason. DeLorean had been rich and was about to be poor, whereas most of the people who had come to the Gold Fair were confident they were headed the other way.

My reasons for going to the fair were less straightforward. Gold had touched my life from time to time since my early childhood, but lately the pace of these intrusions had picked up. A couple of years earlier my friend Bob Crompton and I had started a small company, the Del Norte Chrome Corporation, to try to revive some old chromium mines in northern California. When that attempt stalled — we had a lot of chrome, but it cost more to get it to market than the market would pay for it — we looked around for something else Del Norte might do. Bob is a stockbroker, and his work brings him into touch with a lot of prospectors and geologists. Through these connections he now came up with several blocks of gold claims. One of them was a tract of stunted spruce and bogwater north of Lake Superior, near a point on the transcontinental railway line called Hemlo. Del Norte got the Hemlo claims from Donald McKinnon, a prospector Bob had met through a pair of Vancouver mining promoters, Richard Hughes and Frank Lang. Two years earlier Hughes and Lang had acquired two blocks of gold claims at Hemlo from McKinnon. On one block they had found gold, and on those claims the senior partner they had brought in was now developing a mine. Two other companies were developing mines on the same deposit, one on claims also acquired from McKinnon, the other on claims acquired in disputed circumstances from the estate of an amateur prospector who had died years before in Maryland. Engineers were now reporting that the Hemlo deposit, with its three mines, was the biggest gold discovery ever made in the Western Hemisphere, while brokers were proclaiming that it was incomparably the richest, with gold reserves worth ten billion dollars or more.

Hughes and Lang were at the Gold Fair to get investors interested in their companies. With the story they had to tell, this was easy. Bob Crompton and I were there partly to get investors interested in Del Norte Chrome, and that was hard. Although Del Norte's Hemlo claims were on a spur of the same rocks that were host to the gold discovery — a long strip of greenstone split at one end, like a snake putting out a forked tongue — they were twenty miles away from the three gold mines, and there was no reason whatever to believe that Del Norte's chances of striking gold were any better than those of at least forty other companies that had claims on the same greenstone snake. When I raised this with Bob, who knew a good deal about how to find and finance a gold mine, he brushed me off. "These companies are all the same," he said. "At the beginning, what have they got? An idea and a piece of rock."

So, feeling something like a Seventh-Day Adventist distributing pamphlets outside the Vatican, I pressed Del Norte brochures on everybody who would take them. Few would, and few of those who took one glanced at it, although one middle-aged man who did promptly handed it back to me. I asked him what was the matter.

"I didn't come here to buy a gold mine," he said. "I came to sell one."

His name was Cam McFeeley, and he was the president of a company called Peregrine Petroleum. He had inherited a small gold mine in the mountains of British Columbia, the Mosquito Creek Gold Mining Company Limited, and now he wanted to sell it to somebody who could make money running it.

"Why don't you run it yourself?" I asked.

"At one time I did," he said. "But I left and went to the oil patch. I wanted to work with holes that were too small to go down."

This was doubtless McFeeley's standard joke when he fell into conversation with strangers, but there was an uncomfortable element of truth in the remark as well. Most gold mines follow quartz veins, which never run in a straight line, and their dark crooked tunnels are often cramped and sometimes dangerous. When McFeeley moved on I wrote down what he'd said in a notebook I'd started when Del Norte Chrome took up its gold claims. If we were going to try to find a gold mine it seemed to me I'd better learn something about gold. By the time the notebook was half full I realized that the bond between gold and the people who prize it is perverse and irrational, buried, like a web of quartz veins, deep in the cramped and sometimes dangerous passages of the back brain. My memory groped for, and finally found a scene from my youth I'd altogether forgotten: a street in Hong Kong towards the end of the Chinese revolution, the pavement on both sides lined with folding tables. At each table sat a specialist with an array of sharp steel instruments set out around a small charcoal brazier. The specialist's art was to extract natural teeth from a client's jaw, fit a bridge, and replace the natural teeth with false ones made of gold. Clients, or would-be clients who that day were just looking, crowded the sidewalks and spilled off the curbs into the street. Once I saw a man spit blood and smile, displaying a single eighteen-karat incisor glinting among the white ones. Once a woman turned to her family, respectfully ranged around her, wiped the blood from her lips, and stretched her mouth to show them a new smile that glittered from front to back and top to bottom — two full rows of more or less solid gold.

At about the time I remembered the intense pleasure that radiated from those bloody but dazzling smiles, I decided to extend my notebook into a book, this one. Not long after that, my own back brain started to resist the idea. Although I went to the Gold Fair partly to make notes for the book, my back brain was still telling me to dump it, and I was still asking myself why. Then, when Ian McAvity mentioned the number of people around us who were hoping for a crisis, and the same people laughed too loudly at Rukeyser's joke about DeLorean's comedown, I began to understand what my back brain was trying to tell me about gold. It was much the same thing the American capitalist Otto H. Kahn once said about short sales. In a short sale the trader sells stock he doesn't own, expecting to buy it later at a lower price. There is an elaborate rationale that justifies the practice on the grounds that a short sale acts as a kind of governor that keeps the price of a stock from rising too high too fast. But many people shy away from short selling none the less, for reasons they don't necessarily understand — reasons of the back brain. My friend Bob is one of them; when I once asked him why he never sold short, he merely grimaced and said he was more interested in building things up than tearing them down. Otto Kahn, who was never inarticulate, said this of short selling: "The very root purpose of making a short sale, to profit by the misfortunes of others, tends to make the practice inherently repellant to a right-thinking man."

Buying gold amounts to a short sale of money. Now, with the insight of Otto Kahn and the help of McAvity and Rukeyser, I began to see why my back brain was resisting the idea of working on a book about gold. By this time, though, I had read enough about gold's ancient, arcane history to realize that gold has led to conflict, both inner and external, for well over two thousand years, and it would be unreasonable to expect this double nature to stop with me. Despite my divided mind I stayed at the Gold Fair, and went on making notes.

The full name of the fair is the "Investment Conference of the National Committee for Monetary Reform", but to get tickets you fill out a sheet titled "Gold Club Registration Form" and send money — that year it was

$545 for each "convention delegate", which is what you get called after you pay. Once you get to the ICNCMR, you just call it the "Gold Fair". Later, you can deduct your registration fee along with your travel expenses from your taxable income, provided you use information you picked up at the fair for investment or business purposes. Had you done so the year I was there you could have deducted your capital losses as well, since virtually all the experts who spoke at the fair advised their listeners to buy gold, which was then to be had for about four hundred dollars an ounce. In the short run, the experts said, gold would make modest gains, but by 1986, after a couple of years of steep inflation, the price would rise to a thousand dollars an ounce, or two thousand, or three thousand, or perhaps four. In fact, gold fell to about $320 an ounce soon after the fair that year, and stayed close to that figure for almost three years.

The Gold Fair was the creation of James U. Blanchard, III — his signature was everywhere at the fair, and he signed himself no other way. Blanchard was a bright blond with a Marine haircut and a bland pink face who looked twenty-seven and was said by his press office to be forty. He was confined to a wheelchair as the result of a highway accident, and the combination of his apparent youth and his visible infirmity was evidently appealing to the delegates; he was applauded at every appearance, both before he spoke and after.

This was the Gold Fair's tenth year, and to coincide with the anniversary Blanchard had launched a quarterly magazine called *Wealth*. Copies of the first issue, which had a cover price of five dollars, were distributed free to the "delegates", a benefit for being there. Blanchard's editorial in *Wealth* said much the same thing he said in his keynote remarks at the fair. He spoke of "what I call the megatrend of the twentieth century — the trend to collectivism." The villain, he said, was big government, dedicated to the destruction of wealth by the creation of paper money. There was one interesting and perhaps instructive difference between the conclusion he drew in his speech and the one he drew in print. "What delegates learn here," he said from the platform, "is how to protect their assets against this megatrend." But in his editorial he wrote that *Wealth* was meant "to help our readers profit from the immense opportunities that lie ahead."

I wondered briefly whether Blanchard was one of the people McAvity had spoken of, the people who could hardly wait for the next crisis, and then leafed quickly through the magazine. The longest piece was an excerpt from a book by Robert J. Ringer, a member of the International Advisory Board of *Wealth* and the popular author of *Winning Through Intimidation*. Ringer's new book was titled *How You Can Find Happiness During the Collapse of Western Civilization*. He offered seven rules. Number one began: "Start buying gold now, regardless of the price."

The contributors and advisors to *Wealth* included many of the people who were to appear as panelists or speakers at the Gold Fair. In the ten years of the fair's life Blanchard had aligned himself with most of the stars of the international gold circuit, and created a few of his own. There was Douglas Casey, author of *Crisis Investing*, who said, "Now is the time to get out of paper dollars and into real wealth before a wholesale panic develops." There was Dr. Henry Mark Holzer, a professor at Brooklyn Law School and author of *Sweet Land of Liberty?*, who said, "The government of the United States is solemnly dedicated to plundering private wealth." There was Donald S. McAlvany, editor and publisher of the expensive *McAlvany Intelligence Advisor*, who said, "Fuelled by global monetary, economic and geopolitical dislocations, the final leg of the current gold bull market could carry gold up to two thousand dollars to four thousand dollars an ounce." There were many, many others, but none of them caught the eye and the imagination in quite the way the Aden sisters did.

Mary Anne and Pamela Aden were then in their mid-thirties. They were both dark and slight, with the even-featured good looks of television actresses. They had predicted the buying frenzy that carried the price of gold from the $200-an-ounce range in 1979 to $850 an ounce in January 1981. They had then predicted the timing and the depth of the long slump that brought gold back down to just under $300 an ounce in the summer of 1982. In circles that take gold seriously they had become global celebrities; alone among gold analysts they had forecast both the high and the low with what appeared to be magical precision. No sooner were their faces familiar to readers of the *Wall Street Journal*, the *Sunday Times* of London, and the *Financial Post* of Toronto, than they "shocked the investment world", as the managing editor of *Wealth* put it, by issuing a new prediction.

"We expect gold to double in twelve to fifteen months," they announced, "and then explode up from there to $4,000 by the middle of 1986." A good many other gold analysts had since boarded the Adens' bandwagon, but at the Gold Fair the sisters were the sentimental favourites, drawing waves of applause when they were onstage and some handclapping when they merely entered a room.

Pamela made more entrances of this kind than Mary Anne, who was roundly pregnant and tired easily, and for the same reason Pamela more often stayed to talk. "We were born and raised in Long Beach, California," she told me on one such occasion. "But our mother is Costa Rican, and when our uncle became president of Costa Rica in 1974, we moved there.

His term was up in seventy-eight, but by then we were settled." They both married, Pamela to a Costa Rican lawyer, Mary Anne to an American employed in Costa Rica by an industrial-machinery manufacturer. "He's also involved in a gold mine down south, but right now it's closed down. I'm not sure why, but it is," Pamela said.

In California the sisters had both worked as second-mortgage appraisal officers; in Costa Rica jobs for women were almost non-existent, so they invented one. "We met a gentleman who did market analysis for himself, and we sort of became apprentices, helping him and learning from him for four years. Then, with his blessing, we went out on our own." A mutual friend introduced them to Blanchard, who agreed to publish their *Aden Gold Study* — fifteen thousand copies at twenty-five dollars. They were invited to join the management group of an investment fund, Austrian Advisers, that is based on the tax-haven island, Grand Cayman, but holds its clients' money in Switzerland. And they started the *Aden Newsletter*, a monthly that when we spoke had sixteen thousand subscribers at $195 a year. They were doing many things profitably and well, none of which would have been possible if they had lived a few hundred miles farther south.

"Costa Rica is at the very end of the footprint of the satellite that keeps us in touch with the markets. By satellite we have direct-dialling globally, we have a telex, we have an incoming Reuters wire. We're setting up a computer with a modem to hook us into American and European data banks.

"Without the satellite, nothing would move. With it, well, we'll stay in Costa Rica. The only reason we'd leave would be if something happened to interfere with communications or peace. There's the border with Nicaragua — the Sandinistas are chasing rebels into Costa Rica all the time. But Costa Rica would be quick to run to the U.S. if the Sandinistas tried to cross the border after them."

When I said that Costa Rica nevertheless seemed a little, ah, remote, Pamela said their lives were full, and she couldn't see how they could be any fuller elsewhere. "In the middle of a deadline period we think, 'My God, why am I doing this — fourteen hours a day? Ridiculous.' And I feel like pulling my hair out. But once the deadline's past, it feels good again. If there's any spare time then, the kids take it up." She had two small sons, she told me. "Having a family changed me. If I didn't have the kids, I'd be a workaholic now. But we get out a lot with the boys. You know, considering the way Central America *is*, Costa Ricans live a pretty good life. The restaurants and movie houses are always packed."

She paused, and her slightly stagey prettiness darkened. "But the country's broke, of course, like all those countries. Inflation is running pretty close to a hundred percent, everything going up except incomes." She frowned, pulling her eyebrows together. "Petty thievery is getting worse," she said. "Before, they used to come and steal from you only when you were away. Now they'll come in when you're sleeping. And you don't want to wake up — they come armed. Everybody's getting steel bars built over their windows." She stopped, and her mood shifted again.

"But I can't say it bothers me that much," she said. "We always had steel bars on the windows. And Dobermanns in the garden."

Now I paused, while I asked myself whether she was really as off-hand about the bars and the dogs as her tone suggested. "You and your sister seem to know everything there is to know about the price of gold," I said after a while. "But tell me — do you think gold is important?"

"Yes," she said. "As a last survival aid, I think gold is important."

The notion that gold is important has an ancient and partly honourable history. The written record begins, perhaps, with Moses at the moment when he ran out of patience with the Israelites. According to the 32nd chapter of Exodus he seized their idol, a certain Golden Calf before which they were in the habit of bowing down, and ground it to dust. He then flung the dust upon the waters, where, oddly, it floated. This was all the evidence later generations of alchemists needed to prove that Moses must himself have been an alchemist of no mean accomplishment. Clearly, they reasoned, he could make or unmake gold at will — how else could he cause gold dust to float?

Before long, the alchemists were trying to perform greater tricks than the one Moses showed the Israelites. The object of their science was to change base substances — lead, say, or common dirt, or indeed the dung of dogs or men — to gold. But their art, like anybody else's, soon altered the material they were working on, transmuting base substances into metaphors. By the time Christ came after Moses as a lawbringer, the substance the alchemists were trying to change had become the low nature of man, and the gold they sought was the perfected human spirit. Here is a more graphic description, written in the third century by "an important alchemist and Gnostic" of the time named Zosimos of Panopolis: "The priest, that brazen man, has changed the colour of his nature and become the silver man; and if you will it, he will become the golden man."

Zosimos had seen the brass man become gold in a dream that included a bloody struggle with a dragon: "And after I had seen this apparition, I awoke, and I said to myself, 'What is the cause of this vision?' " The question led Zosimos to a good deal of interpretation, as a result of which he decided that the vision was "the key, which shall open to you the flowers of the discourse that are to follow, namely, the investigation of the arts, of wisdom, of reason and understanding, of the revelations that throw light upon the secret words."

Poring over the secret words of the alchemists a couple of millennia later, the psychologist Carl Jung found in them many of the symbols he and other psychologists were discovering in the unconscious minds of their clients, principally by exploring with them their dreams. Jung concluded from this that in the papers left behind by two thousand years of alchemy there was a sort of confirmation of psychological theory, a seal of authenticity that was otherwise unavailable.

"Anyone who wishes to understand the symbolism of dreams cannot close his eyes to the fact that the dreams of modern men and women often contain the very images and metaphors that we find in the alchemical treatises," Jung wrote. Moreover, these "facts" have practical value, "since an understanding of the biological compensation produced by dreams is of importance in the treatment of neurosis as well as in the development of consciousness."

From the perspective of the couch, Jung saw the vision of Zosimos as the dramatization of the "violent and agonizing process of transformation", which is "experienced as punishment, torment, death, and transfiguration.

"Once again the universal struggle of the hero with the dragon is enacted, and each time at its victorious conclusion the sun rises," Jung wrote, "consciousness dawns, and it is perceived that the transformation process is taking place inside the temple, that is, in the head. It is in truth the inner man . . . who passes through the stages that transform the brass into silver and the silver into gold, and who thus undergoes a gradual enhancement of value.

"It sounds very strange to modern ears," he went on, "that the inner man and his spiritual growth should be symbolized by metals." (Strange to Jung, perhaps, although it strikes me that nothing would sound more commonplace to James U. Blanchard, III, and the idea would cause few delegates to the Gold Fair to raise an eyebrow.) "It seems that nature is out to prod man's consciousness towards greater expansion and greater clarity, and for this reason continually exploits his greed for metals, especially the precious ones, and makes him seek them out and investigate their properties."

Jung found in the writings of the alchemists many of his insights into psychology, as well as the confirmation of his theories that he had been searching for elsewhere with mounting desperation. In 1928, he wrote, he had been "investigating the processes of the collective unconscious since the year 1913, and had obtained results that seemed to me questionable in more than one respect." How to test them? "I knew of no realm of human experience with which I might have backed up my findings with some degree of assurance." Then his friend Richard Wilhelm sent him a copy of *The Secret of the Golden Flower*, a Taoist manuscript about Chinese yoga that includes a treatise on alchemy. It was this, he wrote, "that first put me on the right track. For in medieval alchemy we have the long-sought connecting link between Gnosis [or the rise of mystical thought] and the processes of the collective unconscious that can be observed in modern man."

Jung wrote three monumental books on the associations between alchemy and the subconscious mind, in the course of which he touched on most of the Western alchemists who had left a written record. The one who attracted him most strongly was, like Jung, a Swiss. He was born in 1493 and grandly christened, or so he later said, Aureolus Theophrastus Bombastes Paracelsus Hohenheim. He chose to be known as Paracelsus, and under that name became, again like Jung, a celebrated physician. He was at the same time the most famous alchemist of his day, and at the end of his life the most notorious.

To Jung and most other modern physicians Paracelsus was a towering figure in the development of medicine. He set direct observation of nature against the authority of tradition, and attacked the blinkered obedience to custom of the great medical schools and eminent doctors of his time. "It was an attitude that opened the way for the scientific investigation of nature and helped to emancipate natural science from the authority of tradition," Jung wrote reverentially.

But then Jung needed Paracelsus and the other alchemists. There were many writers who didn't. One of them was the unseducible Scot, Charles Mackay, whose book *Extraordinary Popular Delusions and the Madness of Crowds* was published in 1841. Mackay's book is the indispensable text on money and mania. He wrote clear-eyed accounts of the Great Mississippi Land Scheme and the South-Sea Bubble, the Dutch-bulb craze called "Tulipomania", and the mania for religious relics that in the aftermath of the Crusades created a memorable bull market in splinters from the true cross, the bottled tears of our Saviour, and the toenails of the Apostles. "Many a nail," Mackay says, "was sold at a diamond's price." But his most searching attention he gave to the alchemists.

In his book, Mackay wrote biographical sketches of more than thirty alchemists. He divided them into two types, erring philosophers or wilful cheats. The philosophers, he said, had in mind the good of mankind, reasoning that by creating an unlimited supply of gold they could eradicate poverty.

The cheats appear to have outnumbered the philosophers by about ten to one, and what they had in mind was hustling a buck. Here is an eye-witness account of the technique used by Jean Delisle, a celebrated French alchemist at the turn of the eighteenth century. It was written in 1709 by the Bishop of Senés to the Comptroller of Finance for Louis XIV:

> . . . I summoned the alchymist to come to me . . . and I had him escorted by eight or ten vigilant men, to whom I had given notice to watch his hands strictly. Before all of us he changed two pieces of lead into gold and silver. I sent them both to [a notary in Paris], and he afterwards informed me by letter . . . that he had shewn them to the most experienced goldsmiths of Paris, who unanimously pronounced them to be gold and silver of the very purest quality, and without alloy. My former bad opinion of Delisle was now indeed shaken. It was much more so when he performed transmutation five or six times before me at Senés, and made me perform it myself before him without his putting his hand to anything. . . . A hundred persons in my diocese have been witnesses of these things.

So had the Prior of Châteauneuf, who had written of Delisle to the Vicar of St. Jacques du Hautpas in Paris: "He turns lead into gold, and iron into silver, by merely heating these metals red-hot, and pouring upon them in that state some oil and powder he is possessed of; so that it would not be impossible for any man to make a million a day, if he had sufficient of this wondrous mixture."

All this was more than enough testimony to convince Louis XIV that Delisle might well be a useful addition to the staff down at the Treasury. Three times over six years Louis issued letters of safe conduct under which Delisle was to travel to Versailles. Each time Delisle came up with a reason for delay, until, in 1711, Louis sent a fourth letter. This one was a *lettre de cachet* under which Delisle was seized and carried off to the Bastille — not, it should be noted, for failing to make gold, but for failing to come when the King called. Although Louis sent the good Bishop of Senés to offer Delisle his freedom if he would now transmute a few ounces of lead into gold while the King watched, Delisle declined. He died in the Bastille a few months later, at forty-one.

The Bishop, not to say the Comptroller of Finance and the Sun King himself, might have done well to look up a certain M. Geoffroy *père*, who on April 15, 1722, read a paper on the alchemists' methods to a sitting of the Royal Academy of Sciences in Paris. The prop no aspiring alchemist could do without, M. Geoffroy reported, was a sturdy double-bottomed crucible. The lower of the two bottoms was made of iron or copper. On top of this the alchemist deposited a thin strip of loose gold. On top of the gold he moulded a false bottom of wax, tinted to match the metal of the crucible. When his skill was adequate to sustain the illusion, the witnesses saw only a metal pot in which, when the secret ingredients were added and heat was applied, presto! pure gold appeared without fail.

Now, M. Geoffroy went on, let us suppose the alchemist is too pressed for time to mould a wax bottom for his pot. He will then take his alchemical wand, the one with the hollow end, and into the hollow slip a little gold dust, sealing the gold in with wax or hard butter. Then he will set a pot holding secret ingredients over a bed of hot coals. And then he will stir the pot with his wand.

An alchemist adept in the art could also drill a hole in a lead bar, plug the hole with gold, and refinish the bar's surface so that to the eye the bar was again solid lead. Until, that is, he melted it in his furnace, whereupon witnesses would swear they had seen him transmute part of the bar to gold. Or he could treat gold with mercury in such a way that the gold looked like a lump of base metal — until he changed it back to gold by washing it with alcohol.

Such, M. Geoffroy assured the members of the Academy, were the means by which Jean Delisle created gold before the eyes of witnesses by the hundreds, and such, he believed, were the means used in all the other known instances of alchemical philosophers transmuting base substances into gold.

Which was doubtless true, but which left a nice question: If alchemy was a fraud how was it that the alchemists so often gave away the gold they made, and sometimes even the credit for making it? Mackay set down this appearance of caring little for the product of their art as perhaps "the most cunning of their manoeuvres". It was their seal of authenticity, and with it came "entrance to Royal households, maintenance at the public expense, and gifts from ambitious potentates".

The manoeuvre, though cunning, wasn't foolproof. After Delisle died in the Bastille, his step-son, Albert Aluys, made it known that he had inherited Delisle's secret, the formula for the powder that precipitated the transmutation. "It was his usual practice," Mackay wrote, "to pretend that he possessed only a few grains of his powder, with which he would operate in any house where he intended to fix his quarters for the season. He would make the proprietor the present of a piece of gold thus transmuted, and promise him millions, if he could only be provided with leisure to gather [the ingredients of the powder], and board, lodging, and loose cash for himself, his wife, and his pupil, in the interval."

By this means Aluys seems to have lived well for several years, moving comfortably from one noble house to another. Eventually, though, he caught the attention of the Duc de Richelieu, on whom the manoeuvre worked too well. Not only did the Duke rejoice in telling his friends about the gold Aluys made for him, but he pressed Aluys to turn his pewter plates and mugs to gold. Meanwhile, when Aluys hinted that he could use a little pocket money, the Duke advised him to be content with the honour of the Duke's acquaintance. For how could a man lack money, the Duke inquired reasonably, who could create gold at the flick of a wand? Much the same question later occurred to more than one "delegate" to the New Orleans Gold Fair, where they met many experts who were wonderfully anxious to reveal, for a modest fee, the secret of creating wealth.

Aluys gave up on the Duke and moved on. He encountered in the capitals of Europe no lack of credulity until he was charged with poisoning in Brussels, escaped to Paris, and disappeared. His biographer, Lenglet du Fresnoy, conjectured that he died "in some obscure dungeon".

Jung's hero, Paracelsus, came likewise to a dismal end, according to Charles Mackay, "in a state of abject poverty in the hospital of Saltzbourg". Mackay judged Paracelsus harshly. "This strange charlatan," he wrote, "was a public drunkard and a private demon worshipper." Paracelsus said of himself, "I am the monarch of medicine!" and indeed discovered "some happy cures by means of opium and mercury". At the same time, he "imagined that gold could cure ossification of the heart and, in fact, all diseases" — but for such high medical purposes common gold smelted from ore would not do. The gold that cured all diseases had to be gold alchemically transmuted from a base substance and administered under the correct conjunction of planets.

Of the writings Paracelsus issued in prodigious volume all his life, Mackay said, "Their great obscurity was no impediment to their fame; for the less the author was understood, the more the demonologists [and] fanatics . . . seemed to appreciate him." Jung saw the tortured style of these treatises merely as confirmation, if any was needed, that Paracelsus was suffering from the inner conflict that afflicts most of us, though perhaps Paracelsus was a more acute case than most. "When one unconsciously works against oneself, the result is impatience, irritability, and an impotent longing to get one's opponent down whatever the means," Jung wrote. The symptoms of this state include "a peculiar use of language: one wants to speak forcefully in order to impress one's opponent, so one employs a special, 'bombastic' style full of neologisms which might be described as 'power words'." Jung said he had heard or read this peculiar language not only in the psychiatric clinic and in the works of "certain modern philosophers", but, above all, "whenever anything unworthy of belief has to be insisted on in the teeth of inner resistance. The language swells up, overreaches itself, sprouts grotesque words distinguished only by their needless complexity. The word is charged with the task of achieving what cannot be done by honest means," Jung said. "It is the old word magic. . . ."

"The financial world has gone insane," an expert named Julian Snyder said on the last day of the 1983 Gold Fair. "The world's banking system is collapsing. U.S. Marines are killed by the hundreds in Lebanon. And what happens? The price of gold goes down."

TOWARDS THE END OF THE
Gold Fair Bob pressed a Del Norte Chrome pamphlet on a retired merchant
from Ohio who said his name was Harry. He had been telling us the story of
his forays into the gold markets, some of which had evidently turned out
well for him, judging by the weight of the watch he wore strapped outside
his sweater sleeve. He glanced without much interest at the pamphlet, then
brightened and said, "Hemlo; it says here you've got some ground at Hemlo."
We agreed.

"In that case," he said, "do you know this feller Pezzam?" We did.

"I went to hear him last year," Harry said. "He was here at the Gold Fair,
talking about Hemlo. It sounded *fant*astic."

"It is," Bob said. "Did you buy some of his stock?"

"Pezzam's?" Harry said. "Hell, no."

"How come?"

"He talked too fast. Pitchman like that, I didn't trust him."

Murray Pezim, the "Pezzam" of Harry's story, was the promoter of International Corona Resources, the company that discovered the first of the
three mines on the great Hemlo gold deposit. Pezim was one of the modern
masters of the old word magic. During the thirty years leading up to the
Hemlo discovery he had worked the spell time and again, usually selling
stock in companies that explored where no gold was ever found, much as
alchemists, from Zosimos of Panopolis on, had raised money in laboratories
where no gold was ever made. But throughout the centuries between Zosimos
and Pezim there had been many people who, like Harry, resisted the gold-
makers' magic, as well as a lot of people who didn't. Harry, of course, had
chosen the wrong stock to resist — Pezim's company, Corona, found gold in
very large quantities indeed — but for Harry that was just an accident of
timing.

Harry's attitude to Pezim raised a question: why did the old word magic
work on Harry at some times and not at others, whereas it seemed to work
all the time on many people who were just as intelligent and no less sceptical? Harry, for instance, was clearly no smarter than the Bishop of Senés,

who touted the alchemist Jean Delisle to Louis XIV; if he had been, he would hardly have gone to the Gold Fair.

The solution to this puzzle seems to lie, again, in the back brain, where instinct blends fear and greed and weighs the outcome against ordinary prudence. Who doesn't fear loss, and wish for gain? And does anything but gold speak so eloquently to both desires? Do you fear that inflation will destroy the value of your money? Buy gold to preserve it. Do you covet part of the new wealth others will acquire should the Gold Fair's experts be right after all, and the price of gold soar into the thousands? Buy gold to get it. Do you fear an avaricious tax system, the collapse of the banking system, international terrorism, war? Buy gold.

The moment when fear and greed tilt the scales in their own favour appears to vary widely from one person to the next. The balance is delicate, and fear of one kind can be offset by fear of another. For Harry the fear of making a fool of himself if he went along with somebody who talked as fast as Murray Pezim momentarily overcame the fear of missing a chance to buy into a good gold mine cheap. By the time we met him, though, the moment had come again for Harry when his back brain was telling him to buy gold.

That moment came for Atsuo Iida and Masakazu Yano early in 1981. The revolution in Iran and the onset of war in Afghanistan had destabilized the international order. The price of oil appeared to have no upper limit, and in Japan, where every barrel of oil that burned was imported, the newspapers were solemnly assuring their readers that hyperinflation was just around the corner. Gold was selling at an all-time high, and most experts were predicting that it would soon go higher. Since the terror in which the Second World War ended for Japan, there had seldom been a time when there was more reason for fear and greed to overcome prudence.

This was the moment when a company named Toyota Shoji announced that it had overcome the last barrier to owning gold, the problem of where to store it. The solution was that Toyota Shoji would buy the gold, store it in vaults secure from thieves and disasters alike, and place in the hands of the gold's real owners handsomely engraved certificates to be known as "Pure Gold Family Contracts". Each Pure Gold Family Contract, Toyota Shoji assured its clients, was an "unbreakable claim" on gold bullion held in the company's impregnable vault.

The old word magic has seldom met a warmer reception. Between 1981 and the first months of 1985 more than thirty thousand Japanese, of whom Atsuo Iida and Masakazu Yano were among the first, bought Pure Gold Family Contracts. They paid Toyota Shoji, in all, more than eight hundred million U.S. dollars at the then-current rate of exchange. Most of the thirty thousand clients remained easy in their own minds until early in 1985. Then some of them, including Iida and Yano, reconsidered. In the four years since they had bought their certificates the price of gold had gone down while the stock market and even the bond market had gone up; holding gold, they reasoned, was making them poor. Some of them went to Toyota Shoji's offices and presented their Pure Gold Family Contracts for redemption. The company readily gave them verbal guarantees that their claims on gold were unbreakable, but declined, with grave courtesy, to give them any money. Several clients then said that the company's position was perfectly agreeable to them; rather than money, they would take the gold the company was holding for them. With only mildly impaired politeness the company again declined. Inasmuch as Pure Gold Family Contracts were an unbreakable claim on gold, a company spokesman said, any request to remove gold from the vault was not only unnecessary but unreasonable.

But now the old word magic was losing its power, and the courtesies were almost over. A few investors went to the newspapers; a few others went to their lawyers. The authorities began an investigation, and within a few weeks they closed the company's offices, seized its records, and searched its vault. The vault held no gold whatever and very little money. It did, however, hold many documents, and from these it became clear that Toyota Shoji's founder and chairman, Kazuo Nagano, did not have the same blend of fear and greed that attracted his customers to gold.

A precocious entrepreneur, just twenty-eight when he started the company, Nagano seems to have been more than adequately imbued with greed but to have lacked the proper degree of fear. From the records found in the company's vault the authorities tracked the activities of close to one hundred separate companies Nagano had incorporated during his four years at the wheel of Toyota Shoji. (Toyota Shoji was entirely unrelated to the car company; the name was just another instance of the old word magic.) Every one of these companies was incorporated as a "trading company", but "trade" apparently meant to Nagano what "play" means in a casino. Nagano's trading companies had taken a roll on pork bellies, cocoa, ocean-front real estate, tankers, diamonds — pretty well everything speculators buy or sell. Everything, that is, but gold. As far as the investigators could tell from the records, Nagano had sold close to a billion dollars' worth of Pure Gold Family Contracts and blown the money without ever buying an ounce of gold.

On a Tuesday afternoon in June 1985, more than thirty reporters gathered outside Nagano's door. Several were business writers; here was a man who clearly held interesting views on how to run a financial trust. Police had tracked him to a small apartment he kept in a low-rent district of Osaka. The hall outside the apartment door was narrow. In this cramped space the television crews were elbowing one another for favourable camera angles outside the door, and the areas that were free of people were strung with cables and piled with equipment.

The corridor appeared to be impassable when, late in the afternoon, the investors Atsuo Iida and Masakazu Yano eeled politely but firmly through the crowd and reached the door to Nagano's apartment. Alongside the door a window screened by a thin yellow curtain looked onto the corridor. Iida and Yano rattled the locked door and turned to the window. Reporters, meanwhile, were shouting at their crews. Cameras rolled. That night Japanese television audiences saw this scene:

> Two men smash a window. They push aside a yellow curtain and climb through the opening. The curtain falls back and hangs in front of the lens. On the soundtrack we hear muffled grunts and screams.
>
> Now a hand pulls aside the yellow curtain, and through the broken window the two men we saw earlier thrust the head of a third. The man we are later told is Iida speaks.
>
> "This is Nagano," he says.
>
> Nagano is dead, his features obscured by his own blood. Iida and Yano drop the corpse and withdraw from the window. We hear the rattle of locks and bolts, the camera pans to the door. It opens. Iida and Yano come into the corridor. Yano is carrying a bayonet; the lens zooms to the blood on the blade. Iida holds out a knife and seems to wait for somebody to take it from him. When nobody does, he speaks again.
>
> "Call the police."
>
> Police appear, and we see Yano and Iida taken into custody. Now the camera seeks a glimpse of the two men behind a screen of blue uniforms, and we see only part of Iida's face as he speaks the last line we hear from him.
>
> "We are the ones who did this," he says, making a hand gesture that draws into a ring with him the silent Yano and the dead Nagano. His voice lacks entirely the overtones of guilt or confession. Lest some other claimant come forward, Iida claims for Yano and himself the authorship of their act.

Would Iida and Yano have carried out the same act had Nagano betrayed them over something other than gold — real estate, say? I suppose they might have, but I find it hard to believe that Iida and Yano and thirty thousand others would have given Nagano a billion dollars for claims on real estate or coffee beans that didn't exist. No, these people wanted to buy gold with their money because they feared to lose it; they put their trust in gold, not in Nagano. When he betrayed them the depth of their outrage was a measure of the strength of their belief that a claim on gold would give them security in an uncertain world.

During a six-month period in the early 1980s I collected press clippings describing twenty-three different gold swindles in the United States, Canada, Latin America, the Near East, the Middle East, and the Far East, and then I stopped; why go on? If all these reports were reliable, in that short time perhaps a hundred thousand people had been separated from more than two billion dollars, and there was no way to guess how many similar cases I had missed, or how many more had gone unreported. Nagano, when I first saw the film clip of his death, seemed to be a peculiarly Japanese figure, an expression of that fear-filled time in his then-beleaguered homeland. But once I started collecting similar stories, I found them everywhere. Bullion Reserve of North America, an organization with a name that rang as true as the National Mint's, sold "World Class Precious Metals Receipts" to American businessmen. Bullion Reserve's Receipts, like Toyota Shoji's Pure Gold Family Contracts, were handsomely engraved and guaranteed to be an unbreakable claim on bullion.

"Gold You Can Fold," said Bullion Reserve's advertisements: "Now the safest, least expensive, most liquid way to own gold bullion."

Bullion Reserve was the creation of a long-faced Californian named Alan David Saxon, who was described by his estranged wife as "a shy and gentle man". Saxon sold something like a hundred million dollars' worth of Receipts. In time his clients, too, started asking for their money or their gold. Saxon did not, like Kazuo Nagano, wait for a couple of clients to catch up with him. He switched on a motor scooter, ran a hose from its exhaust pipe into his sauna, and died as he had lived, sweating a little lest somebody look in his vault. When the authorities investigating his suicide did open the vault they found slightly more than a million dollars in gold. The other ninety-nine million was gone — speculation, mainly, with here and there a Lear jet, a Maserati, a Porsche, an ocean-front condominium in Venice, California, with its own sauna.

In Florida, at precisely the same time, William and James Alderdice were in jail facing eighteen charges of conspiracy and mail and wire fraud. Had they beaten any or all of them, they faced another forty charges of fraud brought by New York State. All the charges rose out of the collapse of their

International Gold Bullion Exchange, which had sold thousands of claims on gold that existed nowhere outside their Bullion Certificates.

Investigators for the Securities and Exchange Commission (SEC) in the United States reported at about this time that they had looked into seventy-eight initial public offerings of stocks that sold for less than a dollar, many of them gold stocks. The investigators found that 45 percent "had participants with histories of securities injunctions, violations, fraud or associations with reputed crime figures". Had companies smaller than these been included, the 45 percent might have been closer to 90 percent. In most cases a company that has fewer than five hundred shareholders and raises less than three million dollars is exempt from SEC reporting requirements.

None of these companies, as far as I know, is run by a promoter whose ability to sell what doesn't exist is equal to that of Count Cagliostro, an eighteenth-century practitioner of the old word magic whom Mackay called "the arch-quack of his age". Cagliostro said he could "transmute all metals into gold; that he could render himself invisible, cure all diseases, and administer an elixir against old age and decay". If that wasn't enough, listen to Mackay's description of the girl Cagliostro persuaded to marry him, Lorenza Feliciana. "Beside her ravishing beauty," Mackay said, "she had the readiest wit, the most engaging manners, the most fertile imagination, and the least principle of any of the maidens of Rome."

Together they conquered Brussels, London, Strasbourg, Bordeaux. In Paris, Cagliostro started a rumour that he could call forth from their graves the ghosts of famous men and women. For a favoured client he would arrange an interview with Julius Caesar, say, or for a client of different tastes, one with Lucretia Borgia. These encounters across the barrier of the grave were, however, expensive. "For," as Cagliostro said, "the dead would not rise for nothing."

A Papal Court convicted Cagliostro of heresy and sorcery in 1789, and condemned him to perpetual imprisonment in the Castle of St. Angelo. He died the following year in the castle's dungeon. His wife, the radiant though unprincipled Lorenza, remained faithful to the grave, and beyond. While Cagliostro was alive she "made men her slaves," Mackay said, "without ever granting a favour of which the vainest might boast." Upon Cagliostro's death she immured herself in a nunnery.

In our time marvels have grown scarcer, but among the promoters of his day Murray Pezim, though no Cagliostro, was an acknowledged master of the old word magic. Although there were those, like Harry, who could resist his spell, it was Pezim's gift for raising money that led to the gold discovery at Hemlo. Rocco Schiralli, a member of the grubstake syndicate that sold the Hemlo claims to Pezim's company, Corona, once said to me, "You know, it's lucky for everybody that a guy like Murray had those claims. If I'd had them, I'd have quit after seven or eight holes. I go for results, and most guys are like me."

Pezim raised the money, some of it his own, to pay for seventy-five diamond-drill holes before the seventy-sixth suggested there might be something unusual below the surface. At the New Orleans Gold Fair, where Pezim was a member of a panel on penny mining stocks, he said, with more than a touch of the old word magic, "The risk-taking public can never forgive a quitter. The Pez group of companies will never quit trying." At the time, he was selling stock in something like forty other companies that were turning over the rocks in the same greenstone belt where Corona found gold. Three years later none of them had found anything of value, but that is not to say they never will.

Pezim had come to the Gold Fair in his jet, a Hawker Siddeley that, he said to me, was bigger than a Lear and could easily take one more passenger. He was flying from New Orleans to Phoenix, Arizona, and since I was going that way, sort of, he gave me a lift. Pezim, who is short but not light, sat in a special chair with a table in front of him, and when the plane was in the air he turned to the others in the cabin and said, "How did I do?"

"Okay," a twentyish blonde with very long legs and an unspecified role in the entourage said. "Maybe a little hypocritical, but okay."

"Waddaya mean, hypocritical?"

"A few days ago I heard you cutting up the Vancouver Stock Exchange into little pieces. Then you come on here saying it's the greatest stock exchange in the world. . . ."

"Wait a minute," Pezim said. "Wait just a damn minute. I said there's a lot of things the VSE needs to do better. But it's still the best vehicle in the world for raising risk capital. That's *true!*"

On *true* his voice rose an octave and changed, in a blend of anger and indignation that almost squeaked, and he slammed his palm on the table-top in front of him. A moment later he was telling the blonde, whom he called Susan, a funny story; there wasn't a trace of ill-will in his voice. The incident interested me for a couple of reasons. I had assumed he was the kind of small potentate whose retinue would be chosen partly for their willingness to flatter him, and in accepting this cliché I had obviously made a mistake — Susan was no yes-man, so to say, and when she spoke out he showed anger but no resentment. Then, too, his formula of criticism and praise for the Vancouver Stock Exchange was obviously sincere; he believed what he said about it. This quality of belief was probably the source of his magic in the money markets. Like those alchemists who put more gold into their furnaces than they ever extracted, he was the first among the believers in his art.

At this stage in his life he had lost count of how many fortunes he had made and lost and made and, forever at the head of the file when the believers lined up for another try, lost again. It was a pattern of behaviour that probably began in 1933, at his own bar mitzvah. They were serving ice cream. Everybody came. His mother took Murray aside and whispered to him.

"She said, 'Sorry, son, we haven't got enough ice cream to go around.' What she was trying to tell me was that she and my brother, Norman, and I shouldn't have any; we should leave it for the guests.

"I was so hurt I crawled under the tablecloth to hide, and I started to cry. Thirteen years old, my bar mitzvah, I'm crying because I'm not supposed to have any ice cream. Norman heard me. He pulled me out and said, 'Okay, I'll get you some ice cream.'

"After, my mother had to sell the presents to pay for the party. Handkerchiefs, a pen — you know. Nineteen thirty-three. Who could buy a present worth more than twenty cents?"

In Phoenix he had an office, or rather his holding company, Pezamerica, had an office in a low-rise plaza between a dentist's office and a dental laboratory. The dental mechanic looked in every hour or so to say howyadoin' guys, and smile; I got the impression he was making more money from stock Pezim put him into than he was from dentures, and he was anxious to keep the pipeline open. Murray's brother, Norman, ran the office. He was two and a half years older than Murray, he told me, and I could see for myself that he was a good deal softer — the kind of man people say is "sweet", and mean it.

Norman said his brother had been a promoter practically from birth, and when I asked him what he meant, he said, "Listen. The high school we went to, in Toronto, they made the kids pay a dollar deposit for the combination locks. For their lockers? At the end of the year they give everybody their dollar back, right? On that day Murray runs a crap game in our backyard. Every pass, he drags a dime from the bank — some kid or other is going to win a few bucks gambling, but the only guaranteed winner is Murray. Then he hires the right tackle on the football team to ride shotgun on the game. Nobody's gonna rip Murray off."

"Well, I dunno," I said. "He wasn't that hard-nosed. I heard about his bar mitzvah."

"You mean about the ice cream?" Norman said. "And he's under the table there, crying? I'll never forget pulling him out; it was dark under there. But Murray — I don't know." Norman shook his head. "Did he tell you how he hustled his bar mitzvah in the first place?"

"Come on, Norman," I said.

"No, he promoted the whole deal," Norman said. "It was his mother wanted him to be bar mitzvah. I don't think Murray cared that much, but if his mother wanted it he was gonna do it. You know the ceremony requires the kid to recite in Hebrew? So he's gotta know the language, he's gotta know the lines from the Talmud, he's gotta know when to say them. Kids go to Hebrew school two hours a day, *after* public school, to learn this stuff. Not Murray. He gets bored too quick, so he's been skipping the whole thing for years. But now it's a question of his mother's happiness. So . . ."

"So?"

"Well," Norman said, "she was my mother, too. So Murray came to me and I coached him. Wrote out the Hebrew lines in phonetics, helped Murray memorize them in the right order. During the ceremony I stood next to him, and when it came time for him to say another line I'd nudge him with my elbow.

"Maybe it wasn't the most moral way to do it," Norman said. "But we got by, and our mother was happy."

Marilyn, Murray's second wife, also believed he was a natural promoter. "He had me believing he had no middle name because his family was too poor to give him one," she told me one day.

"Aside from the joke, which isn't that great, why would he do that?"

"For practice," she said.

When I left, Pezim dropped me at the airport. "This lawsuit against Lac," I said when I was getting out of the car. "Why don't you settle?"

"I'll settle with those bastards," he said, "the day they give me back what they stole from me."

In the spring of 1981 a geologist working for Lac Minerals read about a drilling program being carried out near Hemlo by Corona Resources, a company Murray Pezim then had a loose arrangement to promote. Lac was interested. Some Lac people asked for, and made, a visit to the site. They then asked Corona's consulting geologist to talk to them in Toronto, and soon after this they staked hundreds of claims in the area. Lac then wrote Corona, setting out ways in which the two companies might collaborate and asking Corona to make a presentation to Lac of their exploration results. The Corona people did so.

The Corona people had asked the prospector who had sold them the claims in the first place, Donald McKinnon, to buy a separate adjoining block for them. This group of claims was the property of a widow who lived in Maryland but wintered in Florida. McKinnon lost a good deal of time finding her, and a good deal more negotiating with her — he thought her first asking price was too low. In time he and she reached a verbal understanding, but before the letter of agreement was signed Lac found her too. A Lac executive persuaded her to drop McKinnon, turn down a direct bid from Corona, and sell the claims to Lac.

Pezim was outraged. Lac tried again to strike a deal with Corona. First, Pezim said, give me the property you stole from me. The Lac people brushed him off. This time Pezim answered with a lawsuit claiming the property "back" from Lac even though Corona had never owned it — or, alternatively, very large amounts of money. At about the same time, Richard Hughes and Frank Lang, who held an adjoining block of claims also acquired from McKinnon, sold control of their block to Noranda, a mining conglomerate controlled by the non-distillery branch of the Bronfman family. A little later Pezim sold 55 percent of the Corona property to another large mining organization, Teck. During the next couple of years Noranda, Teck, and Lac cut diamond-drill holes by the linear mile. As the samples thus lifted from the rock came back from the assay laboratories it became clear that Hemlo was an authentic bonanza, the most valuable deposit of gold discovered until that time in the Western Hemisphere. The disputed claims in the hands of Lac held the richest part of the deposit, a lode that by itself was said to be worth billions.

Given the speed at which the mills of justice grind, it was not until the autumn of 1985 that Corona got Lac to court. Meanwhile I had been wrestling with the book I had started to write about the peculiar relationship between people and gold, and was losing more falls than I was winning. Although I now understood better the reasons for my reluctance to grapple with the subject, I still hadn't overcome them. But here, in the trial between Lac and Corona, many of the people who among them had found and financed an historic gold discovery would come before a Justice of the Supreme Court and tell him how they'd done it, what it had done for and to them, and what they'd done to each other. The judge would then try to apply reasonable standards to the actions of both parties. The search for reasonable standards is what makes gold valuable in the first place. Since gold is incorruptible — unlike those of us who are interested in it — the back brain tells us that gold remains a reasonable standard of value when all else changes. Not that the back brain is always right; but right or wrong, the search for reasonable standards is always with us.

All this was my story. When the trial opened, I went to court to hear the members of the original cast tell it, under oath.

A Memory

· ·

To tell the truth, I don't know much
about prospecting.
— B. Traven, *The Treasure of the Sierra Madre*

The summer of 1934 blazed. One day I drank from the sweat that pooled
between my mother's palm and mine as she led me from door to door. She
was selling Christmas cards in July. When a door closed on us she would set
her face towards the next one like a navigator setting his bow towards a
landfall, clamp my hand more firmly in hers, and shift the weight of the
sample box in her other hand to counterbalance the drag I increasingly put
on her as the day wore on.

In my memory the answer at the next door is always no, but there must
have been exceptions. On the way home we would buy flat farmer's sau-
sage and potatoes for dinner, and the next morning take the streetcar to the
starting point for that day's walk from door to door. Food and carfare was
costing half a dollar a day or more, and I knew the money wasn't coming
from my father. In the mornings he left our room at the same time we did
and spent his days shuffling forward in the long line-ups of men looking for
work, a foot soldier in the army of the unemployed. That was an army that
seldom won a skirmish and never won a battle; in the evenings he sat on the
side of the bed, muttering curses against the bosses, the system, the times.
He seldom raised his voice, but the undertone of his rage frightened me, and
between the evening meal and time for bed I tried to escape into the backyard. Across the fence lived the family of a Japanese gardener, the only
family I knew who had an entire house to themselves. The children taught
me how to jump off the garage roof and land unhurt in the soft earth of
the flowerbed under the eaves, and they taught me a few words of their
language; I taught my own children to say "chee-chai" when they meant
"small". The gardener himself never said anything, at least when I was
around, but in the evenings he sat on the back steps, sharpening his tools
for the next day's work. In the fading light I watched him spit on his stone

and restore the bright cutting edges to the blades of his shears and mowers. His hand, brown with darker brown spots and pared nails the colour of clay, moved the stone firmly towards the tip of the steel and lightly back, and in the precision of his stroke I felt the same steadiness that showed in my mother's face when she turned from a door that was closing on her to one that hadn't yet opened.

Before nightfall the gardener's tools were ready for work and I was ready for bed. Upstairs my father would stop muttering and raise me in a breathless hug, offering the side of his face in a wordless request for a kiss. The kiss, once a gesture as light and natural as a smile, was now getting harder to give with each asking. On one such night, in the stretched moment before the difficult kiss, I came to see it wasn't my father's anger I was trying to escape from in the evenings, it was his love. What I saw in my mother's face and the Japanese gardener's hand, the ability to find a course and hold it, was missing in my father. Needing love from me he pressed love on me, and the weight of his need was more than I could bear.

There were days when my mother left me at home, perhaps because she had run out of money for the streetcar and knew she'd have to walk farther than my legs would carry me. Towards the end of a day like this I was on the garage roof, getting ready to jump, when a grey horse turned the corner on to our block, led on a rope halter by a man I didn't look at until he and the animal stopped at the curb in front of the house where we lived. Then I took my eye from the horse and saw that the man was my father. My father with a horse? A horse! Joy launched me into the air as though I'd been learning to fly, not jump. I landed without looking at the ground and felt the surge of pain from a twisted ankle, and laughed out loud. When my father reached for me I went into his arms gladly and sat on his cocked hip like a cowboy, watching the Japanese kids jump off the roof after me, landing with flexed knees and springing up like acrobats, pointing and shouting.

"What's that?"

"What does it look like?"

"A horse?"

"My father's horse." For the first time in my life I was proud of my father. It may have been the first time I'd felt pride.

"What's he going to do with it?"

"What do you think? Ride it," I said, secure, superior, the son of a man with a horse.

He never did ride the horse. The horse was only half broken and my father, no wrangler, had all he could do to lead the animal on a halter.

"You can't ride a half-wild horse," my mother said that night.

"I don't want to," my father said. "I don't need a saddle horse. I need a pack horse."

My mother didn't often make jokes, but now she smiled. "For your money?" she said.

"No," my father said earnestly, sounding as though he might indeed have more money than he could carry. "For my gear."

"All the gear we've got in the world weighs less than ten pounds," my mother said, looking bleakly around the room.

"Your brother's lending me his."

"Ingjarl?" she said, surprised. "How is a horse going to help you catch salmon?"

"Walter. Walter's got a job driving cab. He's not going to need the stuff he uses when he goes panning for gold, at least for a while, so he's lending it to me."

They talked late that night and I tried to hear every word they said; that was no night to fall asleep. The horse was a loan from Walter, too, in a way. At the head of False Creek, on the marshy ground known then as the Flats and later as the site of Expo '86, a few small bands of feral horses ranged. My father knew a man who now and then caught one of these horses, broke it to the halter, and sold it for a pack animal. His price was one dollar. My father didn't have a dollar, of course, but he had borrowed one from Walter. A dollar; I had never held a sum of money that big in my hand, but then until that evening I had never held the halter of a live horse in my hand either. The money and the horse were both wonders.

The next day my father went to Walter's place and brought back his picks and shovels and pans and groundsheets and cooking gear and practised tying them all on the horse. Then he led the animal around the backyard by the rope. I came behind, picking up the stuff that fell off, and at the end of each loop around the yard my father tried new ways to tie the stuff back on before going around again. The morning after, he set out to find gold.

All the Japanese kids from next door were out on the curb along with their mother, who until now had never set foot outside their door while I was around. My uncle Walter pulled up in his cab with my uncle Ingjarl beside him in the front seat. My mother stood holding the halter while my father tried to find a way to tie onto the horse's back a couple of paper bags full of berries and fruit, a gift from the Japanese gardener. I waited with one hand on the horse's twitching belly, feeling better than I had ever felt before.

"Well," my uncle Walter said. The word was male code that meant it was time; for my father, time to go. He tugged and the horse moved. Before they reached the corner the load slipped and my father stopped to work on the lashing. While he was pulling on knots my uncle Ingjarl said, "Well," and I watched him and Walter get into the cab and drive off. When I looked back towards the other corner my father and the horse were out of sight.

He came back in the autumn. He picked me up and offered his cheek and I kissed him quickly and easily.

"Where's our horse?" I said.

"He's gone."

"Where?"

"Gone."

Walter told me a long time later that one night that autumn he and my father drank a quart and a half of dandelion wine and while they could still talk my father said, Well, I ate the horse, which was no great surprise to Walter. The horse went down pretty good, my father said, but when the meat was gone and it was time to break camp, he had looked at Walter's gear and realized there was no way in the world he could carry it out of there without help, and he'd just carved the help. So he left most of Walter's stuff in a dry place overhung by a big rock, slung the rest over his shoulder in a bedroll, and walked back. Ten or twelve miles down the creek where he'd been camped to the Fraser, a hundred and fifty miles or so down the Fraser to Vancouver, and every step of the way, my father said, he was back-tracking the route of the famous gold rush of '89, or whenever the hell it was.

"Did you pan any colour?" Walter said.

"What?"

"Colour. Did you find any gold?"

"Well," my father said, "not exactly. Not what you'd call gold."

Nor did he ever find anything else he could take to the bank; not what you'd call a deposit. By the end of the Depression we were forty-four months behind with the rent. Sometimes my father still sat on the edge of the bed and muttered his rage against what was happening to his life. But now he was less likely to fill the room with the feeling that he and we were captives there and might all be dead before we got out. Though I never was able to give him all the love he needed, I no longer pulled away when he reached out his arms. He was my father, after all, and he had shown me that when you've tried everything you can think of and there's nothing left for you but anger, you can still refuse to sit still. You can get up and go looking for gold.

A STRONG SHARP TOOTH

This obligation to perfect fairness and good faith is, moreover, not confined to persons who actually are partners. It extends to persons negotiating for a partnership, but between whom no partnership yet exists.

— *Lindley on Partnership*

THE GUARD STOPPED ME AT
the courtroom door. "Are you a witness?" he asked.

"No," I said. "Just an onlooker."

The guard stood aside, then put a hand on my elbow to stop me again.

"That's too bad," he said. "They tell me all the witnesses in this case got rich."

We smiled at each other, the unamused smile by which two strangers acknowledge that the story of their lives has been repeated and, as always, it was the other guys who got rich. Then the guard dropped his hand and I went into Courtroom 10 of the Supreme Court of Ontario, where Mr. Justice Richard Holland was trying the contending claims of two corporations to the same slab of plain grey rock near the northern shore of Lake Superior. It was October 16, 1985, the second day of the trial, and already the casual spectators who had filled the visitors' benches the day before were gone. Now the big room held only the black-robed officials of the court, the lawyers, clerks, and students fighting the action, a handful of young lawyers taking notes for people who weren't there but had a stake in the outcome, and a financial analyst.

All rise when Judge Holland enters his courtroom. Deliberately and somewhat stiffly he climbs to his chair on the top tier of a three-level dais at the front of the room, while his bailiffs and recorders and reporters and clerks take their places on the lower levels. He bows, and all those who stand before him, on both sides of the rail that separates the spectators from the participants, bow in return. He spreads the tails of his deep blue gown to sit, and when he is settled adjusts the broad orange lapels before he leans back and slides his half-glasses down his nose so that he can look out at the courtroom. Costumed and staged as he is he looks as though he might break into song, but the note of musical comedy ends when he speaks. His voice is light, highly modulated, the pronunciation mid-Atlantic but the choice of words plain and clear.

"Are you ready to open, Mr. Lenczner?"

"Yes, M'lord."

"Then please do."

Feisty as a flyweight at the opening bell and about the same size, Alan J. Lenczner hustles to the lectern on the right side of the courtroom and spreads his papers. For the next three hours he will tell the judge about the "wrongful and unlawful" things done by a big company, Lac Minerals Ltd., to his client, a small company named International Corona Resources Ltd. Should the judge find Lac guilty, Lenczner will ask him to order Lac to "disgorge" eleven mining claims at Hemlo, on the north shore of Lake Superior.

There is gold in those claims. The transfer of wealth (in the phrase OPEC made familiar to lovers of money) that would take place if Lac disgorged the claims and made good some additional damages demanded by Corona has been the subject of several estimates. None is lower than a billion dollars, and one is higher than ten billion. Earlier in the day, in an exchange over procedure, the lawyer leading Lac's defence, John Lorn McDougall, said, "Look, we're not in small-claims court here." He got an appreciative chuckle from both his opponents and His Lordship.

Here is the story Alan Lenczner told Judge Holland.

Early in April 1981, a man named Chris Pegg, district geologist for Lac Minerals in northwestern Ontario, made an overture towards a young woman named Nell Dragovan. Pegg lived in Kirkland Lake, a town that had been one of Ontario's great early gold camps. From there he telephoned Ms. Dragovan in Vancouver. He told her Lac was interested in the claims Corona was exploring at Hemlo; he thought the two companies might work together. Though not the president of Corona, Nell Dragovan was the person holding the company together. She had advanced money out of her own bank account to pay some of its early exploration bills while she looked for other avenues of financing, and she ran the company's paperwork out of her small Vancouver office. But this was her first time out as the principal of an exploration company, and she wanted help in answering questions as important as Pegg's. So she told Pegg to call Corona's consulting geologist, David Bell.

Pegg had much in common with Bell. Less than a year earlier Bell, too, had been a staff geologist for a large company, in his case Dome Mines Ltd. He was now on his own as a consultant, with Corona as his first client. He was in charge of exploring Corona's claims at Hemlo, which were Corona's only mineral prospect and, indeed, only asset. Pegg reached Bell at his new office in Timmins, another of Ontario's early mining camps. He asked Bell whether Corona needed money. Would Corona be interested, Pegg wanted to know, in a joint venture? (When I asked questions like these of the Texans I once worked with on an oil-exploration crew in the Peace River Valley, they would say, "Why, shucks, is a monkey's nose red?") Bell said Corona would be interested, yes, and Pegg asked permission for some people from Lac to visit Corona's Hemlo site in April or May.

Over the next few years Pegg and Bell talked several times on the phone. They fixed the date for the property visit on May 6, 1981, when Pegg's boss, Dennis Sheehan, Lac's vice-president of exploration, could get away from Toronto, and Bell's principal, Nell Dragovan, was due to fly in from Vancouver. On the afternoon of that day they all met at the core shack on Corona's Hemlo property.

Here the nature and purpose of "core" become part of the story. Geologists spend their working lives trying to see into solid rock. This is a task at which they can never entirely succeed; but they have devised a variety of tools that help make their guesses more plausible. The most important of these tools is the diamond drill. At the end of a length of pipe the driller attaches a ring of industrial diamonds, the bit. The drill engine turns the pipe, the bit cuts a ring in the rock, and the finger of rock left inside the diamond ring — the core — is contained within the pipe. To deepen the hole the driller adds another length of pipe at the surface; by pulling the pipe out of the hole, he can extract the core. Interpreting core from a single hole, a geologist can see the rock strata that underlie the drill's starting point on the surface. With core from a second hole he can begin to guess what lies between the two holes, and with each additional hole he can cast a little more light on the dark heart of the rock.

At the Corona core shack on May 6 David Bell asked the site geologist, John Dadds, to empty his bag for Pegg and Sheehan. Dadds showed them lengths of core, drill logs, assay results, sections (drawings of the underground terrain the drills were cutting), the Corona drill plan, surface maps showing all the mining claims in the area. These included an eleven-claim block contiguous to Corona's western boundary, a property known as "the Williams claims". Before Sheehan and Pegg left the site, Sheehan told Bell that Corona should go after the Williams claims. Bell said Sheehan was right; they were working on it already.

Between this May meeting and the last week in July the lines between Lac and Corona were open. Corona gave Lac more information when Lac asked for it, and Lac gave Corona the outlines for "a number of avenues" that might lead the two companies towards a joint development in the Hemlo area. Sheehan described one of his letters to Bell as "further evidence of our sincerity in joining with Corona".

Meanwhile Lac was secretly trying to buy the Williams claims. The block of eleven claims was named after an American radiologist, Dr. J.K. Williams, who acquired them in 1945. After his death in 1953 they lay more or less forgotten in his estate until the spring of 1981. In February that year Corona's geologist, David Bell, asked a Timmins prospector, Donald McKinnon, to try to get the Williams claims for Corona. McKinnon was the prospector who had staked the seventeen claim block that Nell Dragovan had originally acquired for Corona. He traced the ownership of the Williams claims to the doctor's widow. By early July, Lola Williams had come to a verbal understanding with McKinnon. He was waiting for her to return a signed copy of the letter of agreement he had sent her when Dennis Sheehan reached her by telephone.

Sheehan told Lola Williams that McKinnon was a "land dealer" who might resell her property to anybody. His own company, Lac, he said, was a "major" gold-mining company. He made her an offer while they spoke, followed a few days later by a letter setting out Lac's terms. Lac, Sheehan wrote, had "been in the mining and exploration business for years" and was accordingly "quite capable of giving you the very best of expertise. . . ."

Corona, learning that a new bidder had appeared, though still unaware of the bidder's identity, made a new offer in its own name rather than McKinnon's. Sheehan countered with an amended Lac offer. At this juncture the Corona bid was almost exactly double Lac's in both the amounts of cash the widow would receive at each stage of exploration and the size of the royalty she would earn in the unlikely event that a gold mine were actually developed on the property. On July 28 Lola Williams wrote to Sheehan, accepting Lac's offer.

Courts deal with questions of three kinds: questions of fact, questions of opinion — on which only the testimony of experts assumed to be independent is admitted — and questions of law. When Alan Lenczner turned from the facts of this case to the law that governed them, he lost some of his self-assurance. While he was telling the story he was up on his toes, moving around, now and then swivelling his bright bird-sharp gaze around the spectators' benches behind him to measure the effect of his words on his audience. Now he settled down. Lenczner was midway on the trip from blond to bald, with a long, almost fleshless and faintly pocked face and a nose like a blade. This he pointed at Judge Holland, and began to address him as though he hadn't quite finished thinking what to say.

"This case really turns on *reasonable standards.*" He placed equal emphasis on both words. "You'll hear arguments about how businessmen conduct themselves. There's a paucity of cases around — but some cases in England and Australia have been nibbling at the edges."

Judge Holland took his half-glasses in his left hand and started chewing on the earpiece; he kept his gold pen in his right hand but stopped taking notes. I began to wonder whether Lenczner's argument was so thin that he was reluctant to make it. Maybe, now that Corona's case had at last reached court after more than four years of preliminary skirmishing, there was no case. Outside the courtroom Corona had always accused Lac of breach of contract. Yet in Lenczner's telling of the story there was no contract, merely talk about the kinds of contract the parties might enter into, should they agree to do so.

At this moment Lenczner's voice hardened; almost angrily he asked, "Does the obligation for fairness and good faith bind only partners? Or does it bind parties who are negotiating a partnership or joint venture?"

He answered himself by quoting an Australian judge who found that when two parties are negotiating, their duty towards each other arises from their intention, not their eventual contract. "An intending partner," the Australian judge wrote, "like a partner, owes a duty of the utmost good faith." Lenczner's tone shifted from anger to scorn. "The contention that no fiduciary relationship exists before a formal contract has been signed," he said, "is clearly wrong."

The quickest way to get from the Supreme Court building to a fast-food place where you don't have to stand in line is to cut across the top of Toronto's civic square, a route that leads past the City Hall branch of the public library. On the way to lunch I detoured through the library and learned that "fiduciary" is a noun, not as I had supposed exclusively an adjective, and that it means "a person to whom property or power is entrusted for the benefit of another". At the fast-food place one of the other reporters at the table, Kerry Knoll, an intense young man with a black-bearded face lifted from an icon, said the morning in court had given him a new idea of the case. I asked him what idea that was.

"That Corona's got a chance," he said.

"Who have you been talking to up to now?"

He thought for a moment. "Mainly Lac," he said. "They, you know, they flew me up there to the mine, showed me around, told me the story." Knoll was an associate editor of the *Northern Miner*, a weekly avidly read by many of the people who speculate in the stock of companies that look for gold.

"They're nice guys, the Lac guys," he went on. "Unless you get offside with them. One time I got a press release from Corona saying they weren't suing Lac for three hundred million dollars any more, they were going for three billion. Naturally I wrote the story, and it ran with a headline, 'Three-Billion-Dollar Suit Against Lac.'

"So a few weeks later I went to Lac's head office to get an order for printing. We print a lot of annual reports and shareholders' letters and prospectuses and stuff like that for these companies, and it's more or less automatic that they give us their orders. Only this time Ian Hamilton, their main legal guy, reaches into the drawer of his desk and pulls out a copy of my story with the headline about the three billion dollars and lays it in front of me.

" 'Now you tell me,' he says, 'why we should do business with you if you're going to print stuff like this about us?' "

Knoll frowned and shook his head. "It took me a lot of time and a lot of work to get that account back," he said.

After lunch Alan Lenczner went in a single bound from the fiduciary relationship to something he called "the springboard doctrine". Some years ago in England a man invented a better carpet grip and went looking for a company to manufacture it. (A carpet grip — well may you ask — is a grip set on the floor to hold in place a carpet laid on top of it.) One company gave the inventor a hearing and looked carefully at his drawings but in the end rejected his design. Before long the same company began to make and sell carpet grips that looked painfully familiar to the inventor, who sued. The company argued that everybody knew how to make carpet grips. The inventor's lawyer replied that his client's carpet grip was not like everybody else's, and that the features that created the difference had been shown to the manufacturer in confidence. Not so, said the company — there can be no breach of confidence about something everybody knows.

The English judge found the company guilty, Lenczner said. Information, the judge decided, does not have to be secret to be confidential. Anybody can take public information — something everybody knows — and by applying the brain to it, create an idea that might be passed on in confidence. The inventor of the carpet grip had seen the necessity, the judge said, for "a strong sharp tooth" and had passed this insight on to the company in confidence.

"The law on this subject does not depend on any implied contract," the judge wrote. "It depends on the broad principle of equity that he who has received information in confidence shall not take unfair advantage of it. He must not make use of it to the prejudice of him who gave it without obtaining his consent." Much of the information the inventor had given the company was indeed freely available to the public, the judge acknowledged. "Nevertheless, the germ of the idea and the broad principle . . . was I am certain implanted in their minds by the plaintiff, and afterwards subconsciously reproduced and used, if only as a springboard. . . ."

Lenczner spoke of several other cases in which one party's confidential information became the springboard for another party's gain. There was, he said, the three-girl rock'n'roll group who took a program idea to a television network; the network rejected the girls' outline and later broadcast a program based on the same idea. (My marginal note to myself at this point says, "How many people have worked in television for more than six months without getting the fixed idea that somebody, somewhere, is stealing their best ideas?") Closer to the present issue, there was a consulting geologist named Morrison who went to a client's drilling site, looked at the drill records, then staked the surrounding claims for himself. In court he argued that he could have acquired all the information he got on the site by looking up the public record. "But you didn't," the judge said. "You used their information as a springboard for your own advantage." Finally, there was an industrial-design case brought by a company called Cranleigh Precision Engineering Ltd. It was the judge in this case who set out the clearest formulation of what Lenczner had been calling the springboard doctrine.

"As I understand it," the judge wrote, "the essence of this branch of the law, whatever the origin of it may be, is that a person who has obtained information in confidence is not allowed to use it as a springboard for activities detrimental to the person who made the confidential communication. And springboard it remains even when all the features have been published or can be ascertained by actual inspection by any member of the public."

Lenczner had now brushed in the final strokes of his argument's outline. If the faults he accused Lac of were somewhat abstruse, the cure he proposed was simple.

Lac, he said, had committed two distinct breaches of the law. First, breach of trust: Lac made itself a fiduciary for Corona and then broke the trust. Second, breach of confidence: Lac used Corona's own information as a springboard for activities detrimental to Corona. The law says nobody may profit from either of these breaches. So, Lenczner said, the remedy was clear:

"Lac must give up the Williams claims to Corona."

Judge Holland may have been anticipating without relish listening to a claim for damages based on dense columns of figures with tonnage and dollar signs attached to them. He paused for a moment to savour the simplicity of Lenczner's sentence, then delivered a simpler one of his own.

"So your first position is," he said, "you want the property back?"

"Yes," Lenczner said.

Courtroom 10 is on the fourth floor, which makes getting out of the building a three-escalator trip. On the way out that afternoon two of Lac's lawyers were on the escalator step behind me.

"What do you suppose the penalty is for subconscious breach of confidence?" one said.

"You'd have to ask a shrink," the other said. "Maybe you get a guilt complex."

Their spirits were running fairly high; they seemed to think that if those were Lenczner's best shots, he was not going to be able to hurt them. My own feelings were mixed. It was true that Lenczner's argument sounded wordy rather than concrete, and that when he made some of his connections he seemed to be reaching for them. On the other hand, his argument was interesting in ways I hadn't expected it to be. While Lenczner was talking I had the feeling he was making the case not just for Corona but for everybody else who has ever entered a transaction with a bigger, stronger, richer second party and come out feeling badly used — the feeling the phrase "I was shafted" had to be invented to describe. There can't be many people who have never said, "Those guys shafted me," then shrugged and said, "but there's nothing I can do about it."

And now here was Corona, in the person of Alan Lenczner, standing up in court and trying to do something about it, unexpectedly stretching a quarrel between two companies over a division of spoils into an issue that could touch any one of us. The note I wrote to myself that evening said, "There seems to be no statute law that applies here, so in a way Lenczner is asking the judge to make a new application of the case law that Lenczner claims *does* apply. The judge, perhaps, becomes more important than he would be in a different kind of case — a more conventional one."

That night I went to the race-track for dinner with friends, one of whom, Jake Howard, is a distinguished lawyer. Some months earlier Jake had been retained by the firm defending Lac to read the documents in the case and give a second opinion. As he was obliged to do, he avoided telling me what that opinion was, but when I mentioned my notion about Lenczner taking his argument into little-travelled regions of the law and thereby making the judge unusually important to the outcome, Jake looked at me slantwise, as he sometimes does when I have given an opinion about the prospects of a horse.

"Don't kid yourself," he said. "There's only one issue in that trial."

"Lenczner claims there are two," I said. "Fiduciary responsibility and breach of confidence."

"No," Jake said. "One. The issue is, who will the judge believe? Sheehan or Bell?"

O PENING LAC'S DEFENCE,
John Lorn McDougall spoke in a key so low he was almost inaudible, like an
actor who wants all of his upper register to be available when the time
comes to extend himself. Artfulness, indeed, was apparently the impression
McDougall sought to make. He had a tall, lean body and a thin, patrician
face, topped by long brownish hair that fell across his forehead in waves.
Altogether he cut a decidedly English figure, and his manner of speaking,
carefully modulated and highly articulated, reinforced that impression. Like
Judge Holland, he had a mid-Atlantic accent, and they seemed to share a
taste for long words. Early in his opening he made a dismissive reference to
"the seminal theory" of David Bell's, to which the judge replied, "I see you've
been reading the decisions of Justice Laskin — you use that word." (The late
Bora Laskin, for many years the Chief Justice of the Supreme Court of Canada, was a writer for whom no two-syllable word would do if he could say
the same thing in three or more.)

The judge smiled. McDougall said, "Quite right, M'lord," and smiled
back.

In a criminal trial the authorities lay a charge against the person accused
of having committed the crime. The equivalent in a civil trial is a document called "the statement of claim", which is set out not by the authorities
but by the party that claims to have been wronged. Yesterday, before opening his case, Lenczner asked the judge to accept an amended statement of
claim from Corona. Against bitter opposition from John Lorn McDougall,
the judge accepted the amended claim. Today McDougall opened his defence
of Lac by attacking claims that Corona was no longer making.

Corona's first claim was filed with the court in 1981. That was the one,
McDougall said, that "shows the true complaint in this case", which was
that Lac entered a partnership agreement with Corona on May 6, 1981,
and then "fraudulently and negligently" broke the agreement. Between that
time and this the allegation of a violated partnership has disappeared.

The day before the trial opened, McDougall said, "We were dealing with
the amended amended *amended* claim." This latest statement of claim was

an amendment to that. In this distant descendant of the original claim, he
went on, "the gravamen of the plaintiff's case is confidential information."
But this allegation, like the vanished claim of a breached partnership agreement, has no foundation in fact; none whatever.

"You will hear evidence from Mr. Sheehan," McDougall told the judge,
"that he asked Mr. Bell *not* to tell him anything that was confidential." As
to the claim that Bell and Sheehan agreed that Corona was to acquire the
Williams property, "Mr. Sheehan's testimony will be that there never was
any such agreement." Indeed, McDougall said, Lac was trying to get some
kind of agreement worked out with Corona but couldn't even get started,
because "Corona never told Lac what they wanted."

Later, McDougall described a conversation that took place between
Sheehan and Bell on May 6, 1981. After the session in the core shack, the
two men went for a walk on the Corona property. Bell claims that they
discussed areas of interest and that he told Sheehan Corona intended to go
after both the Williams ground and the Hughes claims. Sheehan says absolutely not; Bell told him that Corona was just a small company without
much money to spare, and was "happy with its land position".

Judge Holland broke in on McDougall here. "Does the ownership of a
mining claim," he asked, "give you the right to keep other people off the
claim if you don't want them there?"

"Not in law," McDougall said. "But I've heard of people doing it with
everything from shotguns to bears."

Judge Holland leaned forward. When he is at rest, listening, his features
are heavy and his expression almost sullen. But when he stirs to speak his
eyebrows climb towards the tufts of hair on either side of his bulbed forehead and his small mouth unfolds into a pink budlike smile.

"I'm wondering," he said, "where they get the bears?"

An appreciative murmur ran around the courtroom. By this time I was
beginning to understand that when you spend entire days in court you have
to contend with a physical problem that everybody else in the room shares.
The problem is how to avoid falling asleep, or at least how to doze lightly
enough that when somebody says something you want to hear it will get
through to you. The professionals seem to have a variety of solutions to the
problem including, in a few cases, ignoring it. One of the judge's officials,
an elderly fellow with great white balls of hair above his eyes, mouth, and
ears, falls asleep within minutes of taking his seat and maintains a dignified
upright slumber unless the judge calls on him directly, which seldom happens; he wakes apparently by instinct just before it's time to get up again
and leave by the back door. Some of the lawyers who crowd the large tables
on either side of the space before the judge's dais spend a lot of their time

looking into legal documents. What the judge sees is the fan
blue covers and spiral bindings of briefs or transcripts. What
sees from the back of the room, looking over the lawyers' shoul{
these document covers often come out of the briefcase holding
novels inside them. On the spectator benches there is a fair amount of nodding, but when the nods are followed by heavy breathing there is help at
hand. The guard who earlier stopped me at the door, a merry-faced man in
a blue blazer with a military crest on the pocket, approaches from the rear
and with a discreet grip on the upper-arm helps the sleeper come awake.
Today, on the way back into the courtroom after the morning recess, I
remembered the warning of the ancient Roman lawgivers always to ask
who watches the watchers. Accordingly I stopped to ask the guard at the
door who wakes him when he nods off.

"Nobody," he said. "But I'm usually okay."

"How come?"

"There's this game I play — here, I'll show you." He pulled from his breast
pocket a sheaf of old envelopes, all of them covered with short words printed
in block letters. "I take a long word and see how many short words I can
make out of it. Twenty's a good score, more than thirty's terrific."

"What's your record?"

"I've hit thirty-five a few times, but I've never hit forty. You want to look
for words with a lot of vowels; if you can find one with all the vowels, they're
the best."

"Did you take a shot at 'fiduciary'?"

"Yesterday. It was so-so. 'Unauthorized' was better."

What the word game does for the guard, Judge Holland's remark about
the bears had briefly done for the rest of us. It had blown a change of air —
where *do* they get those bears? — into minds being lulled by the repetition
of legal formulas.

My first stop during the lunch break was again the public library. Finding
the word took ten minutes because I didn't even know how to spell it. I
looked up "gravoman". "gravomen", "graviman", "gravimen", and "gra-
vimon" before I found it. "Gravamen: the part of an accusation that weighs
most heavily against the accused." That "men" on the end of the word is
singular; the plural is "gravamina". Truly.

I went to lunch with a friend who produces movies, a calling whose sur-
viving practitioners learned early to keep their elbows up in the corners. He
asked how the case was going. When I told him, he thought for a moment
and said, "Are you going to bet on it?"

"Probably," I said, "but I haven't decided which way yet."

"Bet Lac," he said.

"Why?"

"Those Corona people, Bell and, what was it, Dragovan? Their first time out, what did they know? They kept talking too long and it cost them. That's not a crime; it's business."

When I got back to the courtroom, the guard was at his place by the door. "What do you think?" I asked him, nodding towards the lectern where McDougall was rearranging his papers. "How's he doing?"

"Who knows?" the guard said. "I'm thinking of trying 'auriferous' this afternoon."

I considered offering him "gravamina", but there weren't enough vowels to make it worth his while, so I went in and opened my notebook.

A trained gunner fires two preliminary rounds, one short and one long, to bracket his target; the third round does the damage. McDougall's manner now suggested he had Corona bracketed. He raised his voice, hardened his tone, and launched a barrage aimed at reducing the Corona case to rubble.

The law establishes four tests that must be met before a defendant can be found guilty of breaching a confidence, McDougall said. First, the aggrieved party must prove that the information really was imparted in confidence. Second, that the information so imparted really was confidential — that it wasn't material anybody could get from public sources. Third, that the recipient made unauthorized use of the material to the detriment of the party that disclosed it. And fourth, that the way the recipient used the information cannot be justified.

Measured against these tests, McDougall argued, the case against Lac ceased to exist. Not only did Corona fail to stipulate that there was anything confidential about the information Lac got, but Sheehan told Bell in so many words that he didn't want to hear anything that was confidential.

"You can't give somebody information and then come along later and say, 'Now this is all confidential.' You've got to say so beforehand. That's only common sense."

As for the second test, the character of the information itself, McDougall claimed there was nothing confidential about it. Indeed, the contrary was true: Corona was going out of its way to press the same information on anybody who would listen. The drill results Sheehan saw in the core shack? A press release went to the Vancouver Stock Exchange every time Corona had a fresh drill result to report, and every report that had any significance was published in a daily market circular called the *George Cross Newsletter*. Corona even flew Bell to Vancouver at this time to make a personal appearance in what stock promoters call a dog-and-pony show — Bell, that is, pressed on a large audience of brokers, investors, and consultants as much information about Corona's Hemlo drilling program as he could get them to sit still for. Information, McDougall argued, has to be withheld from *somebody* before it can be passed on in confidence to somebody else; without an element of secrecy there cannot be an element of confidence.

Corona's case failed just as badly by the third test. What would have happened, McDougall asked, if Lac had made use of Corona's information? Assays of Corona's drill cores indicated that the gold content of the rock "horizon" the drills were probing rose towards the east and fell towards the west. The Williams claims lay to the west; Corona's information, had Lac used it, would have led Lac *away* from the Williams property, where the gold values appeared to be pinching out.

Since the information was useless, indeed downright misleading, the fourth test — was the use made of the information justified? — scarcely need be applied. But the judge would later hear, McDougall said, testimony from some of the most luminous figures in the realm of mineral exploration, men such as the celebrated Dr. David Robertson and the almost legendary Dr. Duncan Derry. From them, McDougall told Judge Holland, he would hear what they or indeed any reasonable man with a professional knowledge of exploration-industry standards would have done in Lac's place. They would have done what Lac did. Corona, on the other hand, is now doing what losers often do, though most of them don't go to court to do it. "They are trying," he said, "to make up the rules after the game."

A Memory

· ·

*For almost a generation, gold bullion was air-freighted
from London to Hong Kong, passing through in
transit to Macao, originally aboard an ancient
Catalina flying boat. . . .*

— Timothy Green, *The New World of Gold*

These are the rules of the gold trade as I began to learn them on the China
Coast at the beginning of the 1950s:

1. There are no rules you can depend on.

2. Information you give somebody else is not confidential unless nobody
wants to listen. Information you get from somebody else is probably a lie.

3. Gold has no nationality, no sentiment, and little practical value outside the practice of the dental arts. None the less, should you lay your hands
on some, somebody will shortly try to take it away from you.

4. Gold moves in the direction of trouble.

In the winter of 1950 Bob Crompton and I left Vancouver to go looking,
much as my father had, though unlike him we weren't looking for gold. We
just wanted to see what the world was like, and we stumbled through the
back door of the gold trade before we knew it was there. Lacking a horse,
we had gone to sea, shipping out of Galveston, Texas, in the MV *Ferncape*,
a Norwegian tramp freighter bound for Hong Kong. The Red Army was
then completing the conquest of China. Among the people awash in that sea
of troubles were thousands of displaced Westerners, many of whom were
engaged in devising new forms of larceny. These, at one stage or another,
almost always involved the movement of gold.

Scott Carr was a gold-mover. We met him, not long after we came ashore
in Hong Kong, at the Foreign Press Club, a Colonial relic even then going

gloriously to seed on the side of Victoria Peak. Carr was an Australian pilot in his early thirties, ten years older than we were, but he formed an instant friendship with us, or rather with Bob. At that time Bob was a rail-thin redhead, six feet four inches tall. He had an amiable face partly hidden by freckles and an absolute lack of the self-consciousness that usually keeps one stranger aloof from another — in the course of an elevator ride I've known him to talk eight strangers into joining an all-night party. Within an hour of meeting Carr, Bob knew the story of his recent life.

Carr had ended the war flying the Burma Hump for General Claire Chennault's celebrated Flying Tigers. He was now piloting Catalina flying boats for the fledgling commercial airline, CAT, that Chennault had organized after the war. (The initials stood for "Civil Air Transport", but had obviously been chosen to evoke the Flying Tigers.) Until this time CAT's activities had not, in truth, been all that civil; most of the line's air miles were flown to move supplies and people for the Chinese Republican Army. With the Republic's defeat Chennault was now trying to negotiate landing rights and contracts with the new government, clearly no easy switch to accomplish and one that in the end was beyond his powers of persuasion, great though these were. While Chennault negotiated, what, we asked Carr, was he doing?

"Still flying," Carr said.

"Where?"

"Here and there."

"Carrying what?"

"This and that," Carr said. "You know."

We didn't know, not yet, but before long we knew other things about Carr. He lived in an apartment on the Peak with a sweep of glass looking down on the city and the harbour, much the same view the Governor looked out on from his mansion along the brow of the hill. To Carr's door women came at all hours, stewardesses who flew for international airlines, singers and dancers booked into local clubs, tall elegant northern Chinese who came and went in chauffeured limousines and who did — what? Somehow we thought it would be rude to ask them and when we asked Carr he shook his bright curls and told us to figure it out for ourselves. My guess was that they were either the mistresses of men who were at home with their wives, or call girls with unimaginable talents and fees. Then a Pan Am pilot who partied with Carr when he was in Hong Kong between flights told me that one of these flawless women was the daughter of a vice-president of the Hong Kong and Shanghai Bank. She was an example, the pilot said, of the powerful connections Carr had on the mainland — even if he was forced down he had friends who could get him out of China. Startled, I asked why Carr would be forced down? The Pan Am pilot looked at me as though I should have known better than to ask, which I suppose I should, and walked away. When I tried to strike up a conversation with the banker's daughter she composed her perfect face into a bland smile and answered in Chinese.

Until those evenings with Carr I don't believe it had crossed my mind that a man might be glamorous. Apart from the pay, male movie actors seemed to have very little going for them; they were obliged to wear make-up on the job and hang around the set for hours before doing a few minutes' work. Some athletes and artists were admirable and some rich or powerful men were enviable, but *Carr*, ah, Carr with his flying boat and glass-walled apartment and seemingly effortless access to these unspeakably attractive, impenetrably indifferent (to me) young women — it was only now, with Carr there in front of me in life rather than on paper or on stage or on screen, that I became aware of male glamour.

We were rolling liars' dice at the Foreign Press Club one night with Carr and some other people who had nothing to do with the press when a big muscular square-headed man whose eyes were a paler shade of blue than his jaw came into the bar. Carr threw an arm around the man's shoulder and they exchanged mock insults. The newcomer was an American sea captain, master of a small tramp freighter that was registered in Panama but traded mainly in the South China Sea. Earlier that day he had reached Hong Kong after many weeks on the coasts of Java and Sumatra. He would be in Hong Kong for a couple of weeks while his ship's shaft bearings were repacked, and then he'd sail for Singapore. By the end of the evening he'd offered to sign us on as members of the deck crew, if we'd give him our word not to do any work — the Chinese deck-hands were touchy, he said, and they'd refuse to work if he put us to work with them. Well, we said, if he insisted, we supposed we could refrain from chipping rust for a week or two.

We thought we might find jobs in Hong Kong for the days before the tramp sailed, but everybody we asked turned us down; we couldn't work beside Chinese, they said, because the Chinese would quit. The last place we tried was a big shop — we thought maybe we could look after English-speaking customers — run by a Goanese merchant. After he had said no, he said, "Let me ask you a question: what will you do if you can't find work?" We told him we were going to sail for Singapore in a small tramp freighter.

"Are you in a position," he asked with consummate Goanese delicacy, "to make a small investment prior to departure?"

"Why?"

"Because there are more profitable avenues of enterprise open to you than finding a job. You are naturally aware that Hong Kong is a free port, but are you aware that Singapore is not? And that there are certain, ah, valuables that command prices many times higher in Singapore than they do in Hong Kong?"

"Such as?"

"What are your thoughts about . . . gold?"

"Why would we think about it? We haven't got any."

"That is regrettable," he said, "but not insuperable." He reached into a display case to pick up one of his Rolexes, dull and heavy as bullion, and let it swing from his fingers by the band.

Climbing the ship's ladder to the deck we placed our feet on the rungs with the precision of Blondin walking a wire in a high wind. Under our jacket sleeves our forearms were strapped to the elbows with watches made, more or less, of gold. Had we set a foot wrong and fallen into the harbour we might well have drowned. At best we'd have rusted out the watches, and on them rested our prospects as the most undercapitalized and surely the least worldly speculators ever to enter the gold trade on the South China Sea.

At sea we fell into the habit of trying to keep the captain talking as late as we could in the evenings. Nautically speaking, we learned, he had been something of a child prodigy, with a younger brother even more precocious than he was. In 1941 they had both been working their way through a merchant-marine officers' school on the Atlantic coast when the United States went to war. At nineteen our friend had already qualified for a second-mate's ticket. He went straight into the navy. By the time he was twenty-two he was made master of a newly launched destroyer. His first assignment was to set a speed record for a west-to-east Atlantic crossing; nobody told him why. He ran the engines at revs that popped rivets all over the hull. He told us he made Ireland from Boston in something under two days at an average speed of something over forty knots. He ran the bearings, burnt out the piston rings, and buckled the shaft. "They had to tear out everything below the shelter deck and throw it away," he told us. "That was the most fun I ever had at sea."

After the war he went back to merchant ships. For a time he was captain of a freighter that ran regularly between New York and Genoa. The Mediterranean basin after the war went through a sort of golden age of smuggling, to which he did his part to add lustre. Preparation, he said, was nine-tenths of successful smuggling; the other tenth was observation. In Italy, for instance, there was a thriving black market in American cigarettes — but how many cartons of cigarettes could you hide from the customs inspectors when you entered the country? However, he had observed that the customs inspectors not infrequently took the cartons they confiscated and sold them on the black market at some risk to themselves. The captain went to the man in charge of the customs patrol boats in the port of Genoa with a proposal to make smuggling simpler for everybody, smuggler and customs officer alike. With his preparations complete he sailed back to New York and began loading his vessel for the return voyage. He instructed his third mate, the officer in charge of stowing cargo, to make a mistake in loading number two hatch. Not a big mistake, just enough to leave room for another six to eight tons. Then, when the longshoremen had worked their last shift, a few trucks rolled down onto the dock and the third mate directed a few members of the crew to offload the trucks and stow the contents in the space left by the mistake in two hatch. The captain himself never laid eyes on this informal cargo until his ship was lying outside the three-mile limit at Genoa. Then he made a radio call to the customs official he was dealing with. Within half an hour three or four customs cutters came alongside, each of them capable of carrying a couple of tons. Under the practised eye of the third mate it took no time at all to offload six or eight tons into the cutters, which then took off, gunning their engines and throwing around a lot of white water. "Everybody goes away happy," the captain said. He thought for a moment and added, "Although it's important to remember that if you're going to stay happy you've got to get the money before they get the cigarettes. Those cutters are *fast*."

When a smuggling run went wrong the fault usually lay in preparation rather than execution. He told us with relish about a plot hatched in New York to smuggle gold to the Middle East, where an ounce of gold acquired for the official price of thirty-five dollars in the United States then would sell for seventy-five or eighty dollars. The smugglers worked out an ingenious plan and took great pains to execute it well. They bought a big Cadillac, stripped off the bumpers, and hired a skilled foundryman to make exact moulds from them. Then they melted down gold bricks and cast replicas of the bumpers. They chrome-plated the gold replicas and bolted them to the car, whereupon the car sagged on its springs until the bumpers touched the concrete. They returned to the drawing board and designed a way to reinforce the Cadillac's suspension with heavy-duty truck springs. Then they sent the car to the pierhead to be loaded aboard a passenger liner as the personal baggage of a middle-aged couple destined for Istanbul on what they described as a combination of business and pleasure.

The Cadillac never got on the boat; the customs inspectors confiscated it on the dock. What went wrong? we asked our friend.

"Lack of preparation," he said. "If they'd shipped the car as cargo they'd have been fine — it's a flat rate for the space. But personal baggage, that goes by the pound. Everything goes on the scales. So all of a sudden these guys are standing there, the longshoremen and the union guy and the customs guy, and they're all staring at a Cadillac that weighs about as much as a Sherman tank. The judge gave the guy eighteen months, suspended sentence on the wife, and confiscated the bumpers. As far as I know they got to keep the car."

The story rattled us, and a day or two later we told the captain we were up to the elbows in gold watches.

"Rolexes?" he asked.

We told him we couldn't afford Rolexes but we had all these other makes, some of which we'd heard of before, and anyway what did it matter? The merchant we bought them from gave them to us at cost, so we couldn't go wrong — could we?

"This merchant, what's his name?"

We told him, and asked if he knew him.

"Never heard of him," he said. "But I'll tell you one thing. That guy can really sell watches."

The tramp's starboard bow was off the North Vietnamese province of Cochin China, a French colony few English-speaking people had then heard of, when the captain came into the saloon one morning with a long wireless message in his hand. He told us there was bad news about Carr. His flying boat was down, somewhere outside Macao, and he was in the hands of the Red Army. We asked what would happen to him.

"They'll lock him up and eat the key," the captain said. "Unless they shoot him first."

"He flies for CAT. How can they lock him up for that?"

"Oh, for God's sake," the captain said, shifting his anger over his friend's trouble to us. "Don't you guys ever know what's going on? Carr flies for CAT some of the time and some of the time he flies for himself. You didn't think he could live the way he does on what Chennault pays him, did you?"

"Yes." We were both worried about Carr. We'd known him less than a month but we'd been taken with his brightness, his generosity, his glamour. Now the captain was telling us Carr was a gold-courier. He ferried gold in large ingots from Hong Kong to Macao, where they were melted down and recast into small bars called *taels* that found their way to every part of China where there was trouble, which was to say every part of China. Carr had flown scores of gold shipments, the captain said, and had refined the technique until the risk was close to zero.

"Then how come he got caught?"

"He must have flown for greedy people."

"They're all greedy," I said, which was more than a little hypocritical given our investment in gold-plated watches.

"You know nothing, and now you're insulting as well. If they were all greedy he'd have gone to jail the first time he flew for them. That's the way it works. Somebody sells you some opium, some smack, some gold — whatever. The next thing he does, if he's greedy, he turns you in. Then he collects the reward."

The captain liked to use bureaucratic language for ironic emphasis. "They call it 'information leading to the confiscation of contraband'," he said. "The reward varies from place to place. In China for gold it's half. You give them information leading, and they give you half the value of any gold they confiscate. So, if you two can follow the logic, when the people you're dealing with don't turn you in you can be pretty sure you haven't run into the greedy people. Not yet."

"Come on — they don't turn in their own customers."

"For another fifty percent? You bet your ass they do."

We didn't quite believe the man who could really sell watches would have turned us in for half the three hundred dollars we'd spent with him. But we were coming to see that there were a lot of things we had no very clear idea about, and this might be one of them.

Ships calling at Singapore drop anchor first well offshore, in an area known as the Outer Roads. Customs and immigration officers come alongside by launch to clear the vessel and crew, and the ship then moves to the Inner Roads. Not until this second anchorage is the vessel free to discharge and take on cargo, and the crew free to go ashore.

Clearing a ship the size of the little tramp we were in takes perhaps three hours. Two full days after she dropped anchor in the Outer Roads we were still there. The ship had scarcely stopped moving when the first cutter came alongside and many small men in oddly formal double-breasted blue suits swarmed aboard, smiling like Barbary pirates taking a fat prize without firing a shot. Some set up guard posts on deck at points from which they could see anybody who tried to slip into the water. Others set up a long trestle table in the saloon, where they began to question and search members of the crew. Bob and I both worked hard to avoid showing on our faces the things a rush of strong juices was doing to our stomachs. We still couldn't believe all these people were here to confiscate some cheap watches, but if they weren't why were they here?

We went below and took the watches out of Bob's club bag. Now what?

There aren't many hiding places in a seaman's cabin: steel bulkheads and floorplates, thin mattresses, a couple of drawers. In the end we stuffed the watches into our work boots, jammed dirty socks on top of them, and left the work boots out on the floor. How were the customs people to know we were under orders never to do any work?

When our turn came we went to the saloon, where the immigration people looked at our Panamanian seamen's tickets and Canadian passports and stamped both. The customs people asked us where we'd been and where we were going, then searched us without finding anything that interested them. When we got back to the cabin we couldn't tell whether it had been searched or not, but the watches were still in the boots. We put them on our arms, pulled long-sleeved shirts over them, and never took them off until we left the ship.

Not long after we changed shirts three customs officers did search the cabin. They ignored the boots and us, but they measured all the walls with steel tapes and checked their figures against blueprints they were carrying. Later we saw them making similar measurements all over the ship — the saloon and the galleys, the wheelhouse, the engine room, even the corridors and companionways. They carried small steel hammers, and now and then one would whack a bulkhead, either because he liked noise or because he thought the echo might tell him something. We heard loud noises from the hatches, where other customs people were shifting cargo. On the second afternoon a larger launch came alongside, our donkeyman was asked to hoist aboard a set of acetylene and oxygen tanks, and a welder started cutting openings in the metal masts. We asked the customs officer in charge of searching the deck why he was cutting up the masts. Smugglers, he said, often opened metal masts, taped packages inside the hollow, and welded the opening shut again. Then they'd grind the welded seam flat and spend days, if necessary, rubbing the surface smooth by hand before giving the entire mast a fresh coat of paint. From outside, he said, it was impossible to tell whether such a mast has been tampered with; all you could do was cut your own hole and take a look.

Late that night a clangour of steel on steel woke us. It came from somewhere up in the bows of the ship, and in the morning all the customs people were gone. We looked for the captain, but he was on the bridge, getting ready to move the vessel to the Inner Roads. We were packed and ready to go ashore, forearms dragging, before we got him alone for a few minutes. The customs people, he told us, had received information from Hong Kong meant to lead to the confiscation of contraband, just as we'd guessed. But this time they hadn't been told where to find it, and they'd almost given up looking. Then they had a shift change at midnight. Somebody on the fresh crew said what the hell, we may as well try everything, so they went up to the forecastle and started running out the anchor chain.

The water in the Outer Roads isn't all that deep. With the anchor holding there were still a few tons of chain piled up in the locker. When they got it all run out they found a steep plate at the bottom of the locker, wedged into the V of the bow. Under the plate there were four blocks of opium wrapped in oilskin. They took the opium off in the cutter at about four in the morning, and a little later they took off two deck-hands from Shanghai. Their names had reached the customs people in Singapore less than an hour after we cleared Hong Kong harbour.

"The deck-hands claim they've never seen the stuff before," the captain said. "But the people in Hong Kong say they sold it to them, and that's enough to convict them. Singapore pays thirty percent for information leading to dope."

"How much for gold?"

"Twenty. But don't let that fool you. The greedy ones will turn you in for ten."

Singapore was slower and hotter than Hong Kong. We tramped the streets for a few days, sweat running from our armpits down past our elbows to collect under the watchbands. The skin there started to turn green, and since we'd found nobody who wanted to buy the watches, we took a "loan" of about half what we'd paid for them from a merchant who said he'd hold them till we got back. Not long after that we found a ship that was making for the west coast of Australia, and sailed out of the South China Sea.

We never heard of Carr again. Two or three years later I read a two-paragraph story in the *New York Times* that said an American merchant-marine captain with the same name as our friend had been captured by a Chinese gunboat while sailing his yacht in Chinese territorial waters. He appeared to have been blown off course, the report said, but the Chinese claimed to have confiscated a large amount of contraband gold hidden aboard his yacht. They intended to make an example of him by imposing a particularly severe jail sentence. Perhaps three years after that the *Times* carried an even shorter story in which he was reported to have been pardoned by the Chinese and was soon to be released. I wrote to him care of the Foreign Press Club in Hong Kong, but heard nothing back.

McKINNON

"We have to go where there is no trail. We have to go where we can be positive that no surveyor or anybody who knows something about mining has ever been before. The best spots are those where you feel sure that anybody who is paid for his job would be afraid to go and would not think it worthwhile to risk his hide for the salary he gets."

— B. Traven, *The Treasure of the Sierra Madre*

"The best place to look for gold is where gold is known to be."

— Donald McKinnon

MR. JUSTICE RICHARD Holland enters his courtroom slowly, climbs the short staircase to his raised bench one step at a time, and lowers himself by degrees into his chair. He sits stiffly, as though any movement might cause him acute discomfort. The impression he gives of momentarily apprehending the onset of pain is strong enough to make itself felt on the spectator benches. Early in the trial I inquired about it, and his law clerk told me that a few years earlier the judge had injured his spine in a car accident. He is now subject to pain from almost any quick action or even from prolonged inaction, such as sitting in one place for a long time. Since this is a form of inactivity no judge can escape, he often feels pain he tries not to reveal. No doubt this is why he appears to be more than ordinarily sensitive to the comfort of others. As each new witness completes the oath, for instance, the judge turns to the witness and points out in tones of the gravest courtesy that there is a stool at the back of the box. The witness may sit or stand, entirely at his own pleasure.

For Donald McKinnon, sitting is out of the question. McKinnon's stance, the way he sets himself in order to face the world, is intended to place him at eye level with anything or anybody he may confront. He is a combative man. Northerners often nourish an inward belief that they belong to a type, a northern breed that is independent, self-reliant, able to endure in conditions that would defeat softer people, by which they mean people who live to the south of them. Northerners have a settled conviction that it's in their nature to *act*, in those situations when coming out ahead, or even coming out alive, depends less on thinking than on doing. McKinnon is of the type Northerners believe they belong to.

He has made some outward changes since I first ran into him towards the end of 1982. Bob Crompton introduced us one evening in a big hotel-lobby lounge in Vancouver. McKinnon then looked like a small-town hardware merchant, his thin straight hair closely barbered by a hard hand, his dark brown suit taken down from a long rack. He was recovering from a skin condition that had been diagnosed as cancerous, though not malignant, and from time to time he passed his fingertips across a patch on his forehead where the natural freckles had been bleached almost white. Sitting, he looked his age, a few years over fifty, but later, when we walked to the street, he moved with the ease and force of the athlete he once was. Although Bob introduced him as the prospector responsible for the gold discovery at Hemlo, there was nothing about him to suggest that here was a most unusual man. His contribution to the round of jokes that precedes conversation in the ritual of the barroom was a standard mining-man story. (Yes, there are mining-man jokes, though like other vocational jokes they are not much told outside the trade, for reasons not far to seek.)

"What's the difference," he asked, "between a black hooker and a geo-physicist?"

All shrugged.

"Her black box works."

Everybody laughed but me. McKinnon looked at me doubtfully, moved his chair closer to mine, and told me in a low voice that the prejudice mani-fested by the joke was directed against geophysicists. (The instrument used by a geophysicist to record the electromagnetic imprints of rocks is known familiarly as a black box.) McKinnon left school in grade ten; he is impa-tient with the theoretical speculation and much of the elaborate classifica-tion of data that fleshes out most geological reports. When he digs such a report out of the archives, as he often does in the course of researching mineral prospects, he reads the summary at the beginning, the conclusions at the end, and skips "all that bullshit in the middle". Like the earlier joke, this remark struck me as fairly standard inverse snobbery, and it wasn't until he started talking about his problem that he caught my full attention.

"They've offered me a hundred million dollars," he said. "Payable in any currency, deposited in any bank in the world."

"That's your *problem?*"

"I wish it was. My problem is that my partners don't want to take it."

In 1982 McKinnon had three partners, John Larche, Rocco Schiralli, and Claude Bonhomme. Larche, another prospector from Timmins, had turned up at Hemlo soon after McKinnon began staking at the end of 1979. On the spot they formed a hand-shake partnership to pool their claims and share whatever might come of them. Some of the claims they pooled that day became the Corona mine. Later they wanted to stake more ground. They formed a grubstake syndicate with two financial partners, a Toronto lawyer, Rocco Schiralli, and his associate in a southwestern Ontario oil-drilling scheme, Claude Bonhomme. Schiralli and Bonhomme put up fif-teen thousand dollars, McKinnon and Larche put up the claims they had already staked and added, over a period of time, a hundred and fifty more. They sold these claims to Richard Hughes and Frank Lang, who in turn sold control of them to Noranda, and Noranda developed on them the mine affectionately known as "the Golden Giant". McKinnon and his partners retained an interest in both mines.

The partners' agreement with Noranda entitled them to 15 percent of the net profit for as long as the mine produced gold. Although this figure was in dispute — Noranda wanted to cut them back to 7.5 percent — McKinnon was now telling me that a merchant bank had offered to buy their share of the Golden Giant's profit from them for a hundred million dollars. If the deal went through his partners would realize a profit on their fifteen-thousand-dollar investment that was beyond my mental ability to calculate. Why, then, did they decline to sell? He shook his head.

"They think the price of gold might go up, the tonnage might go up, the grade might go up, I don't know what all might go up. The idea is, they think they might get more money."

"What do you think?"

"I've been in this game for a long time now, and nobody ever offered me a hundred million dollars before."

In Rocco Schiralli's Toronto office about a year later I listened to Schiralli talking about the pressure he and Claude Bonhomme were under from their southwestern Ontario oil-drilling project. By now they had expected to be pumping oil out of the ground. Instead, they were still pumping money into it and trying to think of a way to reverse the flow.

"The oil play could be worth more to us than Hemlo," Schiralli said. "There's that potential. But in the meantime every hole costs us a hundred and fifty thousand dollars and we're still drilling."

In that case, I said, why not take the hundred million?

"What hundred million?"

"For your interest in the Golden Giant. The New York offer?"

"I never heard of it. Where did you get that?"

"From McKinnon."

Schiralli, a short wide dark man who tends to slouch behind his desk, sat straight up.

"If he had an offer like that and didn't tell me, I'll shoot him." Schiralli laughed, and I reminded myself that what had sounded like a firm offer to the prospector McKinnon may have had so little substance that the lawyer Schiralli couldn't even remember it.

Before I met Donald McKinnon, most of what I knew about finding gold came from reading *The Treasure of the Sierra Madre*. The book made a splendid movie, but they both got prospecting backwards.

"Here on this map," the old prospector Howard told the newcomers Curtin and Dobbs, "I can't make out properly whether it's mountain, swamp, desert, or what. But that shows that the makers of the map themselves don't know for sure what there is. Once on the spot, all you have to do is to wipe your eyes and look carefully around you."

Wrong; going where nobody has ever been is not how gold prospecting works. To see how it does work — how McKinnon, say, led the way to the Golden Giant — you really have to start at the beginning. Between the last days of the ice age and the first days of the twentieth century almost nothing happened on the Pre-Cambrian shield that didn't involve bark or fur. But the laws of history have their loopholes. On the shoreline of a small lake not far from Lake Temiskaming, the Indians of the region sometimes picked up lumps of native silver. With their customary generosity they showed the silver-gathering place to the first white man who passed by, Pierre de Troyes. De Troyes, a captain in the French colonial army, left Quebec in the spring of 1686 in command of a hundred men with orders from the governor to throw the English out of Hudson Bay. Near Lake Temiskaming an Indian guide the French called Coignac took de Troyes on a side trip to the shore of a small lake. There, de Troyes wrote in his journal, he saw a silver vein a hundred feet long. He worked a few samples loose from the vein — "it was hard to do," he noted in his journal — and sent them back to Quebec with Coignac. Nothing whatever came of Coignac's journey, and de Troyes died two years later of scurvy while defending Fort Niagara from an Iroquois siege.

During most of the next two hundred years if the Indians in the vicinity of Lake Temiskaming spoke of silver, nobody showed much interest. Then in 1850 a speculator from Ottawa named E.V. Wright bought timber rights in the area and came across de Troyes's vein, or one just like it. He found a couple of American mining men for partners and drove an adit — a kind of horizontal shaft — into the vein. They took out about ten tons of ore but seem not to have liked what they saw, because they dropped the claim. Two or three other groups later tried working the same ground, with the same result.

By now there had grown up among experts, particularly British mining engineers, a widely held conviction that the Pre-Cambrian rocks of the Canadian Shield were more or less barren of minerals, at least in the quantities that might make somebody rich. It is true that in 1883 engineers building the Canadian Pacific Railway made some rock cuts near the northern extremity of Georgian Bay and found in the rubble a sulphide compound that bore interesting amounts of both nickel and copper. The interest was largely academic, though, since at the time nobody knew how to recover either metal from the sulphides at a reasonable cost, and so it was a good many years before anybody began stripping nickel from the rockbeds at what later became the site of Sudbury.

In the spring of 1900, a new Liberal government in Ontario seeking to shore up a fragile majority decided to set out once again on the old Canadian path to glory, the development of the frontier. By 1900, "frontier" meant the regions between the CPR mainline and Hudson Bay, regions where the great surveyor-explorers had drawn in the twisted lines of the waterways on maps that were otherwise blanker than Voltaire's snowy acres. Before the blackflies started biting that year the government had ten survey crews camped out on the blank spaces. Among the early reports they sent back was a glowing description of a forested flatland near Lake Temiskaming, a hundred miles north of North Bay. Stripped of timber, the surveyors said, the flatland would yield a million acres of rich clay loam for farming. Then came reports of a second flatland, north of the first and sixteen times larger. The survey parties had discovered the silted beds of two great meltwater lakes left by the retreating glaciers. Delighted, the Liberals proclaimed a new northern empire consisting largely of the two lakebeds, renamed the Little Clay Belt and the Great Clay Belt. Early the following summer the government ran a free excursion, by rail and lakeboat, to the Little Clay Belt. A hundred and sixty would-be farmers took the nine-day trip, and a hundred and twenty-five of them took up homesteads on the loam.

That year the Liberals announced plans to build a new railway to the clay belts, both Little and Great. The new line was to be a spur running north from the CPR mainline at North Bay to reach the timber and arable land of the clay belts. But to arrive at the good lands the railwaymen had to cut a line through the badlands, the hundred miles of gnarled and pitted granite that lay between North Bay and Lake Temiskaming. Late in the summer of 1903 the line-cutting crews reached Long Lake, a small lake about four miles southwest of Lake Temiskaming. Two lumbermen walking the right-of-way in search of timber for railway ties stopped and looked up for a moment while they were passing the lake's southeast corner. High on the cliff face they saw a pink stain.

This was the key that unlocked the first great underground treasure vault on the Pre-Cambrian shield. As youngsters both lumbermen had sought their fortunes in the California goldfields. Though they returned with no more money than they took, they did bring back a fair idea of how prospectors worked. They took samples from the pink streak on the cliff face, sent them away for assay, and staked their claim to the ground. Then they went back to work on their timber contract. Within weeks the blacksmith who sharpened drills for the rock-blasting crews staked two more claims on the same side of the lake. Soon after this the province's first official geologist walked in from Lake Temiskaming to see for himself what was going on. Fred La Rose, the blacksmith, was glad to see him. La Rose was trying to melt down in his forge some of the pink-tinged rock from the veins he had staked, which he took to contain copper. The geologist, Dr. Willet Miller, was able to tell La Rose that the pink veins contained no copper but a lot of nickel and a little cobalt, a much rarer mineral that develops a "decomposition bloom" when it's exposed to the air. The bloom is usually pink. Though Miller was not much given to lyrical language, he called the cobalt bloom "beautiful" in his field report. Miller told La Rose that the weather-blackened rocks he had been tossing aside while he gathered the pink ones were chunks of native silver, tarnished by exposure. Some of them, Miller wrote, were as large "as stove lids or cannon balls". Three of the four veins La Rose had staked were similarly rich in silver; the one that had attracted his attention in the first place was a compound of nickel.

Before Miller left for Toronto he crossed the lake with another French Canadian, a railway worker named Tom Hébert, who just the day before had come across yet another exposed vein, this one on the east shore. It was perfect, Miller wrote later, "a text-book vein". Then he went south for the winter.

By spring Miller expected to lead a staking rush north to Long Lake. All winter he churned out pieces for the newspapers and mining journals and carpet-bagged his grab samples, heavy with silver, to every convention and meeting that would let him in the door. Hardly anyone paid attention. The professionals had seen rich grab samples many times before; virtually every mining scheme the amateurs had ever heard about that was located on the Canadian Shield had ended with the exposure of fraud. When Miller went north again in early spring there were only two young men with him, and he was paying both of them. He pitched his tent near La Rose's forge, and the next thing he did was rename the lake. Moved perhaps by the same impulse that had overcome him the previous autumn when he included the word "beautiful" in a geological field report, he now painted on a board the misleading title "Cobalt Station". The nearest station was a hundred miles away and the new track wouldn't reach the camp for months, but the name stuck to both the lake and the town that grew up on its shore.

Within a year there were four mines on the margins of Cobalt Lake; a year after that seventeen; eventually, more than a hundred. The village grew to a shanty city of twelve thousand, suffered the fire that sooner or later devastated most such log-and-tarpaper mining camps, and rose again, this time with an opera hall at the end of the main street. For a time Cobalt became one of those totemistic words that have the power to call forth buy orders on the stock market whether the actual value of the stock is going up or down. Philip Smith, the authorized historian of mining in Ontario, reports that on Wall Street mounted police were called out at one point to "control the crowds clamoring to buy Cobalt stocks". So compulsive was the lure that the seven Guggenheim brothers, who at the time held imperial sway over the Western Hemisphere's copper supply, sent John Hays Hammond to Cobalt. Short of Queen Victoria there could scarcely have been a more august arrival in a town that was still two years away from laying its first sidewalks. To say that Hammond, a mining engineer, worked for the Guggenheims is much like saying that Cardinal Richelieu worked for Louis XIV; he did, but he had a lot going for himself on the side. Hammond was a front-rank celebrity, better known, as celebrities often are, for the size of his income than the scale of his accomplishments. The Guggenheims paid him a quarter of a million dollars a year to look at mining prospects; when they bought a property on his advice, they paid him an additional 25 percent interest in the property. All this made Hammond, as everybody knew, the highest-paid employee in the United States.

Hammond rolled into Cobalt in his private railway car, dressed by his own valet, fed by his own chef, and irrigated by his own wine steward. He was there to look at a mine called the Nipissing Mine — known to mining men in Cobalt as "the Big Nip". Not long after Hammond entrained to go south again the Guggenheims negotiated an option to buy four hundred thousand shares of the Big Nip at twenty-five dollars each. They took down the first hundred thousand shares right away. Quickly the stock went to thirty-five dollars. Then the Guggenheims dropped the option and the Big Nip crashed, losing twenty dollars overnight and another ten within a few months. Meanwhile the mining engineers who were at work evaluating the actual amount of silver in the Big Nip's foliated vein structure were raising their estimates every day, and the Big Nip went on to pay dividends for forty years. Nobody ever found out what it was that had spooked the Guggenheims, if indeed they were spooked. Nor did anybody ever come forward with evidence to support the Toronto rumour that the Guggenheims — or Hammond, their high-priced help — had been industriously selling the Big Nip short at thirty-five dollars, thereby making more money faster than they could conceivably have done by exercising their option at twenty-five.

Conspiracy theories seem to enter mining camps at the same time the first cheque gets back from the smelter. They persist partly because belief in the corruptibility of others is a widely held article of faith, and partly because events often confirm this belief. At Cobalt there were lawyers, Philip Smith writes, "who stored sheafs of charter applications in their desk drawers, and all the promoter had to do was fill in the blanks" before he started cashing other people's cheques. Between Cobalt and Hemlo much changed in the mining camps, but this did not.

Most of the rocks at Cobalt were bare of glacial debris, and the silver-bearing veins were either at the surface or close to it. A dozen years after Dr. Miller's long winter of vainly trying to give away this bonanza, the veins of Cobalt had been bled of almost three hundred million ounces of silver. Much of it had been easy to find and simple, if backbreaking, to mine. As a consequence far more money came out of the ground than had gone into it. For almost the first time since the fur trade a group of Canadians made a lot of money without being forced to raise capital by going into hock to British or American bankers. Having gambled and won, many of them were more than willing to gamble again; nobody will buy more lottery tickets next week than the winners of this week's draw. So the new rich of Cobalt financed a native Canadian mineral-exploration industry.

As much as any of the so-called cultural industries that proclaimed their own importance a few generations later, this was a talent industry. Prospectors, engineers, geologists began to learn skills here that were known to very few others anywhere. They learned how to find and unlock some of the deepest vaults in the Pre-Cambrian shield and strip them of their treasure. They were practising a craft, to be sure, but they were also contributing to the creation of a pool of talent that from time to time has achieved almost magical effects.

Within a few years of the discovery at Cobalt, talent trained there followed the railway to the Great Clay Belt. As the politicians had promised, agriculture was possible here — barely. Settlers had cleared a few farms, and were now struggling to balance the fertility of the soil against the hostility of the climate. Timber companies were logging the first-growth pine and hemlock and cutting pulpwood on poorer tracts of soil. But the chances of drawing people in any numbers to this bleak prospect were dim.

The first arrivals from the mining camp at Cobalt made the outlook no brighter, since there wasn't much a prospector could do with the tools of the time to get at whatever treasure might be buried under two hundred or three hundred feet of post-glacial mud. Here and there, though, a ridge of the underlying rock broke through the clay. One such outcrop broke the surface just west of Porcupine Lake, about a hundred miles northwest of Cobalt. A prospector named Reuben D'Aigle staked seven claims here in 1906, judging the quartz outcrop to show some promise of bearing gold. D'Aigle was a New Brunswicker who had made his way to the Klondike at nineteen, found nothing, gone on to Alaska, and was working a good claim there when word came of the bonanza at Cobalt. He sold his claim and walked out of the backwoods, pushing his bagged gold dust ahead of him in a wheelbarrow. When he reached Cobalt, though, the camp already felt crowded to him, and he kept going till he reached Porcupine Lake. Samples from his quartz outcrop yielded enough gold to encourage him but not enough to mine. From spring to autumn the next year D'Aigle cut trails and striped his claims with trenches, but found nothing. He abandoned the outcrop and never came back to the Porcupine. Two years later another pair of young prospectors from Cobalt, Alex Gillies and Benjamin Hollinger, reached Porcupine Lake and found all the ground around it staked — earlier that year a group led by a prospector named Jack Wilson had discovered a huge arch of gold-bearing quartz that soon became known around the world as "the Dome". Pressing past the staked ground that already surrounded the Dome, Gillies and Hollinger found a few miles to the northwest an old trail that led to an open pit. They had rediscovered Reuben D'Aigle's claims, though they hadn't yet found his old corner posts, and they now began restaking them. Gillies later wrote that he was cutting a discovery post while Hollinger pulled moss off the rocks a few feet away, when "suddenly he let a roar out of him. At first I thought he was crazy." Gillies went over to see what the shouting was about: "The quartz where he had taken off the moss looked as though someone had dripped a candle along it, but instead of wax it was gold."

According to Noah Timmins, who had arrived in Cobalt to keep store and departed a mining magnate, "news of the strike at Porcupine travelled like wildfire". Among the places the fire reached was Montreal, where Timmins and his brother Henry had gone into conspicuous retirement after selling their holdings in Cobalt to such newcomers as Bernard Baruch, the American financier, statesman, and scholar. Now Timmins made the first rail connection he could to the Porcupine and started again. He took a $330,000 option on the claims staked by Gillies and Hollinger, with $2,000 down and the rest to come. The mine he developed ran without stopping for more than half a century and yielded gold worth more than half a billion dollars at thirty-five dollars an ounce or less. Hollinger gave his name to the mine. Noah Timmins gave his name to the city of thirty-five thousand people that eventually grew up around the Hollinger and the Dome and the score of mines that followed them. The name of Reuben D'Aigle was largely forgotten.

Among the prospectors who swarmed from camp to camp in the great staking rushes at the turn of the century, an American, Harry Oakes, was one of very few who had trained for the trade, a qualified professional among enthusiastic amateurs. Oakes graduated in engineering from Bowdoin College in Maine, and spent his journeyman years tracking gold strikes from California to Australia, the Philippines, Mexico. He was in Alaska, searching for placer gold, when he heard rumours about Kirkland Lake, an area not far from the already famous Porcupine camp.

Oakes struck out for Kirkland Lake, but on the way he made two stops. One was to the Bureau of Mines in Toronto, the other to the mining recorder's office at Matheson, where staking records for the Kirkland Lake area were filed. He picked up whatever had been recorded about the area, including the location of a claim on the south shore of the lake that was soon to lapse for non-performance of the required assessment work. As soon as he reached the camp he staked this claim in a nominee's name, and later added two adjoining claims that were thrown open for the same reason.

Oakes staked his claims on the shore of Kirkland Lake in 1911. By the summer of 1912 he had staked or bought two more adjacent claims. Now, with his "land position secured" — a phrase that would recur like a chorus in the dispute over the claims at Hemlo — Oakes set out to drill his own ground. He worked compulsively, sinking all the money he could lay his hands on into the rock under the lake, missing the vein by inches and coming back to drill again. At one point his mine manager, whose salary Oakes had been paying partly in stock, is reported to have sold every share he had for ten cents each.

Oakes seems to have been fixated on owning his own gold mine, a state of mind that usually ends in bankruptcy. For Harry Oakes it led to the Lakeshore, in its day one of the richest gold mines in the world. Not long after the end of the First World War the stock his manager had sold for a dime was quoted at sixty-four dollars. Oakes, in the words of mining historian Philip Smith, had become "one of the few prospectors in Canadian history to stake the claims, raise the financing, and develop a mine to the production and dividend-paying stage without losing control of it."

Now Oakes went on to acquire a string of mansions. He built the first on top of the tailings from the Lakeshore; built another in Niagara Falls; bought a third in England, where a grateful monarch made him a baronet; built yet another in the Bahamas. Here, midway through the Second World War, somebody killed him, thereby making the most celebrated prospector of his time the victim of the most notorious unsolved murder.

What followed was less operatic than either the life or the death of Sir Harry. Jack Allen, a Toronto stockbroker, flew to Nassau and bought the Lakeshore mine from Sir Harry's widow, largely with the Lakeshore's own money. On this foundation he assembled a mining group that eventually became Lac Minerals Ltd., of which in 1980 his son Peter was president and Dennis Sheehan was vice-president in charge of exploration.

L ATE IN 1983 DON McKINNON
and I got up one morning before first light reached his house outside
Connaught, a village not far from Timmins. Stumbling now and then in
the dark I carried my bag out to his van and went back inside to pick up a
video camera and portable recorder that were a recent gift from McKinnon to
his wife, Stephanie. She was still asleep, as were their infant daughter and
his two sons from an earlier marriage. Moving quietly to avoid waking them,
McKinnon brought out a box of files and maps and loaded them into the
van alongside his overnight bag. When he started the van we still hadn't
spoken. As he backed and turned, the headlights picked out the second-
storey addition to the house where he was installing a new computer and
the electronic data system that went with it. Then the lights swung across
the small lake behind the house, came to the old barn where his boys stored
their motorcycles, and passed on to the new barn where his wife stabled her
horses. Whatever the headlight beams fell on, the bare poplars and the
skin of ice on the lake, the roofs of the buildings and the old grass in the
paddocks, the unmoving animals and the machines — everything we saw
became silver and then, like a scene from an old, old television show, faded
to black. When we entered the long gravel lane leading to the road he broke
the morning silence.

"There's no reason for me ever to leave this place," he said. "I think I'll
die here."

We were retracing McKinnon's first staking trip to Hemlo. A mile or two
down the gravel road, a left turn and half a dozen miles on the two-lane
blacktop, and we were at another intersection. "Over your right shoulder,"
he said. "You see it?"

"See what?" I still wasn't altogether awake.

"The Kidd Creek mine."

I looked again. Against the dark horizon there was an irregular rectangle of
denser black. It might have been a mill.

"That's the Texas Gulf discovery," McKinnon said. "Now look over there."
He pointed towards the horizon beyond the profile of the mill. "Along that
treeline? About three miles south. Those are the Windfall claims."

The Windfall Affair, as it came to be known, was probably the noisiest stock-market scandal in Canadian history.

"Windfall was the first time out for me," McKinnon said. "And the truth is, until Hemlo it was the best time."

The Texas Gulf Sulphur Company was an American multinational that true to its name had grown rich and powerful producing sulphur, first on the American coast of the Gulf of Mexico and later in other sulphur-rich parts of the world. Towards the end of the 1950s the men running Texas Gulf decided the time had come to adopt the corporate fashion of the day and diversify. They saw little need, however, to stray far from the stuff they knew best. Sulphur is not an entirely sociable substance, particularly for anybody who happens to be downwind of it, but it does have an easy-going ability to combine with other minerals. Compounds so formed are called sulphides, and they often contain valuable concentrations of lead or zinc, copper or nickel, silver or gold. The host for most of the silver at Cobalt was a sulphide compound, as was the host for the nickel deposits at what later became Sudbury. Finding a sulphide deposit is far from finding a mine, but it can be a promising start. The Texas Gulf people now set out to take an inventory of the sulphide deposits in Eastern Canada.

At ground level the job would have taken longer than any of them had left to live, but as a legacy of the recent wars there were among them men capable of getting the job off the ground. Their chief geologist, Walter Holyk, had spent the Second World War in the Royal Canadian Air Force, and their chief geophysicist, H. Van Donohoo, had practised his trade in the U.S. Army during both the Second World War and the Korean War. Between them, they devised an airborne electromagnetic survey and a set of helicopter-mounted instruments to carry it out.

By 1959 Texas Gulf had mapped hundreds of magnetic anomalies from the air. At a few they had already started drilling, at others they had sent men in to look around on the ground. One of these anomalies lay just seventeen miles outside Timmins, almost within eyesight of the headframes at the Dome and Hollinger mines. They and several other mines of the storied Porcupine camp were still producing gold but in dwindling amounts, and it seemed that the mines, and Timmins itself, had entered their last long decline.

Texas Gulf sent a young Canadian geologist named Kenneth Darke to look at the Timmins anomaly, which was located on the map sheet named "Kidd Creek". Darke sketched the area and took his sketch down to the registry office, where he found that the rock structure he was interested in lay beneath three different private lots. Two were owned by the estates of Boer War veterans, to whom the Ontario government of the time had offered free lots. The third was owned by a subsidiary of the Curtis Publishing Company, which harvested wood pulp in the region.

Texas Gulf immediately made offers for all three lots, proposing the usual option in which modest cash payments would be followed by a share of the profits — in this case 10 percent — should further exploration of the subsurface lead to the development of a mine. But with two sets of trustees and one set of publishing executives, along with their lawyers and consultants, all arguing the fine print of the Texas Gulf proposal, the negotiations stretched until late in 1963.

Texas Gulf moved the first diamond drill onto the anomaly in November of that year. Before Christmas, executives in New York had seen the assay report on the first hole. The rumour mill now began to overheat, and before long it seemed that everybody who could sharpen the end of a pole was staking claims on the featureless grey plain, including a thirty-year-old logging crew foreman named Donald McKinnon.

"I was the walking boss for the company that owned the ground. The ones that had the *Saturday Evening Post?* Curtis — that's it. So I knew that ground, every inch of it. Texas Gulf, we'd seen them flying their helicopters in there for two, three years. All in back of that treeline there."

McKinnon swept his right hand towards the skyline on my side of the van.

"Curtis owned most of the timber lots, but some of the other lots, when the owners had cut the timber off them they thought they were worthless, so they let them go for the back taxes. That's how I started prospecting, staking some of those lots that had come open.

"What did I know about staking claims? Damn all. I got a prospector who lived in Timmins, a friend of mine named John Larche, to show me. Some of the claims we went into partnership on, John, me, sometimes another guy, Fred Rousseau, and sold them together. They knew prospecting, I knew the ground, every inch. I knew where the steel posts were, I'd opened up the township lines. I'd been logging in there for three years, and when you're logging you can't go across the property line because then you're cutting somebody else's wood. You *better* know where you are."

The winter of 1963-64 passed. Helicopters chartered by Texas Gulf flew back and forth above McKinnon's head. McKinnon sold a few claims in partnership with Larche and Rousseau, and a few on his own. He made more money than he spent, but he saw no reason to quit his day job. He heard the rumours of a rich strike, he heard the denials, he heard the rumours again.

Darke's drill was down no more than one hundred and fifty feet when the drillers pulled a core that Darke could see with his unaided eye was a sulphide compound bearing copper and zinc. Immediately he started taking security measures. Until the hole was complete, he held the core under lock and key and then quietly sent it all the way to Salt Lake City for assay. He piled brush over the discovery hole. Then, revealing a stage-magician's talent for misdirection, he moved the drill to the far corner of the property, off the anomaly altogether, and hid nearby a pile of core that contained absolutely nothing of any value. He hid the core pretty well, but not so well that anybody who trespassed on the property to spy on the drill results couldn't find it and draw his own, mistaken, conclusions.

Although Texas Gulf held the assay report for this first hole in secrecy until April 1964, Darke and some other Texas Gulf people had it in their hands before Christmas 1963. The drill had cut through about six hundred feet of sulphides. Of this, something more than 1 percent was copper, 8 percent was zinc, and four ounces of each ton was silver. Although the anomaly this core came from was hardly farther than McKinnon could throw a bush axe from some of the most prolific gold mines on the continent, there was no gold. Darke scarcely noticed the absence of gold; at thirty-five dollars an ounce, the price of gold had for some time been well below the cost of mining it. Virtually all the nearby gold mines with the depleted veins and the glittering pasts were running, like opera companies, on subsidies. But copper was the bright new star that had come onstage as gold faded. If those first assays were to be confirmed by later drilling, Texas Gulf was about to raise the curtain on a bonanza.

During the Christmas season of 1963 rumours flew over the old Porcupine mining camp like reindeer in a Disney film. By April the mining recorder's office was trying to deal with the paperwork on more than ten thousand new claims that had been filed since the beginning of the year, months in which the recorder would normally have had to cope with fewer than two hundred. Of the ten thousand claims the Texas Gulf people staked about two hundred and fifty. At the same time they struck a deal with the Curtis Publishing Company that gave Texas Gulf the right to explore fifty-five thousand acres that Curtis owned. Darke and his associates now controlled the mineral rights to every anomaly in the area that their airborne surveys indicated might contain something of value.

Or so they supposed.

That left more than 9,750 claims that were staked by people whose reasons for joining the rush were based on the rumour mill, which was grinding very hard indeed. For several hundred square miles around the Texas Gulf drillsite not an acre of bush was left unstaked. The prospectors dealt their claims to the promoters, who fed the financial wire services with stories about the "strategic location" of their acquisitions while the Toronto stock market churned tens of millions of shares in their companies every day. In Timmins speculators drank in the promoters' stories along with their beer in the bar of the Empire Hotel at night, found a floor to sleep on, and in the morning lined up on the street outside the brokers' offices before opening time. There they waited in line, while ice stiffened their nose hairs, to get through the doors first and make their trades before the uninformed public caught on to the inside dope they'd picked up in the bar the night before. The opera was in full throat and the fat lady might never get a chance to sing.

Among the professionals there was some quieter activity. During the winter a firm of geophysical consultants from Toronto moved a crew into Timmins with a contract to fly an independent electromagnetic survey of the region. By early spring this crew had outlined scores of electromagnetic anomalies underlying the bland surface of the clay plain. Now they were grading these conductors according to the degree of probability that they might bear minerals of value. To each grade the geophysicists assigned a colour code.

At the end of February 1964 Darke sent a contract crew out to stake a block of four claims a few miles east of his discovery hole. He gave the foreman a small aerial photograph marked with the location of the four claims. The landmark by which the crew was to locate the claim block was the east-west township line. Along this line, according to the note Darke made on the aerial photograph, ran a clearly defined road. The crew was dropped by helicopter close to this road, and staked the four claims precisely where Darke had marked them on the photograph. These claims, and a handful more the same crew staked during the next couple of days, were entered at the mining recorder's office in Timmins towards the middle of March. As Darke and his colleagues interpreted their own airborne surveys, these were the last claims Texas Gulf needed to lock up all the promising ground in the district. In the phrase that sooner or later appears among the judgement calls made in every exploration program of this kind, Texas Gulf was now "satisfied with its land position".

"I knew about a couple of other lots that might be coming open in there," McKinnon said. We were miles west of Timmins now, nearing the lip of the Great Clay Belt where the worn old roots of the Pre-Cambrian mountains rise like the backs of sea creatures from the plain. McKinnon was driving the big van carefully, watching for the stretches of black ice that lay in ambush on the asphalt, but now he glanced at me to see if I was paying attention.

"I wanted to have a look at those lots, and the best way to get in was to follow the township line. It was getting late in spring, April, the snow was turning mushy and it was hard going, so I had to get out early in the morning.

"I walked out on the township line. After a while I started thinking there was something wrong. It took me a while to figure out what it was, and then I said, 'Jeezus, where's the posts?'

"Texas Gulf staked four claims right where I was walking, I seen the papers myself at the recorder's office, and now here I am, there's no posts. I kept walking out the township line, looked over the lots I came to see, and finished up around three o'clock. On the way home, when I got to the Texas Gulf ground I turned off the township line and paced off the width of a claim. Now I'm at the next corner. *Still* no posts.

"Next morning I said to myself, 'What the hell's going on?' Then it come to me. If you were looking at an aerial photo of these lots you'd see a road. I should know — my crew cut it, it was our hauling road. We ran it into the bush about half a mile south of the township line.

"On the township line itself there was no road. So," McKinnon said. After twenty years the story still tasted good to him. "So, their fuckin' claims were to hell and gone down by our road. They weren't on the property *ay-tall.*" He laughed and hit the steering wheel with both hands. The van bucked and steadied.

McKinnon and his partners, Larche and Rousseau, went out with their snowshoes at seven the next morning and staked the four claims Darke thought his crew had staked. They were back in town before noon to file the claims at the recorder's office. Before they left, they asked the recorder for an inspection of the claims. The recorder signed the inspection order the same day, and within a week he had cancelled the claims recorded by Texas Gulf and entered the ones staked by McKinnon and his partners.

When Darke and his boss, Walter Holyk, heard that their claims had been cancelled, they phoned the mining recorder to ask if there was anything they could do to correct the mistake. He said no.

"There was no dispute. No argument. They came to me," McKinnon said, "They wanted to buy the claims back. I told them, forget it."

Some time later Darke and Holyk both said they weren't "greatly concerned" about losing the four claims. Texas Gulf was interested, they said, only because the claims lay alongside some privately owned land on which their aerial survey showed an anomaly. On their rating scale they ranked the lost claims at the third level of priority, just above the cut-off point. Holyk said he wouldn't have paid more than five thousand dollars for them. That was perfectly all right with McKinnon; he knew people who would pay more.

McKinnon was starting to learn the other half of the prospector's trade. He had been a quick study at the first half, finding and staking claims. Now he was moving on to the half in which the prospector, something like an alchemist, tries to turn the rock into money. How does he find a buyer? What's a fair price? Can he get some money now, and still get a share of the profits later, should there be any?

There is a distinction to be made between wanting a chance to gamble, and needing one. Although Texas Gulf wanted the claims McKinnon had snatched away, the company already had all the property it needed. Moreover, Texas Gulf had been paying dividends to its shareholders for more than fifty years. Such companies make their profits by producing and selling minerals, not pieces of paper, and it follows that the price Texas Gulf was willing to pay McKinnon was based on the reasonable expectation of mineral production from the ground McKinnon had taken from them. The degree of expectation was very modest indeed, as we have seen, and so, therefore, was the amount of money Texas Gulf was willing to pay McKinnon and his partners.

But Timmins that April was also the instant temporary capital of the Western world for mining promoters. For a promoter, the wants and needs of established mining companies are turned inside out. Promoters make their money by selling stock certificates to speculators. Many of them want to find mines, of course, but a mine is not what a promoter needs. What a promoter needs is a story, preferably one that can ignite the gambling impulse in his customers. To go with the story he needs one or more mining claims where he can spend some of the money he's raised. The price of his stock will go up, in proportion to the appeal of his story, and the promoter will sell some or all of his own stock into this rising market. (In most cases. There are some promoters, as we will see, who get so worked up by their own stories that they become their own best customers. Very rarely there is a case, as we will also see, in which a promoter who has sold his stock then finds that his field crew seems to be in the process of discovering a real mine, and has to go into the market to buy his stock back at rising prices. These are the cases that should gladden the heart of anybody who has ever bought stock from a promoter.) Eventually, there comes a moment when the promoter has to drill some holes. Almost always the drills puncture the story about that particular piece of rock, and the promoter starts looking around for a story about another piece of rock on which to raise more money with which to do the whole thing again. The nature of the promoter's calling puts him in much the same position as a straying husband. He needs a better story every time out, in order to overcome the residue of suspicion left by the last one.

While the claims McKinnon now had for sale were a third-priority property to Texas Gulf, to a knowing promoter the story that went with them was priority one or better. Of the ten thousand claims for sale in the area, only these four had been chosen and staked by Texas Gulf. By itself this was a story that would drive any promoter's stock up. But McKinnon had a kicker. In his hands he had a geophysical map clearly showing the anomaly that bordered his claims, a map nobody but Texas Gulf yet had.

"You've lost me," I said. "Where did you get the map?"

"You have to understand these guys," he said, easing up on the accelerator but avoiding the brake while the van traversed another patch of black ice.

"What guys?"

"The guys flying the geophysical survey. They were going nuts, eh? Money flowing like water all around them and these guys, working for wages there, they must've thought everybody was getting rich but them. So this one guy, a geophysicist, comes up to me, I won't mention his name 'cause he's still around, he comes up and says, 'You want a copy of that map, I'll sell it to you. Five hundred bucks.'

"I says, 'Okay, it's a deal.' So I pick up the five hundred and come to get the map, they've got this little black hole of an office, no windows, nothing, downstairs in the Empire Hotel, right in the basement. I come in, and the guy says, 'I changed my mind. It's gonna be a thousand.'

" 'Okay,' I says. 'That's fine. Shove it.'

"This was a Friday. The guy says, 'Make up your mind. It's the long weekend, we're taking off this afternoon, won't be back till Tuesday.'

" 'I made up my mind,' I says. 'Screw you.'

"So he puts the map back in the file. I'm watching him, not really thinking about the map, just thinking okay, you bastard, that's the kind of deal you give me, that's the kind of deal I give you.

"I made sure they all went to the airport and got on the plane. Then I went to the bellhop. The night man; Italian guy. 'Lookit,' I said to him, 'you want to make a hundred bucks?'

" 'What do I have to do?' he says.

" 'Get me the key to that office.'

" 'How long you gonna keep it?'

" 'Two minutes,' I says.

" 'What're you gonna do in there?'

" 'Nothing,' I says, 'Just have a look around.'

"So I got the key. Went in, there it was, right in the cubbyhole where I watched the guy put it. So now I've got the map, but I can't give the key to the bellhop yet because first I gotta copy the map and then put the original back where I got it. He's waiting in the bar for the key, so I go out the basement door with the map.

"I've got my key to city hall in my pocket, but now I need the guy who runs the copying machine."

McKinnon often goes too fast for me, and I suspect for a lot of other people as well. The key to city hall? What did he do, bribe the mayor as well? No; in 1964, he told me, he had been after the mayor's job himself. A few years earlier, an old, once rich gold mine had shut down. The mine's discharge pond was close to the heart of the city and there the owners intended to leave it. Untended, the pond would become a cesspool. That was the city's problem, the company said; let the taxpayers deal with the pond.

McKinnon and a lot of other taxpayers objected, but the city council of the day seemed to accept the company's decision. Most of the disaffected citizens wrote angry letters to the local paper; some complained to their member of parliament. Complaint is another thing that makes McKinnon impatient. He set out to nail the company with the cost of cleaning up the pond. To give himself a base in politics he ran for a seat on city council and won. By the time the next election was called, he reasoned, he would be able to defeat the mayor and go after the mining company.

This was not quite the way it turned out. On council McKinnon found he could form alliances, becoming in the process something of a self-taught authority on urban renewal. McKinnon and his allies stirred up enough trouble in and out of city hall to force the company to reconsider. The company cleaned up the discharge pond, the mayor kept his job, and by the time the next election came around McKinnon was far away, staking mining claims.

Thus, the key to city hall he was carrying in his pocket the night he lifted the map was there for entirely proper reasons. What he needed that night

for less proper reasons was a couple of people to help him do things he
didn't know how to do himself. As he had said, he needed the man who was
in charge of the big, messy copying machine at city hall. These machines,
gone but never to be forgotten by anybody who ever grappled with one,
required a fresh application of ammonia for every copy they made; in the
room where the machine was kept, there was seldom a dry eye. McKinnon
also needed a geologist to tell him how to interpret the colour codes that
rated the anomalies recorded on the map.

The geologist was easy to get. For the second hundred-dollar fee of the
night McKinnon hired a free-lance geologist who had come to town with
one of the promoters. With this man in tow McKinnon went to the rooming
house where the copying-machine operator lived. His landlady said she hadn't
seen him since breakfast.

"He was out on a drunk," McKinnon told me, holding the van steady
with one hand and drinking coffee from a thermos with the other. "Every
half hour or so I'd phone the rooming house. The guy finally came home
about three in the morning, dead drunk. We get him down to city hall, he's
still drunk, spilling ammonia all over the machine, you've never seen such a
mess. Guy takes hours to get three copies made.

"The bellboy's still over in the bar at the Empire, all alone, going out of
his mind because he hasn't got his key back. By this time the geologist is
getting scared too, and I'm telling him he can't leave until he finishes
colouring in the codes on the first copy of the map.

"I don't know what time it was when we got finished. It felt like high
noon to me, but I remember it was just getting light when I got back to the
hotel. The bellhop's still there, ready to jump out the window he's so scared. I
put back the original of the map, give the bellhop the key and another
hundred bucks, and go home to bed with three copies of the map in my
pocket, one of them with the colour codes on it so I can copy them on to the
other two over the weekend."

In my bag in the back of the van there was a copy of a document called
*Report of the Royal Commission to Investigate Trading in the Shares of
Windfall Oils and Mines Limited*. The night before, I had sat up reading
the report after the others in McKinnon's house went to bed. As a result,
many of the details that had faded in his mind were fresh in mine. I knew,
for instance, that the newspapers had at last published confirmation of
the Texas Gulf discovery on Thursday, April 16. That week a man named
M.W. Rennick, a scout for the big mining conglomerate Noranda, asked
McKinnon's partner Fred Rousseau whether the four claims plucked from

Texas Gulf were for sale. As the Royal Commission later reported these events, Rousseau said yes, but the price would be high. The partners weren't interested in the kind of deal by which they'd get a big cash payment a year later, but only if by then the buyer had found a mine. What they wanted was stock, and not stock that was tied up in escrow, either; they wanted stock that could be sold right away. Rennick merely listened. Rousseau then told Rennick he could have a right of first refusal on the claims. This did little for Rennick but it gave the partners yet another lever to use on other bidders.

The party that made the winning bid came to McKinnon, Larche, and Rousseau's office, Suite 358 in the Empire Hotel, late in the afternoon of April 18. It was a party of two, Viola and George MacMillan, a husband and wife. They had been prominent among the promoters and developers of Canadian mines for more than a quarter of a century. Viola was the incumbent president of the Prospectors and Developers Association. Their activities had left them rich, respected, and not a little envied — they maintained a country estate outside Toronto, a large townhouse in mid-Toronto, and a glass-walled penthouse atop an office tower in downtown Toronto, half a block from Bay Street. They were also, although this was as yet known only to them and possibly their lawyers, bold and arrogant manipulators of the stock market.

When the MacMillans arrived at Suite 358 McKinnon was out in the bush with his logging crew. His partners, Larche and Rousseau, told the MacMillans the partners had forty claims for sale. The MacMillans, who could recognize a priority-one story when they heard it, said they had "a particular interest" in the four claims originally staked by Texas Gulf. They bargained until one-thirty in the morning, when the partners sent for their lawyer. The document he drew up transferred the four former Texas Gulf claims, along with eight others nearby, to Viola MacMillan. There was, however, a condition: she agreed to option the claims within thirty days to Windfall Oils and Mines Limited. She was to pay the partners $100,000 in cash and 250,000 free shares of Windfall, "free" meaning shares the partners were free to sell whenever they chose. (The royal commissioner, an Appeal Court justice named Arthur Kelly, later wanted to know whose idea it was to option the claims to Windfall. Ours, the partners told him. They had insisted on the option, they said, along with the free shares, so that if the transfer of the claims sent the price of Windfall stock up, they would be able to participate in the gain by selling some or all of their free stock. Such a sale would give them a capital gain, which at the time was not taxed, unlike the hundred-thousand-dollar cash payment, which was.)

Six days after Viola MacMillan signed the agreement with McKinnon and his partners, she was invited to a meeting of the Windfall board. The invitation was hardly surprising, since her husband, George, was a director and president of the company and Viola herself, in her own name and the names of companies she controlled, was the dominant shareholder. She told the board she now owned the former Texas Gulf claims, and proposed to sell them to Windfall. The company, she said, was to pay her two hundred thousand dollars in cash, three hundred thousand Windfall shares, and a royalty based on the value of any metals that might be recovered from the claims.

Apparently none of the board members questioned the imperial presumption with which she instructed them to give her twice the money she'd paid McKinnon and his partners a week earlier, along with a big share bonus and a royalty. Windfall's minute-book merely records that the board voted to buy the claims on Viola's terms, and immediately sent the details of the transaction to the Toronto Stock Exchange with a request for approval.

Now the exchange stepped out of character, rejecting the request on the grounds that the price was too high. Viola glared back at the exchange through a red haze. Her ire, according to the Royal Commission report, was of long standing. She felt strongly that "if the exchange disagreed with any of her personal decisions, this constituted an unwarranted interference in the management of her affairs". After weeks of bitter negotiation she and the exchange compromised on a deal that gave her only the $100,000 and 250,000 shares she'd paid McKinnon and his partners for the claims, but left her the royalty on future production. She took it but they couldn't make her like it; from now on she would do everything in her power to frustrate the exchange's attempts to find out what was going on at Windfall.

Blatant disregard for the rules of the stock exchange was just one of the things that was going on. There was also manipulation of the market on a scale that had precedents on Wall Street but none on Bay. The MacMillans displayed a sense of theatre that was highly developed even for mining promoters, among whom the enterprising application of stagecraft is no rare thing. There come moments in the unfolding of most dramas, for instance, when the strongest form of speech is silence. At these moments the script will usually direct the actor to hold a beat (or two beats or three or at times even more). A moment like this came for George MacMillan at noon on July 4, which that year fell on a Saturday. During the night shift that ended at seven that morning the drill crew putting down the first hole at the Windfall site had seen that the sludge coming back up the hole from the drillhead had turned black. This was a sign that the drill had cut into the conductor that was its target. One of the drillers told the core-grabber that the sludge looked like sludge he'd seen from the ore zone at a nearby gold mine.

At noon, the day-crew foreman showed George MacMillan the black sludge, and MacMillan said . . . nothing. He held the silence for a beat, two beats, three — and then the foreman showed him several lengths of core that had been pulled from the same section of the hole the black sludge came from. Still George said . . . nothing. Nothing, that is, about what the core might contain. Instead, he told the crew to load all the boxes holding core from the target zone, about ninety feet in all, into the trunk of his car without opening the boxes again. Then he drove back to the newly opened Windfall office in Timmins, where he locked the boxes in a storeroom. Rocky Szetu, the consulting geologist in charge of exploring the Windfall claims, phoned MacMillan at the office between one and two to ask what was in the core.

"Graphite and sulphides," MacMillan said. This was another way of saying nothing. The graphite was worthless and so were the sulphides, unless they were host to something of value, which was precisely what Szetu was trying to find out.

The beats marking MacMillan's silence stretched to Monday morning. The market for Windfall shares opened at one cent over a dollar, up from fifty-six cents at the close on Friday. The buying pressure that almost doubled the price over the weekend came almost entirely from a northern mining town called Rouyn-Noranda, where the owners of the drilling company that had the contract to drill the Windfall claims lived. They, and members of the crew who were doing the actual work, had made up their minds over the weekend that George MacMillan's silence could mean only one thing. Those among them who didn't know MacMillan personally knew him by reputation; he had a broad and successful background in every aspect of mining. An expert with these credentials could tell at a glance whether core he was looking at held commercial quantities of copper or zinc. (A Dr. Buffam later told the Royal Commission that any competent mining man could have estimated the copper and zinc content of the core within 0.5 percent, merely by looking at it.) Where a core-puller is employed, the drillers themselves get only short glimpses of the core, since it comes out of the hole encased in a steel barrel. But the drillers had been only a few yards away when George MacMillan examined the Windfall core, and to them the reason for his silence was clear enough to bet their last dollar on, as some of them now did.

Among them the principals of the drilling company, the drillers, their brokers, and their friends bought something like a quarter of a million Windfall shares as the market opened Monday morning. Toronto brokers, an eye on the ticker-tape and an ear on the telephone, quickly traced the buy orders to the Windfall drill crew. The brokers started to buy, at first for themselves — within half an hour of the opening trade brokers in Toronto had bought 130,000 shares for their own accounts — and later for their customers. At the end of the day the price of Windfall was two dollars, and more than 1,500,000 shares had been traded. Of these, 433,900 were sold into the market by companies largely owned and exclusively operated by the MacMillans.

At about the time the market closed that day a Toronto laboratory phoned Viola MacMillan to report on two samples of core she had taken in for assay earlier in the day. The samples contained nothing of value. She and George told nobody. Nor did they pass on to anybody else the opinion of a Dr. Ambrose, an eminent mineralogist from Kingston, Ontario, who examined the Windfall core that evening at George's invitation and said it appeared to be worthless.

In truth the MacMillans were doing too well by holding their silence to stop now. By July 10 the price of Windfall shares had doubled again, to close at four dollars. The MacMillans or their companies had unloaded another four hundred thousand shares at prices up to $4.20. That day's trading, the Royal Commission later found, "removed from the market any semblance of order and reduced it to a scene of uncontrollable speculative frenzy".

The Toronto Stock Exchange, no friend to frenzy, issued a stern demand to the MacMillans to disclose their drill results by Monday morning or face a suspension of trading in Windfall. They replied with a few more beats of silence. Well after the Monday deadline Viola had a Windfall director named Cole send the exchange a letter. Cole's way of saying nothing was a little wordier than the MacMillans' but no more informative; he made soothing sounds and nowhere mentioned a fresh fact. The exchange subsided, its menace exhausted by a single exhalation that in retrospect sounded less like the roar of the tiger than the bleat of the goat. For many speculators the failure of the exchange to suspend trading in Windfall tended to confirm the rumours that the MacMillans were keeping secret a rich core — why else would the exchange drop its demand for information?

Meanwhile the director of the Ontario Securities Commission, a former oil-company house lawyer named John Campbell, dived head and shoulders into the MacMillans' bag. In public he berated the stock exchange for the tone of its demand on the MacMillans for disclosure, and lobbied the provincial government's minister of mines to get the exchange off the MacMillans' backs. When the royal commissioner later asked him why he showed such a strong personal interest, he said, "You just don't go to Viola MacMillan and say, 'I want this,' or 'We are going to do that.' I mean, you don't do that to Viola MacMillan."

Privately, Campbell seems to have had a more relaxed notion of what you could go to Viola and say. On the evening of July 12, for instance, in a corridor at the Constellation Hotel where for some reason the MacMillans had a suite although they owned three different residences, all within a cab ride of the hotel, Campbell asked Viola for some Windfall stock to help cover a short sale made by his wife. Viola led him back to her bedroom, took out of her purse certificates for three thousand shares, and handed them to him.

"Not enough," Campbell said. (The Royal Commission report says he "protested" that the number was too small "to do him much good".) She opened her purse again and gave him certificates for two thousand more. During the next couple of weeks Campbell opened several brokerage accounts under other people's names. He dealt exclusively in Windfall stock, always selling short and covering later. By July 10 he had accumulated a profit of about fifteen thousand dollars. That day Windfall closed above four dollars, revived by rumours that the assays of the first core had at last been delivered, reporting high values of copper and zinc.

The MacMillans were still saying nothing to the stock exchange, but they were holding their silence for the last beat. For three weeks they had delayed the assay, first by locking the core up in the trunk of George's car and running it up and down the highways in the name of "security", next by halting the drilling in order to build a lockable core shack on the site, then by ordering the drillers to extend the hole hundreds of feet beyond the lower edge of the target. When at last they delivered the core to the assay laboratory at Swastika and it seemed they could delay no more, they left instructions that no results were to be reported by phone. When the assays were complete, the report was to be sent to Toronto by mail.

The report reached the city on the afternoon of July 30. The stock exchange waited for the close of trading and then put the contents on the news wire. The core contained nothing of value beyond a faint trace of copper; nothing at all. Windfall opened the next morning at eighty cents, very close to the level it had started from almost a month earlier.

During the next few days John Campbell bought back the five thousand shares he owed Viola MacMillan, paying for them not much more than a fifth of what they were selling for on the day she let him have them. He picked up the certificates and phoned Viola, who told him, as always, what to do. He took a cab to Heath Street West, some miles from where either of them lived or was likely to be recognized. He found her waiting on the curb and put the Windfall certificates into her hands. Then he left her, the Royal Commission reported gravely, "standing under a street light".

Backlit by more than twenty years, the Windfall scandal looks smaller than it did at the time, and more than a little silly. John Campbell cannot have come out ahead by more than ten thousand dollars, for which he paid with his job and his reputation. Financially the MacMillans did a little better. Companies they controlled held options on a million shares of Windfall at prices between forty cents and seventy cents. They sold them all during the buying frenzy of mid-July, tilting about a million and a half dollars into the treasuries of these companies and another half-million into the treasury of Windfall itself through the exercise of the options.

Despite the Royal Commission's finding that the MacMillans had "offended every element of company law", neither was brought to court over the Windfall affair until almost five years later. Then they were charged with fraud and placed on trial. They were defended by both Joseph Sedgewick and J.J. Robinette, who were incomparably the most able Canadian trial lawyers of their day. In acquitting the MacMillans, the judge held that they had been within their rights in holding back information about the Windfall core until it had been assayed.

Exonerated in their own eyes by their acquittal, both the MacMillans insisted ever after that they had been victimized by the stock exchange. Rereading the Royal Commission report it is very hard not to conclude that the reverse is closer to the truth — the stock exchange had more to gain by keeping them out of court than by getting them in. There was no way to bring George and Viola MacMillan to trial without exposing to public gaze the conduct of the stock exchange, the securities commission, and indirectly the attorney-general's department, which is responsible for the securities commission.

Indeed, in simple fairness if not in law, it was a nice question whether the stock exchange wasn't more culpable than the MacMillans — for shirking its responsibility to suspend trading in Windfall after the MacMillans evaded the exchange's demand for clear information. Called to the witness box, the president of the stock exchange, an ample retired lieutenant-general named Howard Graham, would have had to acknowledge that a trading suspension would have reduced the commissions Windfall was generating for the members of the exchange. Nor was the chairman of the securities commission likely to have much of an appetite for testifying under oath about the recent antics of the commission's director, John Campbell. These were issues of reasonable standards, and nobody was anxious to face them.

Thus the attorney general, wisely no doubt in the eyes of his peers,
for years before bringing either of the MacMillans into court. So
after their acquittal Viola was tried and convicted of a different o
wash-trading. The stock involved wasn't Windfall's but that of another
company she controlled, Consolidated Golden Arrow.

Wash-trading is a form of free-market onanism in which the trader
becomes his own — or her own — best customer, buying ever-larger amounts
of his own stock from himself at rising prices. The idea is that sooner or
later other buyers will be attracted by the illusion of a buoyant market.
Viola seems to have taken to wash-trading as naturally as Kareem Abdul-
Jabbar took to jumping. She was sentenced to nine months in jail, of which
she served three weeks. Many opposition politicians and not a few editorial
writers saw in her early release evidence that the justice system was distorted in
favour of the wealthy. I remember thinking that if she had been poor and
unknown, which she wasn't, in addition to frail and middle-aged, which
she was, nobody would have noticed or cared if she'd been discharged in a
week. But by this time my own attitude had been somewhat distorted in
Viola's favour. One evening while both her Windfall trial and her wash-
trading trial were still pending I'd gone to a cocktail party at the penthouse
she and her husband, George, maintained downtown. She was short, slat-
thin, and very tightly wound. I was prepared to dislike her, both for her air
of tension and her guest list, which was made up mainly of men wearing
ties that cost more than my suit. She won me over not by arguing about
Windfall but by reminiscing about the Depression years. Early in the 1930s,
she told me, there came a bad moment when she and George were out of
work at the same time. Both of them refused to sit still. George went north,
to the old Porcupine camp, to look for gold. Viola sold Christmas cards
from door to door. The story she told me differed hardly at all from my
mother's and father's, except, of course, in the way it came out.

During the years that followed the Windfall drama the lawmakers rewrote
the legislation that governs the sale of securities in Ontario. The securities commission reformed its regulations and replaced its director, John
Campbell, who was to be tried on conflict-of-interest charges. The Toronto
Stock Exchange, stung beyond endurance by hearing itself criticized in public
for its impotence during the Windfall affair, made clearing the prospectus
for a speculative mining issue so protracted and painful a job that almost
nobody did it any more. Though some members of the exchange mourned
the loss of the low-priced stocks that had been celebrated as penny dreadfuls,
those who belonged to the board of governors congratulated one another
for their overarching sense of responsibility.

The times were right for piety in the marketplace. A year after the Texas Gulf Sulphur discovery at Kidd Creek the Securities and Exchange Commission in New York accused thirteen officers and employees of Texas Gulf Sulphur of illegally doing the opposite of what the MacMillans had done. Whereas the MacMillans had sold stock without telling the buyers their drill hole was barren, the Texas Gulf Sulphur people were said to have bought stock from sellers who didn't yet know that Texas Gulf's drill holes were rich with copper, zinc, and silver. After some years of trial and appeal, eleven of the thirteen were acquitted. The other two were convicted of breaking the rules governing insider trading. In all they bought about thirty-five hundred shares between them, barely enough to make a bulge in Viola MacMillan's handbag.

"Straight — were the promoters straight?" McKinnon said. The van was pulled off the asphalt and we were standing on the gravel shoulder, backs to the traffic, about half way between Timmins and Hemlo. I had suggested a stop at the next service station and he'd laughed and said there wasn't one until we got to Manitouwadge; ahead of us there was another couple of hundred miles of the same low scrub and scoured, reddish rock.

"Dealing for ground, they were straight — the ones we dealt with, anyways. What they said, they did. The deal with Viola MacMillan? She paid the money when she said she would, she handed over the stock when she said she would. All free stock, straight out of the box.

"They all did the same thing. They were supposed to file papers in Toronto, asking for approval to issue stock from the treasury. It would have taken months, the play would have been over. So instead they just reached in their box and gave it to us under the table.

"Why not? What did it cost them — three cents? In those days, for three cents a share they could buy all the stock they wanted. They did a deal with us, next day the stock is a dollar. We've given McKinnon a couple hundred thousand shares? What the hell do we care, we've got a couple of million left.

"They all did the same thing. There was four claims we sold to Gulf Lead. Ten thousand cash, twenty thousand free shares. Same thing — Glickety-glick just reached under the table and pulled them out of his box. Within a week Gulf Lead sold at fifty times its capitalization."

"Who's Glickety-glick?"

"Didn't I ever tell you about Earl Glick? Glickety-glick and his rose boy?"

We were back in the van, rolling again. McKinnon was enjoying himself. Like George MacMillan, he knew the dramatic value of holding his silence for a beat or two. He held it. Then he told me that compared to Glick, the MacMillans had been buttoned-down business people.

"Glick was the big shooter. He flew into Timmins in his private plane and gave us the royal treatment — which we weren't used to. He asked you to eat with him, he'd send the plane to Toronto, fly back with a fancy meal.

"Every day he had dozens and dozens of roses sent in on the train. There was a young guy working for him, learning the trade, one of his jobs was to go down to the station, pick up the roses. Wherever Glick went, this guy would stand behind him, handing out roses to the ladies. Nice young guy, I don't remember much about him from that time except he was always smiling and pricking his fingers. Glickety-glick's rose boy; Murray Pezim, his name was."

(In the after-eddies of Windfall, the Toronto Stock Exchange spiked the guns of the shooter Earl Glick. Glick went to Los Angeles, where among many other things he bought the Hal Roach Studio. He turned the back lot into a real-estate development, and the studio's backlist of old films into the bonanza his mining companies had somehow missed. His rose boy, Murray Pezim, went to Vancouver, where in time he came to be thought of as something of a shooter himself.)

McKINNON SWITCHED ON the van's headlights at about three in the afternoon, and by four night was pinching out the view of scrub and rock on either side of the road. With nothing to look at beyond the headlight beams, McKinnon let his mind stay in the past, and I nudged him now and then with questions about the years that led him from Windfall to Hemlo.

Early on, he said, he realized that the most promising ground a prospector could cover lay in the archives kept by government geologists and mining recorders, and he became adept at his own foreshortened version of academic research. At the same time he carried into the bush the instincts that in his youth he had carried into the corners of semi-professional hockey rinks in places like Toledo, Ohio, where there are no trophies awarded for sportsmanlike conduct. In the Sturgeon Lake staking rush he beat competitors by appearing to negotiate a joint operation for three days, secretly sending his crews out to stake several hundred claims while the other guys' crews stayed in camp to talk and drink McKinnon's beer — of which he made sure there was a steady supply. At Val d'Or he tied up every telephone line in the exchange an hour before officials there released a set of government-financed aerial surveys of the Malartic region. Like his competitors, he had the pilots of chartered helicopters waiting by the phones in Malartic. McKinnon took his time on the phone calls, telling his pilots where to fly his staking crews to get the most valuable claims, while his competitors made rude noises at the telephone operator. One New Year's eve he spent in jail in the State of Maine for trespassing on a mountainside where the mineral rights were to come open on New Year's day. (McKinnon had been under the impression that the then-governor, Edmund Muskie, was in on the deal, but if this was the case the members of the local border patrol didn't know about it. McKinnon was on the mountainside with his friend and frequent collaborator Peter Ferderber, a geophysicist from Quebec, when the patrolmen opened up on them with shotguns. Cover was just a jump away from McKinnon, but Ferderber was caught on open ground, and scampered away crouched almost on all fours. "You couldn't blame them for shooting at him," McKinnon said. "He looked exactly like a big red fox.")

In those years, with and without partners, McKinnon staked claims at La Sarre and Gaspé in Quebec, Pine Point in the Northwest Territories, Ungava in Labrador, and Ellesmere Island in the High Arctic. "Look at any major staking rush in Canada in the last twenty-five years," he said. "See who had the most claims on the best ground. Ask anybody: the most and the best."

He made a living, and something more. Where the ground could be reached by conventional means and the terrain covered in a reasonable length of time, the cost of staking claims in blocks of, say, a hundred, was about fifty dollars each and the selling price might be five to eight times that. At Sturgeon Lake, for instance, he had an open order for as many claims as he could get. He staked almost four hundred. His cost was fifty-five dollars, his selling price three hundred.

So there was usually some money left at the end of the season. Which was just as well, because early in the 1970s his wife died of cancer. McKinnon was more deeply affected than might have been expected from a man whose work had taken him away from home for the greater part of their married life. For a time his will for combat dulled, and at the same time he realized that he would either have to stay at home for a while or leave his boys, both of whom were still under ten, in the hands of strangers. For the next four or five years he chose to stay much of the time with his sons, living mainly on money he had put aside during the great staking rushes of the past, and prospecting close to home when he went into the bush at all.

Sometimes in the evenings he filled in an hour reminiscing with Walter Baker, a retired prospector for whom McKinnon had both affection and respect. Baker had reached the age when he had relinquished the competitive pleasures of guarding his own secrets in favour of the social pleasures of sharing them. One story he told several times was about "finding gold in the sands" not far inland from Heron Bay, on Lake Superior, when he prospected over the area in the early 1940s. Baker had also drilled three shallow holes with a portable rig called a packsack drill. One night McKinnon brought a map, and together they marked the area Baker remembered as having "a lot of merit".

Now McKinnon started, he told me, to "look into it". This is not unlike saying of a piece of piano music that Horowitz started to play it; McKinnon seems to have an abnormally acute instinct for digging mineral prospects out of geological archives. For this he is often described as the first of a "new breed" of prospectors, though seventy years earlier Harry Oakes did the same thing on his way to Kirkland Lake. McKinnon's friend John Harvey, the president of the exploration arm of Noranda Inc. and himself a notable finder of wealth in the ground, has said you can lock McKinnon in a room full of files and he'll come out with a mine. This time the first thing McKinnon came out with was the information that somebody else had already staked the ground Walter Baker was high on. For the time being at least, the claims were in good standing.

McKinnon dug further. Among much else, he unearthed a paper most prospectors would surely have restored to oblivion at the back of the filing cabinet with scarcely a second glance, but which McKinnon, a closet romantic, saw as confirmation of Walter Baker's story.

Now as McKinnon drove and talked, I leafed through a photocopy he had given me the night before. The document, titled *The Nipigon Gold Expedition into Northern Ontario, Canada*, was written in 1937 by an Alfred F.A. Coyne. In seven pages he gave his readers the history of mineralogy from 1494 on; the history of gold exploration north of Lake Superior starting in 1662; and the logic that would compel a prudent investor to lose no time in joining the group he himself was even then in the act of forming, "by private introduction only", to finance his expedition.

"The Nipigon Gold Expendition," he writes, his spelling perhaps revealing more than he intended, is "possibly the greatest gold quest ever."

What did he have in mind? "The acquisition of a whole gold field by a quiet *coup d'état*, a real adventure impregnated with immense potentialities financially."

How did he propose to go about this? "Mr. Coyne offers you the privilege of having a few acres staked on your behalf. Your acres will be pooled with Mr. Coyne's."

To what end? "A gold bloc is created and a complete monopoly established automatically. The administration of this enormous gold bloc becomes at once an ordered affair. Something entirely new in goldfield practice and unheard of or even undreamt of in the whole history of gold discovery."

Would the bloc make money? "All are more or less familiar with the large fortunes made by those lucky enough to have discovered and staked a single gold claim. The aggregate wealth of any goldfield as divided amongst the many claim stakers and multitude of speculators has never yet been tabulated, but it can well be surmised that it always runs into untold millions."

Yes, indeed. Always. Beyond doubt Alfred F.A. Coyne belonged to the class of citizens known in Timmins in 1964 as shooters; if he'd walked into the bar at the Empire Hotel, Earl Glick would have known him on sight for a competitor, and there is a good chance Glick would have instructed Murray Pezim not to give Mrs. Coyne a rose. Alfred himself, I suspect, would have made Mrs. Coyne no better than eight-to-five in the race for the roses at the Empire bar. There is strong internal evidence in Coyne's brochure that Alfred was wise in the ways of the turf. "After all," he writes, "the price of one acre in the Nipigon Gold Expedition will break nobody's back. The risk is attractive enough. The amount risked is infinitesimal. Many have placed more on a dud horse, at the paltry odds of ten to one. Here the figures are about fourteen thousand to one and up."

What are the chances of finding gold? "If the evidence . . . could be published, it would stand out as an easy even money bet that the expedition will be successful."

Here Alfred is being too modest; he has placed some of the evidence in front of us. "In the year 1662," he writes, "the famous French explorers Radisson and Groseilliers reported gold and precious stones on their return from Hudson Bay, via the Albany River, through Lake Nipigon, thence through Lake Superior to Montreal. They were the discoverers of this route, and at one point of some two hundred miles in length, they did *not* disclose the trail they took. In this undisclosed portion lies the gold and precious stones."

This is the kind of archival trace that appeals to McKinnon, combining as it does a long-forgotten reference to wealth in the ground with a story that might be worth money to a promoter. He checked and found that there is indeed a passage in Radisson's journal where he speaks of gold and precious stones. McKinnon, whose appetite for making things happen is a lot like Radisson's, enjoys telling this story, and from him it has found its way into most accounts of the great gold discovery at Hemlo.

The story is scarcely less interesting for apparently being untrue, a fiction written by Radisson. He and his brother-in-law, des Groseilliers, did indeed make an epic voyage by canoe to the western end of Lake Superior and back. The story of this journey begins in August 1659, when the two men slipped away from Trois Rivières, and ends with their return in August 1660. Radisson says that in the spring, before paddling back to the St. Lawrence, they made a side-trip to the shore of Hudson Bay and back, and it's in this part of his narrative that he speaks of gold and precious stones. True, he fails to disclose their trail when they came upon the treasure, but it's also true that his entire account of the side-trip to Hudson Bay is vague, the only part of the story that lacks vivid detail. Historians long ago concluded that the story is vague because the trip to Hudson Bay did not take place; in the time available, the trip was physically impossible. By the spring of 1662, when Alfred Coyne has Radisson on his way overland to Hudson Bay,

Radisson was actually in Boston trying to find a ship-owner willing to risk an attempt to reach Hudson Bay by sea.

Radisson's biographer, Grace Lee Nute, says he made up the fictitious overland journey to Hudson Bay in 1669, lying "rather shamelessly" because, at the time, he and des Groseilliers were trying to attract backers in England for a fur-trading venture in Hudson Bay. Radisson was writing here in the role of financial promoter. In this he succeeded, for in 1686 he was in Hudson Bay working for the men who eventually founded the Hudson's Bay Company; they paid him in both money and stock in the company. That was the year when the young French captain Pierre de Troyes was despatched from Quebec to Hudson Bay to root out the English. His orders were to capture as many of the interlopers as he could, especially Radisson and his people. De Troyes captured three forts but missed Radisson, and was on his way back to Quebec when the Indian guide, Coignac, learned from local Crees about the native silver at Cobalt and took de Troyes there to see the silver for himself.

Reading Alfred F.A. Coyne delighted me almost as much as it did McKinnon, though for somewhat different reasons. With Alfred's help, the line that passes from shooter to shooter could be traced back to Pierre-Esprit Radisson. Like most of the great treasure-seeking promoters, Radisson took the information he had and reworked it in his own imagination, creating a story he could sell to investors. When Radisson wrote his narrative he was trying to promote financing for an expedition to go after furs, but who could tell whether a few words about gold and gemstones might help raise the money? It didn't take long for the English to see that he was right about the furs, but three centuries passed before the long line that led from Radisson's journal to Hemlo was fully drawn, and it was plain to see that although Radisson had invented part of his story, he had been right about the presence of gold and precious stones. The great gold deposit at Hemlo is less than two days by canoe from several prolific amethyst mines.

And what of Alfred F.A. Coyne? Although he often sounds as though he can't be much better than even money to stay out of jail for fraud, he has his own place in the long line that led to Hemlo. Along with his mistakes and outright misrepresentations he makes a number of claims that are not only accurate but, in some cases, prescient. He says there is "geological evidence" that "points to a reef formation", an idea that was unheard of at the time but is now accepted by some academic geologists. The deposit, he goes on, "not being an ore vein, will be widespread, consolidated and ought to be prolific." This is as accurate a description as any corporate geologist has written since. Lest "parasitic strangers" get their hands on part of this treasure, Alfred says his staking plan will "more than cover the visible gold and the whole geological structure containing the invisible gold". At the time, the idea of invisible gold was fairly recent and was yet to be applied to any site in Canada, although it is now routinely applied to the Hemlo deposit. Alfred's instinct was telling him things nobody else found out for another fifty years.

In the greying light of mid-afternoon McKinnon was concentrating on the road, where the shadows pooling in the hollows might conceal black ice. I closed Alfred's pamphlet and laid it on the dashboard.

"How did he make out?"

"If he ever filed a claim," McKinnon said, "there's no record of it."

No matter, I thought. In some things the spirit counts more than the act, and among promoters the spirit of the shooter has rarely been stronger than it was in Alfred F.A. Coyne.

From Walter Baker via the archives and Alfred F.A. Coyne, McKinnon was now hard on a paper trail that led him next to Trevor Page, a geologist at the college that later became Lakehead University in Thunder Bay. Like many geology teachers Page staked claims for himself when he came across ground he thought might have some value, and he often contracted his services to others as a geological consultant.

Towards the end of the 1930s, at about the same time Alfred F.A. Coyne was last heard from, Page had begun looking into the history of mineral exploration in the Hemlo area. He found that in 1869 an Indian named Moses Pe-Kong-Gay led a group of whites to a pair of quartz veins near the village of Heron Bay. They sank a few shafts and shipped out some gold ore, but the veins soon pinched out. During the 1920s a few people dug pits and trenches north and east of the railway station at Hemlo, but nothing came of them.

This was the full sum of recorded activity in the area until the Second World War was ending. Then Peter Moses, an Indian from Heron Bay, showed some rock samples from a gold-bearing outcrop he had come upon in the bush north of the railway tracks to Harry Ollman, the Heron Bay storekeeper. Ollman had the rocks assayed. They ran. ("To run," in the language spoken by field geologists, means "to return significant values of gold in an assay." When a geologist waves a sliver of core in front of your face and says, "This might run," he means that if you have the rock assayed, it may well prove to contain an economically interesting quantity of gold.)

Among Ollman's acquaintances was a radiologist, Dr. J.K. Williams, who lived in the State of Maryland but spent part of his summers prospecting for gold north of Lake Superior. In 1945 the two men formed a partnership. They staked eleven claims in Williams's name, and retained Trevor Page as their consulting geologist. Their activity attracted attention; among the outsiders who came to prospect the area was Walter Baker, who found "gold in the sands" on the claims to the west of the eleven that had been staked by Dr. Williams.

Page, meanwhile, was in touch with another Indian from Heron Bay, Moses Fisher. Fisher had previously led white prospectors to a big base-metal deposit at Manitouwadge, forty-odd miles to the north, and he now led a staking party that included Page, another geology professor, Mel Bartley, and the enthusiastic amateur from Maryland, Dr. J.K. Williams, into the wilderness five miles east of the CPR station at Hemlo. Starting at the eastern boundary of the Ollman-Williams claim block, they staked more ground directly to the east. Trevor Page then went on and staked in his own name a larger block in the shape of a square bracket enclosing three sides of the first block, the sides to the north, east, and south.

Page finished staking these claims in the spring of 1946. All the ground that overlies the Hemlo gold deposit had now been claimed. I am not sure what the most fitting comparative description might be, but the *New York Times*, more magisterial than I, has called it "one of the planet's richest gold mines". In the same story, the paper quotes the president of a sizeable Toronto investment house who says, "Hemlo is the best gold mine, bar none, outside South Africa." (There are in fact three mines on the one deposit.) Of the men who first claimed the ground below which this concentration of wealth lay hidden, only Mel Bartley, the head of the geology department in which Trevor Page taught and a member of the party that staked the first Hemlo claim block, was still alive when I started tracing the story. Bartley was confined to his bed in Thunder Bay when I called him, but we talked for a while on the phone. The great staking rush that followed the Corona discovery was then at its height, and I asked Bartley whether there were claims he'd still like to go out and stake himself.

"Certainly," he said, his voice hoarse but otherwise sounding like a young man's. "And I will, as soon as I'm back on my feet."

"Where?" I asked, mainly to keep the conversation going.

"Son," he said, "I'm going to tell you something about the game you won't find out in the archives. Prospectors are like trout fishermen. They never tell you where to find their best holes."

Well said, I thought, and doubtless true. But later that night, going back in my mind over the trail that led Page and the others to stake their claims to the Golden Giant, it seemed to me there was a notable exception to the truth of what Bartley had said. From Radisson on, every white man who had so much as thought of looking for gold at Hemlo had been led to the idea, or to the ground itself, by an Indian. Among the Indians there appeared to have been none of the defensive secrecy, not to say competitive greed, implied by Bartley's aphorism. Rather, the Indians seemed to have been quick to share their best holes.

Trevor Page wrote several papers and field reports about the mineral prospects at Hemlo. From one of them McKinnon learned that in 1947 all the claims staked by Page and the others, with the exception of the eleven Ollman-Williams claims, had been sold (mainly for stock) to Lake Superior Mining Corporation Limited, a company formed for the purpose of exploring these claims. During the next four years the Lake Superior company did about six thousand feet of diamond drilling. In 1951 an established company, Teck-Hughes Gold Mines Limited, took an option on the property and drilled several more holes. By 1961 Teck-Hughes had dropped the option, and after some additional fitful effort Lake Superior Mining was dissolved in 1965.

The claims were now open again, and over the next several years they were staked, held for short periods, and dropped by four different individuals. Then in 1973 a company named Ardel Exploration Limited picked them up and drilled three more holes. Ardel's consulting geologist estimated that the dozen and a half drill holes put down on the property since 1947 had outlined 150,000 tons of rock bearing 0.21 ounces of gold to the ton. This is enough gold-bearing rock to be interesting but not enough to make a mine, and the Ardel company, too, dropped the claims.

More than a year later Roy Newman, a prospector who then lived in Kirkland Lake, restaked the old Lake Superior claims. Newman also staked an additional block of claims to the west of the intervening Williams block — the same claims where Walter Baker had found "gold in the sands" in the 1940s. After much effort, Newman found a company called Copper Lake Mines that was willing to take an option on the ground. Copper Lake now tried a new tactic: rather than drilling more holes in the target that had been drilled so often before, Copper Lake hired a consulting geologist named Bob Schaaf to conduct a geochemical survey on the outlying claim block to the west. In a survey of this kind the geologist takes samples of the soil and analyses them for traces of mineral content, traces so small they're usually expressed in parts per billion. Schaaf not only reported fairly rich traces of gold on the western claim block, he commented favourably on the geology of these claims as well. But Copper Lake took its exploration of the ground no farther, possibly because the company and Roy Newman, the prospector who had sold the company the claims, were now threatening each other with lawsuits. Before they reached the courts Newman, who had both financial and marital troubles, seems to have departed the country. Copper Lake then decided not to spend the few dollars needed to keep the claims in good standing. The original Lake Superior block lapsed at the beginning of 1978, and the block to the west, where Bob Schaaf had reported strong geochemical results, lapsed at the end of July 1979.

Again the richest square mile in the Western Hemisphere lay open to anybody who might take the trouble to claim it.

McKinnon came away from meeting Trevor Page with some of Page's bullishness reinforcing his own growing interest in Hemlo, and with some notes and reports that Page took from his own files and passed on to the younger man. From this time forward, McKinnon says he kept an eye on the status of the Hemlo claims at the mining-recorder's office.

"The ground came open once, a couple of years later, but I was away somewhere, maybe in Ungava, and I missed it. But this last time, in 1979, I watched it real close, and staked part of it, eight claims, the day it came open."

"Why eight?"

"Those were the key claims, the ones that had most of the work done on them and showed the potential." When McKinnon said "work", he was talking about the geochemical and geological surveys carried out in the mid-seventies on the western claim block by Bob Schaaf, not the drilling done earlier by Trevor Page on the claim block to the east. The margin for error here is clearly very wide, and the confusion it invites has in fact entered most published accounts of Hemlo's history. The eight claims McKinnon first staked were not the claims where the gold discovery was made — the discovery was made to the east, where Page and others had drilled.

"Anyway, eight claims is about all you can get staked in a day. *That* day, the kind of day it was, I was lucky to get eight."

McKinnon and his helper, an elderly but — luckily, as it turned out — still agile prospector named E.B. Neill, had driven out of Timmins in the afternoon, on the same road McKinnon and I were now travelling. The temperature that afternoon was ten degrees above zero and the sky sparkled. They reached Manitouwadge before midnight, checked into a motel, and left a call for five the next morning. Snow fell heavily overnight and the temperature dropped to twenty-five degrees below zero on the Fahrenheit scale. Two hours before daybreak McKinnon and Neill reached the take-off point on the highway, tied on their snowshoes, and struck off across country to locate the claims.

"The trees were just hanging with snow. And the ground — I knew that was rough terrain in there, but I never knew how rough.

"We had to tie on to the baseline of the patented claims. The line was near the top of a cliff, not high, maybe a hundred and fifty feet, but steep. We start up, it's pitch dark and the snowshoes, you get a foot up and slide back three. So now we've got the snowshoes off and we're crawling up the rockface on all fours.

"I don't know how long it took us, but we got up, found the steel posts — they were all there, quite visible, and we tied right on to them and paced off our lines. On most of them, we were within twenty-five feet of where we should of been, all the time."

"I'd get lost."

"Yeah, well, you've got the topographical maps, to start with. You've got a power line in there, on one boundary. And you've got some old roads. I never have trouble locating myself in any of these areas.

"Two hours after dark, we walked back out to the road. We came out right where the van was parked, all right, but we were almost whacked out. Frozen and starved. We'd packed some tomato juice and stuff for lunch, the whole thing was just a block of ice; all we could do was suck on it. I'll tell you, that van looked like comin' home."

Memories alter, like rocks. Later, when he testified at the trial between Corona and Lac, McKinnon said that when he checked his map after staking the eight claims, he saw that "by mistake I'd done something wrong locationwise". Somehow he had started in the wrong place, thereby missing the four claims that adjoined the Williams block.

Less than two weeks later, he came back to stake the four claims he'd missed. This time he brought his two sons, Don and Duncan, who were in the middle of their Christmas break from school. The boys wanted to help their father; they walked into the bush with him. On this day too the cold bit into the bone. (The first town on the highway to the east of Hemlo displays a big roadside sign that says, in an odd manifestation of civic pride, "Welcome to White River, Home of Canada's Coldest Temperature, 66 degrees below zero".) Before long the cold drove the boys out of the bush, back to the van. McKinnon slogged on, tying the four new claims to the baseline of the Williams block, and to the eight claims he had staked earlier. The job, which he had thought he could finish in less than four hours, took more than six. Again he walked out in pitch darkness.

He found his sons "running up and down the road, windmilling their arms, trying to keep from freezing". The boys had been sitting in the van all afternoon with the heater and the radio on. The battery died. They couldn't start the engine.

Neither could McKinnon. Now the wind was coming up, the cold was biting through the bone to chill the marrow, and in the black night all three of them were running up and down the road whirling their arms like leg-break bowlers. A car came down the road and passed them by. There was an edge of anger in McKinnon's voice when he told me this, but judging by his description of the scene, the driver's timidity was easy to sympathize with. They ran some more. The best part of half an hour dragged by. McKinnon was now trying to hide from Don and Duncan the onset of serious worry.

"The snow was coming down pretty good and it was starting to blow. In storm conditions, people in that country don't travel much at night in winter. You get out there on the road, it's easy to see why."

Their legs were starting to cramp from running when they saw a second pair of headlights. This vehicle stopped for them. The drama lapsed into an ordinary roadside incident, and they were soon back at the Sharl Inn, the only motel within twenty miles. Here there followed one of those coincidental meetings that stretch belief too far and hence are banned from credible fiction, though not entirely from life.

At the Sharl Inn, McKinnon and his sons met John Larche and his son, David. Larche and McKinnon were not precisely partners, but they were certainly friendly collaborators. In the years since together they had sold the notorious Windfall claims to Viola MacMillan, they had pooled their interests in more than one staking rush.

Moreover, their reasons for bringing their sons with them on this trip were similar. McKinnon's wife had died of cancer and he now tried to spend as much time as he could with the boys. Larche's wife, too, had been found to have cancer. She was now confined to her bed; he was trying to occupy as much of his son's time as he could. Although neither man would have said so to the other, between them now lay an uncommonly strong bond of shared experience.

Larche told McKinnon he had come to stake the former Newman—Copper Lake claims, which he understood were now open.

"You can't," McKinnon said. "I just staked them. Twelve of them, anyway."

However strong the bond of sympathy between them might be, Larche knew McKinnon well enough to take nothing for granted when there was a staking race on, even if it was only a two-man race. Indeed, Larche had heard a rumour before he left Timmins that McKinnon had already staked all the open claims in the area. He had decided to ignore the rumour, largely because he thought it likely that the rumour had been planted by McKinnon himself to discourage competitors.

Accordingly, the first thing the two men did in the morning was walk into the bush along the western baseline of the Williams claims to check some of McKinnon's new claim tags. With the evidence in front of him that twelve of the claims were already McKinnon's, Larche said he'd stake the old Lake Superior drillsite instead, the site where Trevor Page and others had once outlined 150,000 tons of gold-bearing rock.

"You can't stake that either," McKinnon said.

"Why not?"

"It isn't open."

"The hell it isn't," Larche said. On the way to the Sharl Inn the day before he had stopped off at the Lake Superior site, where he saw no sign of line cutting or any other exploration work. These claims, he concluded, must have lapsed as well. McKinnon was just as sure they had not lapsed. His judgement was based not on a look at the ground, but on a look at a document called a claim map. When a claim lapses, the mining recorder is required to strike the claim number off his map of the area. But when McKinnon had checked the claim map in the recorder's office in Thunder Bay, he'd found the claim numbers in place on all the old Lake Superior claims. This was documentary evidence that the claims were still in good standing, and this is what he told Larche. The two men agreed to disagree, loudly.

Larche now phoned Timmins and spoke to a man named Mike Pickens. Like Larche, Pickens was a claim-staking contractor — for a fee, that is, he would go out and stake claims for other people. "If somebody came to me with a contract I couldn't handle," Larche told me much later, "I'd pass it on to Pickens. Contracts he couldn't handle, he'd pass on to me."

This time, Pickens had passed on to Larche a contract from Bob Schaaf, the geologist who had done the geochemical survey of the western claim block for Copper Lake Mines. Since that time Shaaf had been keeping an eye on these claims, just as McKinnon had. When Schaaf had learned the claims were about to come open he made a contract with Pickens to stake eighteen of them for him — the eighteen claims on which his geochemical survey had picked up the strongest traces of gold in the soils, and where he believed the geology favoured concentrations of gold in the rock. He went back into his files, dug out his map, and marked on it the locations of the claims he wanted. This he passed to Pickens, who had meanwhile concluded that he was too busy to handle the contract himself. Pickens passed the staking contract, and Shaaf's map, on to Larche.

On the phone that morning, Larche told Pickens that McKinnon had beaten them to twelve of the eighteen claims marked on Shaaf's map. Should he go ahead and stake the other six? Pickens said he'd talk to Schaaf. When he called Larche back he said no, Schaaf wasn't interested in winding up with just six of the eighteen claims. He'd told Pickens to drop the contract.

The call released Larche from his obligation to Schaaf. He was still quite sure that in the argument over whether the Lake Superior claims had lapsed, he'd been right and McKinnon had been wrong, no matter what McKinnon said about the claim map. If he went home now, he'd have come a long way for nothing. So the next morning Larche and his son David got up in the dark and went out to start staking the old Trevor Page Lake Superior drillsite.

That morning, while Larche was in the bush, McKinnon was on the phone to the mining-recorder's office in Thunder Bay. He described the discrepancy between what he'd seen on the claim map and what Larche had seen on the ground. The recorder said he'd look into it. The day was well advanced when he called back and told McKinnon there seemed to have been an oversight. No work had been done on the claims and they were, accordingly, open. But somebody had inexplicably forgotten to strike the numbers off the claim map. Larche was right, the official claim map was wrong.

By the end of the day, this was the situation: McKinnon had staked the claims Larche had contracted to stake; Larche had staked the claims McKinnon had believed to be unavailable for staking; and each of them liked the ground the other had staked. That evening they agreed to revive their partnership of fifteen years before. They would share equally in the claims they had already staked at Hemlo, and any others they might later acquire.

McKinnon pulled the van off the highway at Manitouwadge, and we checked into the motel there. It was a Friday night, and at two in the morning the walls of my room were still being sucked in and blown out by the amplifiers in the lounge, where a group well endowed for the job was playing some kind of northern rockabilly. On Saturday morning, when I walked through the place looking for a cup of coffee, I was walking on glass. I had a quick sharp memory of what it was like to be twenty, working in a mining town where you could tell whether everybody had a good a time Friday night by measuring the depth of the broken beer bottles on the floor on Saturday morning. The night before had been a good night in Manitouwadge.

We reloaded the van and drove south. When we came to the Sharl Inn we turned right on the Trans-Canada Highway. A few kilometres to the west, where two years earlier there had been nothing but a rock ridge, a small lake, and a few stunted spruce, there was now the high headframe and huge hangar-like main building of a new mill; then another; then a third — Noranda, Corona, Lac. We turned off the highway onto the gravel road that led to the Noranda mill. A hundred yards up the road we were stopped by a steel-mesh gate with a small guardhouse beside it. McKinnon, showing his pleasure at the exchange, told the security man his name, and he passed us through the gate.

Beyond the gate the road branched around either side of a low rock outcrop, then the branches rejoined. McKinnon pulled the van off the road and we walked together to the outcrop. At its crest there was a professionally lettered sign, half the size of the rock. The sign said, "Mt. McKinnon. Elevation 1.37 Metres".

"That's the stuff," McKinnon said, laying his hand on the outcrop. "Quartz sericite schist, they call it — the host rock to the gold. There used to be outcrops all through here, but they started knocking them down and burying them as soon as construction got going. When I saw they were going to get rid of them all, I asked them to save the last one for me."

Like a clergyman in a B movie the rock was grey and smooth and had no visible character. If you came upon a seven-mile ridge of this stuff you would pass it by, and this is what the engineers who blasted the roadbeds of both the Canadian Pacific Railway and the Trans-Canada Highway had done.

"Get up there," I said. "I'll get the camera." I went to the rear door of the van and hauled out the case holding the portable video camera and recorder that had been a recent gift from McKinnon to his second wife, Stephanie. She wanted a shot of her husband standing on Mt. McKinnon. Remembering that for years I had produced television programs, she had asked me to take her new camera along on this trip and get the shot for her. I had told her it would be no trouble at all.

Not that I took the assignment lightly; like a professional cameraman on location I had taken the power unit into the motel overnight to top up the charge on the battery, seeking to avoid all risk of a power problem on the day. Now I got the gear out of the van, cabled the camera to the recorder, checked the power level, and directed McKinnon to take a more intrepid stance. He stood like Hillary on the summit of his mountain, and I turned to the equipment case for the videotape cassette.

There was no cassette in the case. I did all the things you do in these situations: I rummaged around inside the case, dumped everything out of the case and turned it over once, emptied my overnight bag, got my leading man to make a descent from Mt. McKinnon and empty his overnight bag, and crawled into the back of the van to search the floor under the seats. There was no cassette. I uncabled the gear and repacked it in the van, more than a little annoyed that somebody had forgotten to bring the blank tape. We drove on, met some Noranda geologists, toured the mill. At the end of the day McKinnon took me to the dirt airstrip that had been bulldozed alongside the highway, and I got into a light plane for the first leg of the trip back to Toronto.

McKinnon phoned about a week later. He gave me the answers to some questions I'd asked about geology. Then he said, "You remember the missing cassette?"

"How could I forget? Did you apologize to Stephanie for me?"

"I think you'd better do that yourself," he said.

"Don't tell me you found it?"

"Stephanie found it."

"In the van?"

"In the camera."

"Ahhhh," I said. For some time I said nothing more. Then I said, "I guess you'd better let me speak to Stephanie."

THE WITNESS BOX IN COURT-
room 10 of the Supreme Court of Ontario is about a foot and a half farther
above ground level than the summit of Mt. McKinnon. Standing in the box
two years after our trip by van to Hemlo, McKinnon looked like a different
man. He was wearing a grey-blue glen-check suit set off by a well-bred
Paisley tie, and a pair of rimless designer glasses that he wiped, now and
then, with a handkerchief that matched the tie. For a witness at an important
trial, the ensemble was flawless; McKinnon looked mature, expensive, and
discreet, like a banker who had come here to reassure a big depositor.

Alan Lenczner led McKinnon quickly to the winter and spring of 1980.
He implied that he was mildly surprised that McKinnon and Larche made
an immediate, unwritten agreement to share their claims at Hemlo.

"I've sold hundred of claims," McKinnon said. "Hundreds and *hundreds*.
And I venture to say no more than ten were sold by written agreements.

"I've talked to most of the known prospectors in Canada and the United
States — that's the way we work. You've got to work that way." During this
speech Judge Holland made word-for-word notes, his gold pen flashing as
he tried to keep up. McKinnon was now speaking with passion, his old
combativeness starting to assert itself even though he and the lawyer examining him, Alan Lenczner, were on the same side.

With the Hemlo claims staked, Lenczner asked, what did McKinnon do
next — try to sell them? Yes. To whom? To anybody McKinnon thought
might buy them, starting with some of the biggest and best-financed mining companies in Canada.

He went first to Esso Minerals, the metal-mining arm of Canada's dominant oil company, where he made his presentation to the exploration manager, Fenton Scott. (Scott, I recalled, had been one of the experts called by
the Windfall Commission.) As was his practice, McKinnon made his pitch
in the form of a fully documented package: claim maps, geological maps,
reports of previous exploration programs, drill results, assessment files. Esso
said no.

He made the same presentation to Mattagami Lake Mines. In 1975 and

'76 this company had held a three-mile block of claims that started about a mile east of the claims McKinnon was trying to sell. The company's geologists had spent a lot of money exploring this ground to no effect. Now they looked carefully at McKinnon's material, and said no.

He presented the project to Northgate Exploration. The people there said no the next day. Amex, a very large exploration company, said no. Asarco said no. The list of established companies that turned down the Hemlo proposal lengthened to include most of the companies where McKinnon knew somebody to see. He was still adding names to the list when Lenczner broke in to ask whether he'd spoken to David Bell. McKinnon said yes. Lenczner asked why.

"I've known Dave Bell for years," McKinnon said. "Our families were neighbours; his family were railroaders, my family were railroaders."

As spring neared summer in 1980 David Bell was still working full time as an underground gold geologist for Dome Mines, but he was doing some after-hours consulting for a company called Bronson Mines. This was one of a shelf of small start-up companies run from Vancouver by Richard Hughes and Frank Lang. McKinnon had by now concluded that since he was getting nowhere trying to sell the Hemlo project to the big companies, it was time to try the small ones. He asked Bell to look at the Hemlo package and showed him everything he'd shown the big companies. Bell was interested, but Bronson was almost broke; Bell needed the last dollar in Bronson's treasury to complete the exploration program he was working on in his spare time.

There was one thing Bell could do for McKinnon, though; he could introduce him to his friend and college classmate, Donald Moore, the industrial commissioner for Kirkland Lake. This he did, and Moore in turn introduced McKinnon to "a hot-shot promoter he knew". The promoter's name was Steven Snelgrove. On Snelgrove's assurance that he could deal with the claims quickly and profitably, McKinnon and his partners "sold" part of the Hemlo package, the part where Trevor Page and others had found 150,000 tons of gold-bearing rock on the old Lake Superior Mining drillsite, to a numbered company owned by Snelgrove.

The quotation marks around "sold" in the last sentence are there to emphasize the kind of sale this was. No money whatever changed hands; Snelgrove paid for the claims in promises. The partners were to get a blend of money, stock, and royalties, in the event that Snelgrove could strike a deal with a mining company for the claims. Now Snelgrove took the Hemlo package on the road. For several months he did no better than McKinnon had. The summer waned. Snelgrove had little time left to make good his promises before the claims he'd paid nothing for would revert to McKinnon

and his partners. Snelgrove took the documents McKinnon had given him
and flew to Vancouver.

While McKinnon testified about the months he had spent carpet-bagging the
Hemlo claims from one major mining company to another, I had been wondering how John Lorn McDougall, the lead lawyer for Lac, would get out of
the forked stick this testimony placed him in. For Lac to erect a plausible
defence, McDougall would have to convince the judge that Dennis Sheehan
and Lac's other exploration people learned all they needed to know about
the Williams claims from documents that were freely available to anybody.
McDougall would in fact go farther than this; he would claim that Corona
not only gave Lac no confidential information, but had no information
worth giving that wasn't already part of the public record. Yet here was
McKinnon telling the court that he had gone on the road with the most
persuasive documents he could lay his hands on, starting with Trevor Page's
early reports and coming forward to the most recent publications of the
government geologists. He had presented this material to many of the most
knowledgeable mining executives in the country. They had all said no. How
would McDougall try to get Lac out of the fork in the stick? Would he seek
to show that Lac alone could see what all these other companies could not?
Would he attack McKinnon's ability to recognize the significant documents,
implying that McKinnon couldn't tell anybody else what he had because
he didn't know himself? Or would he look for a third line of attack?

When McKinnon was handed over to McDougall for cross-examination,
McDougall simply ignored the long list of companies where McKinnon had
presented his package. He made a feint at McKinnon's competence without
raising a serious challenge. When he mounted his attack it came from a
third direction, and began with an apparently innocuous question.

"When did you learn the line of strike?" Earlier in the trial McDougall
had spent some time defining for the judge various geological terms,
including this one. Most rock formations are considerably longer than they
are wide, thus drawing a sort of irregular, intermittent line; the direction
this line takes is known as the line of strike. From surface outcrops Trevor
Page had traced the strike line of a rock formation he called "the Lake
Superior shear zone" for a distance of about seven miles. Wherever he had
tested the shear zone, he reported, he found gold, albeit usually in small
amounts. The Lake Superior shear zone, like most other structural elements
of the rocks at Hemlo, trends roughly east and west.

McKinnon answered that he had learned the line of strike "from the mags",
by which he meant the subsurface contour maps drawn from electromagnetic

readings. "Which," McKinnon added, "is a very unprofessional view."

"Well," McDougall said, "I wouldn't know that."

"Well," McKinnon replied, "I'm telling you."

Despite his new bankerly appearance and the advice his lawyers had no doubt given him to avoid argument, he had lost none of his natural will to combat. "From the mags I had my own way of forming an opinion about the strike."

McDougall dropped the line of strike. "You met Trevor Page?"

"Yes."

"What did you get from him?"

McKinnon said he believed Page had given him a copy of his, Page's, map of the Williams property, but he couldn't be certain.

"Did he tell you about the geology?"

"Some. I have a limited knowledge of geology," McKinnon said. "I'm a prospector. My mode of doing research is, I see what was done, and I read the geologists' conclusions. At Hemlo there was gold in the area. It's been known for years. Yes."

"So the information you got was all on the public record?"

"The holes Walter Baker drilled weren't on the public record." Earlier, McKinnon had told the court about the leads he'd got from Walter Baker. In addition to finding gold in the sands at Hemlo, Baker had drilled three shallow holes there. Baker had given McKinnon the locations of these holes, and told him that in the rock fragments brought up by the drill he'd seen visible gold.

"Other than this, the information you got was all on the public record?"

"Not all, no. I got a lot verbally. The key information that got me there was not public."

McDougall changed subjects. "You must have an extensive library?"

"I have," McKinnon said, "and it's getting better. My philosophy is, you look for gold where gold is known to be."

"I'm sure," McDougall said under his breath; he seemed to be losing patience with McKinnon, but trying not to show it. "How did you select the first twelve claims you staked?"

McKinnon said he'd used the information from Walter Baker, along with the report of Bob Schaaf, the consulting geologist who had found high geochemical values on the claim block to the west of the Williams property, and had later asked Mike Pickens to pick them up for him. It was Schaaf's request that, through Pickens, sent John Larche to Hemlo. McDougall extracted Schaaf's report from the pile of documents in front of him and started to leaf through it. A silence followed that McKinnon may have taken to be an unspoken question.

"I saw an article in the *Northern Miner* that referred to a lawsuit between Newman and Copper Lake," he went on. Roy Newman was the prospector who had once held the western claims and had optioned them to Copper Lake Mines. "I figured that people mixed up in a lawsuit might fail to renew their claims."

"When you staked, you tied on to the Williams claims?"

"Yes."

"And you had the geologist's report on the Williams claims?"

McKinnon said he had the report, all right, but it disclosed the presence of gold in only trace amounts. "Not enough," he said, "to interest anybody but me."

"Well," McDougall replied, "some gold is better than no gold."

"That's the way I look at it," McKinnon said. "Yes."

McDougall crossed the floor at the front of the courtroom and picked up a large blow-up of the Hemlo claim map that was resting against the wall. He set the map on the easel. Outlining the various claim blocks with his hand, he showed the court that if the old Lake Superior drillsite was regarded as the centre of the then-known structure, McKinnon had staked the westerly extension first, then, some time later, the easterly extension. Of the easterly claim block McDougall asked, "You were covering the down-dip extension?"

"Yes."

McDougall digressed briefly, then turned back to McKinnon's staking pattern. "But from the very beginning the Williams property was the key piece of the package?"

"It was not." McKinnon spoke as sharply as McDougall had. On the old Lake Superior ground, he said, "The grade was point two seven. On the Williams ground the grade was point zero something."

"If you'd known the Williams ground was available, you'd have staked it?" This was a purely hypothetical question, since title to the Williams claims had been securely in the hands of Lola Williams, but McKinnon answered it.

"Yes, but only to fill in. There was nothing there I could sell."

"Wasn't the geology the same on the Williams claims as on the claims you did stake?"

"You can have ten miles of favourable geology," McKinnon said, "but that doesn't mean you've got a gold mine."

"Look at the Skimming report." There is an elaborate indexing system that allows the recorder of the court to lay his hands quickly on any document that has been entered in evidence. From among a mass of papers ranked in binders that filled twelve feet of table-top, the recorder extracted a copy of the Skimming report and handed it to McKinnon. In 1980 Thomas Skimming, a consulting geologist based in Toronto, had been retained by Steven Snelgrove to write a report on the old Lake Superior drillsite. In doing so, McDougall pointed out, Skimming had also recommended acquiring the Williams claims and the down-dip extension. Again he asked McKinnon, "You staked the down-dip extension?"

"Yes."

"So you reached the same conclusion Skimming did?"

"I suppose so."

"But Skimming also recommended acquiring the Williams claims," McDougall said. He asked a few subsidiary questions, then concluded, "Now, we have been trying to establish why you didn't immediately try to option the Williams property."

"As a prospector I liked it," McKinnon said. "But when I couldn't sell eighty-thousand-odd tons of point two seven, there was no way I could sell the Williams claims."

McDougall had now taken McKinnon through all the effective staking he and Larche had done at Hemlo — all the staking, that is, that led to the discovery of gold. Although they eventually staked another twenty thousand claims in the greenstone formations of the region, on none of them has gold yet been found in significant quantities.

I looked over McDougall's shoulder as he swept his hand across the claim map of the discovery area. The map shows the Lake Superior shear zone stretched along a more-or-less east-west line that roughly parallels both the Trans-Canada Highway and the main transcontinental line of the Canadian Pacific Railway. This is, of course, no coincidence; the engineers who surveyed both routes conformed to the natural contours of the major rock formations rather than trying to cut across them.

On the western flank of the discovery area, where McKinnon staked his first claims, the ground first became the property of Golden Sceptre Resources, one of the many small mining companies operated by the Vancouver partnership of Frank Lang and Richard Hughes. (Let us call this block one.) Although rock samples bearing gold in very rich concentrations indeed have been taken here and there from the Golden Sceptre ground, no mine has yet been developed. Moving east, the next block (block two) is the Williams property, acquired from the doctor's widow, Lola Williams, by Lac Minerals. According to most estimates, the mine on this ground contains roughly half the gold in the entire Hemlo deposit. Moving east again, the next block (block three), the old Lake Superior Mining drillsite, is now the Corona mine, which has a smaller but higher-grade ore body than the Lac mine. And moving to the north and east again, the ground (block four) went to a company called Goliath Gold Mines, another of the Hughes-Lang shelf of companies.

McKinnon and his partners retained interests in blocks one, three and four. Early in the exploration of their Hemlo ground Hughes and Lang combined the Golden Sceptre and Goliath properties in a single joint venture. Soon after this, they sold control of the joint venture to the giant mining conglomerate, Noranda, which then developed on the Goliath property (block four) a third mine that ranks in size midway between the Corona and Lac mines. This is the part of the deposit that McDougall referred to as the "northern", or "down-dip", extension, which simply means that the rock formation that hosts the gold is here tilted at a sharp angle that extends the deeper part of the formation off the Williams property on to the Goliath property, a down-dip to the north.

How much is a down-dip extension worth? That depends on how far down the extension dips — and on whether there are miners around willing to go that far down to dig the gold out. South African miners in the 1980s go down two miles and come back up alive, if not lively. But that is partly the accomplishment of recent technology. At the end of the 1940s, the deepest mine in the world was just over a mile below the dun-coloured dust of the Western Australian desert.

A Memory

. . . .

"I have sometimes thought that I have never seen demeanour more manly, more noble, or more gratifying than that which I have met at the bottom of the shaft of a gold mine."

— Anthony Trollope, *Travels*, the Australian chapter

We jumped ship in Fremantle and just kept going, looking over our shoulders until we were past Perth and well into the desert on the road to Kalgoorlie. Seamen who stay ashore without being discharged from their vessels and admitted by the immigration authorities are said to have jumped ship. Properly speaking they are fugitives, though it's not often anybody bothers to chase them. We had sailed from Singapore to West Australia as supernumeraries, which meant that while we were listed as members of the ship's crew, we didn't get paid. But we thought we knew where we could make some money quickly. Four hundred miles out in the desert lay Kalgoorlie, where the gold mines outnumbered the barber shops. So we had been told by beached seamen in both Hong Kong and Singapore. They said anybody could get work in Kalgoorlie for high wages — Kalgoorlie was built on The Richest Square Mile on Earth.

Yes and no. When a truck dropped us off in Kalgoorlie a few days later we found that the town itself was built on a couple of the poorest square miles on earth, a patch of the featureless gravel desert. The streets were broad gravel strips between the gravel yards of the buildings. These were all much alike, single-storey structures with wooden walls and corrugated iron roofs. The entire town reflected the sun's heat in breaking waves of air that looked denser than water.

We went into a pub and asked about the gold mines. The barman took us out into the street and pointed us towards one of Kalgoorlie's major public works, a jitney railway with open-sided tramcars. The trams ran on narrow-gauge tracks a few miles through the desert to a place where grey rock outcrops showed through the dun and ochre gravel. Long before the end of the line we saw the headframes of the mines rising above the rock. We counted half a dozen, the largest with the name "Lake View and Star" painted in letters ten feet high on the siding that enclosed the headframe. The tram stopped at a turning circle with a pub on either side. The space between the pubs was filled by a billboard that said, sure enough, "The Richest Square Mile on Earth".

We went to the Lake View and Star, where the man in charge at the hiring hall told us we could start the next morning as long as we showed up with a medical clearance. We told him we had no money to pay a doctor.

"You'll be right, mates," he said magnanimously, giving us to understand that the Lake View and Star would pay for the examination.

Hitchhiking from the coast we had both started to pick up the language from the drivers who'd stopped for us. "Good on you," we said, more or less in chorus.

The doctor hit us with his rubber hammer in the usual places and shone his light into the customary orifices. Then he signed two certificates, slipped them into envelopes, and handed them to us. We were outside before we could open the envelopes to see what he'd said. Everything was all right; he had certified us to be free of more than twenty complaints, among them "silicosis of the knee", which, the certificate explained in brackets, meant "(miner's knee)"; silicosis of the elbow "(miner's elbow)"; and silicosis of the lung "(miner's lung)".

In Kalgoorlie we found a landlady willing to take Bob's leather club bag as a security deposit against the rent for two beds, and not long after dawn we rode the narrow-gauge tram back to the mine site. The stores clerk took our medical certificates and gave us in return a pair of miner's hardhats with lamps and batteries. Then he showed us where to find the changing room, and we opened a wooden door on a scene Hieronymus Bosch would have found weird.

The room was long and narrow, with a shower stall off the far end. A dozen benches ran from wall to wall, with rows of clothes hooks above them. The benches were filled by sitting men, a hundred or more. You could see the men at your shoulders clearly enough, but the ones farther away were indistinct, and those at the far ends of the room were shadows. The room was lit at intervals by naked bulbs hung from the ceiling by their own wiring, but the bulbs at the ends of the room were faint and seemed farther off than they were, like beacons in a fogbank.

These effects were brought about by clouds of bright grey dust that quickly invaded the nasal passages and grated between the teeth. There were blowers at both ends of the room, driven by large fans, and I waited for them to clear the air. I don't know how long I waited before I realized that the fans were not there to suck the dust out of the room; they were there to blow the dust in. I turned around to leave, and found Bob talking to the man behind him.

"Faughken alu minium," the man said.

I didn't know what language he was speaking. "Come on," I said urgently. "Let's get out of here."

"Faughkers blow it in, everybody gotta sit here, breatha faughken alu minium. You don't breatha faughken alu minium, you don't go downa faughken mine. Faughkem."

The language he was speaking, we learned over the next couple of weeks, was Australian miners' English. Most of the men who worked underground had come to The Richest Square Mile on Earth from Eastern Europe by way of the displaced persons' camps that gave temporary refuge to stateless men and women at the end of the Second World War. When they spoke English their pronunciation was characterized by the thickened vowels of the Slavic languages. Their vocabulary was based on the indispensable word "faughk", which could fill in for any principal part of speech whatever, verb, noun, adverb, or adjective, and not infrequently do the job better than the original. I remember my boss one afternoon saying, "Faughker's faughked," from which I clearly understood that the pneumatic machine he was using at the time had broken down and he couldn't fix it himself. Faughkit.

A second man joined the conversation, then a third. The dust that darkened the air and partly choked each of us, they said, was finely ground aluminum. The authorities had ordained that no man would be allowed to work underground without first breathing the dust for a minimum of ten minutes. The idea was that the dust would coat the outer tissue of the lungs with a fine layer of aluminum. Inasmuch as aluminum discourages the deposition of silica in the laboratory, lungs layered with aluminum might be expected to resist the ravages of silica in the mine. When an Australian miner develops silicosis of the lung, a progressively disabling and finally fatal condition, his friends say he has been "dusted". The medical authorities had persuaded the management of the mine that aluminum dust could drive out silica dust in much the same way that witch doctors sometimes use poison to drive out evil spirits.

Craziness. In a calm and orderly fashion a hundred men or more were sitting around coating their lungs with finely ground metal particles. I felt a flutter of panic; trying to see through the murk I thought I could make out a dim light at the end of the room, and it was the lambent grin of lunacy. Bob clamped his hand on my arm.

"Take it easy," he said. "Some of these guys have been working here for five years and they're still walking around."

"Come on," I said. "Ten minutes of this, we'll be as crazy as they are."

"How about two weeks?"

When we'd asked how long it would be before we got paid, the man who'd hired us had said two weeks.

"It'll be a long two weeks," I said, but at that point I had no idea how long.

(Several years later I wrote a magazine article about the death rate at the time among Canadian miners, which was tragically high. In mitigation, various head-office people spoke with pride about measures they were taking to reduce the risks their men were running. One such measure, installed at considerable cost by several progressive mines, was a system for blowing aluminum dust into the miners' changing rooms.

When I first heard this I had a baleful memory of that dark swirling room at Kalgoorlie, and made a note about the witch doctors inheriting the world. Before long, though, I learned that the system hadn't originated in the Australian desert, as I'd assumed, but at the Banting Institute in Toronto. Doctors there developed convincing experimental evidence that aluminum dust created an envelope around silica particles, making them less harmful to lung tissue. The treatment was tried first on humans at the McIntyre mine in the Porcupine camp in 1943; in Australia it was still a novelty when we came across it at Kalgoorlie in 1950. It may even have worked, but the evidence was statistical and like most medical statistics subject to contradictory interpretations. Rightly or wrongly, the unions were against it from the start, perhaps instinctively as I had been in Kalgoorlie, perhaps wisely. They argued that the mine owners should be improving ventilation and rockface techniques to get rid of the silica particles before they reached anybody's lungs, rather than looking for an antidote after the miners had inhaled the silica. Then, in the mid-1970s, doctors investigating Alzheimer's disease discovered surprising quantities of aluminum in the brain tissue of Alzheimer's victims. Nobody could say what role the aluminum played in the disease — it could as well have been a symptom as a cause — but it was all the miners' unions needed to mount a campaign against the treatment. By 1980 aluminum dust had been banned from miners' locker rooms in most parts of the world, including the Porcupine and Kalgoorlie.

In Kalgoorlie, remembering Ben Krasner's remark about our gold-plated watches, it had crossed my mind that somebody must have passed through town who really knew how to sell aluminum dust. Now it seems more likely to have been one of those not-infrequent instances of malevolent goodwill, in which groups of people will do anything they're told to do by somebody in authority, provided they're told it's for their own good and assured that many other people are doing the same thing. When a scientific rationalization comes along with the instructions, hardly anybody ever says no. Most officials get involved in instances of malevolent goodwill at one time or another, usually to their sorrow, but some seem particularly prone to the condition. Health officials who license drugs that are meant to be benevolent but turn out to be damaging are only the most obvious example; consider the case of acid rain, or the disposal of nuclear waste, or . . . but the list is too long to go on with. Consider, if you like, the case of Ronald Reagan, whose undeniable goodwill has malevolent overtones almost every time he exercises it.)

At the head of the shaft the foreman told us to come with him. About two dozen miners were pressed together on a wooden platform slung from a double cable; the thing was a sort of medieval elevator, called a skip. We crowded in among the men and the skip fell away from the surface of the earth, dropping faster than a falling parachute. After a thousand feet it started to slow down. The screech of the brake on the cable overhead sounded like a derisive comment on the skip's ability to stop short of the rock at the foot of the shaft. But the screech faded, the skip stopped, and a handful of men got off. The skip dropped and stopped once more, then again, and at the third stop the foreman took us both by an elbow, said, "Come on then, you lot," and led us off.

We were standing in a chamber perhaps thirty feet wide and ten deep, with a vaulted roof cut from the rock twenty feet overhead. Here we could see that the shaft was twinned, the second shaft parallel to the first. Unlike the open shaft the skip ran in, this second shaft had a cover, a grate made of steel rods the diameter of cannon barrels set just close enough to one another so that a man's body couldn't slip between them. The grate was called a grizzly and was cunningly designed to probe for the breaking point of the human spirit, to say nothing of the body, but I wasn't to find that out for another couple of days.

Tunnels opened off each end of the landing chamber. Narrow, crooked tracks ran along the floors of the tunnels, and on a siding of these tracks at one end of the landing chamber there were half a dozen ore cars. The buckets of the cars were about six feet long and three feet across at the top, with the sides converging to join at the bottom, giving them the shape in cross section of a capital V. At either end of the buckets there were round pins that slid into sockets on the endframes of the cars, so that the buckets could swing freely in both directions. The foreman pointed at one of these ore trucks, said, "Bring that," and disappeared into one of the tunnels. We followed with the truck, pushing awkwardly. In the way of first journeys to strange destinations we seemed to keep going indefinitely, and when he called a halt we'd passed several branch turnings. Neither of us would have sworn we could find our way back, but as it turned out the distance was short and the work here was easy.

We were on the eighteen-hundred-foot level, the foreman told us. Some years earlier, the vein this tunnel was following had dwindled in size and grade, and the miners had moved on to richer locations. Now they had followed the high-grade veins as far as they could go, he said, and they were starting to double back to pick up veins like this one. You could never tell; this vein might open up again and the gold values improve.

"That's the way you run a gold mine," he said. "Get on the ore, and stay on the ore."

We didn't recognize it, but he had just given us the distilled wisdom of the entire history of gold mining. Then he told us what to do and left. The job he gave us was to clean up the crooked old railbed, getting it ready for the ore cars to run over it again. There had been some seepage from the rock ceiling and walls, and a fair amount of rubble had fallen on the tracks. But the damage was slight, the rubble was composed mainly of small pieces of rock, and the job looked untaxing. It was; we worked at an easy pace for two full shifts before we saw the foreman again. He came down the tunnel, looked around, seemed content with what he saw, and asked us, in the ubiquitous Australian phrase, if we were right.

"Sure," Bob said.

"Well," I said, "we're *right*, sure, but I was hoping, you know, to learn a little more about mining."

The foreman looked at me. He looked at the ore truck, which we'd about half-filled with rubble in two days. He shook his head, and said, "Right, then. You" — jabbing his finger into my shoulder — "you come with me."

"Right," I said. I looked at Bob. We both shrugged, and I followed the foreman back to the shaft. This time the skip seemed to go into a free fall, with the cable running out so fast it gave off a high moan, and when the brake took hold at last the screech I'd been waiting for was so far overhead I could barely hear it. The foreman stepped out of the skip and motioned at me to follow. The landing chamber was the twin of the one where we'd been working, with an identical grizzly covering the second shaft to the right of the lift shaft.

"Fifty-eight-hundred-foot level," the foreman said, much like the elevator operator announcing the floor in a department store.

"My God, that's more than a mile," I said, as though I thought he might not have figured this out for himself. "How far down does this thing go?"

"Six thousand feet. Deepest mine shaft in the world."

He moved off past the grizzly and entered a tunnel that opened to the right of the chamber. I put my hand on the rock face. The rock in the tunnel where I'd been working earlier was slightly wet, and cold. The rock here was dry and warm, and on the nerve ends of the fingertips as they came away from the rock there seemed to be the afterimage of a tremour, as though somewhere deep inside the rock there were life. I hurried to catch up with the foreman.

There was certainly life in this tunnel, unlike the one where I'd left Bob. Alongside the sections of track underfoot snaked a compressed-air hose that hissed at its joints. Ahead there was a clangour of grinding, banging, and hissing, along with an interplay of light and long shadows. As we got closer I could make out a short, wide man at the side of a machine more squat than he. At his command the machine bucked forward against a heap of broken rock at the end of the tunnel, snorting out gasps of compressed air and attacking the rock with a metal scoop fixed at the front of the machine between two steel arms. When the scoop was full of rock the man pulled a lever and the arms swung the scoop upward and backward to dump the rock into an ore car hitched to the machine's tail.

"Bogger," the foreman shouted above the clanging of rock on steel and the hiss and snort of the venting air.

"Is it not," I shouted back.

The foreman reached forward and twisted the shut-off ring on the air hose. "The machine," he said in the ringing silence, "Mechanical bogger. Does the work of three, four men."

The man running the machine was also called a bogger. His job was to come in after the shot man had detonated his charges and load the freshly blasted rock fragments at the end of the tunnel into ore cars. I was now assigned to be the bogger's helper. My job was to push the loaded ore cars out to the landing chamber, tip the load out onto the grid of steel bars called the grizzly, and go back for the next load. The rock falling through the grizzly would be collected on a lower level of the mine in a bigger bucket and hoisted to the surface, to be crushed and ground in the mill.

"Right?"

"Right."

The foreman left. I got behind a loaded ore car and pushed. Nothing. Pushed again. No apparent motion. Got down at a forty-five-degree angle to the back of the car, wedged my boots and stiffened my spine, and gave it

all I had. Slight motion. Kept pushing. More motion. I was breathing hard
and feeling the strain in my joints, but, all in all, this wasn't so bad.

Within a few yards the ore car was gaining momentum and I was starting
to cruise. *Hey, buddy, what's the track record here?* The car slowed. I pushed
harder; the car rolled slower. When I was pushing as hard as I could, the
car stopped. What the hell? I straightened up to uncramp my legs, and the
car began very slowly to roll back towards me. A nerve twitched in the
lining of my stomach. I bent and pushed again, and the car pushed back.

I'd been pushing so hard I'd stopped thinking. Now my mind stirred and
suggested that the track couldn't be level. I'd started on a downslope, and
now I was stuck on an upslope, both slopes so gradual that in the deep
shadow of the tunnel my eye had failed to pick up either. I squeezed past
the ore car to the opposite end and pushed. The car rolled. I kept pushing
as hard as I could, picking up momentum, for a moment almost running.
When the car started pushing back I eased up and let it roll to a stop.

With any luck I was at least half-way back up the first slope I'd come
down. For a few minutes I leaned against the car in the dark, catching my
breath. Then I squeezed past it again, bent, and shoved. The car moved, I
moved faster, together we accelerated down the slope. This time when the
car rolled through the dip and started on the upslope, I could feel the car's
weight start to press back and I pushed harder, trying to maintain the
momentum carried over from the downslope. The car slowed, my boots
dug for purchase and slipped, the car stopped.

The second time I tried it, it worked.

At the top of the upslope there was level track, not easy to push the ore
car over but not impossible either. There was another bad moment when
the track swung around a corner and joined the track from a branching
tunnel. The wheels almost stuck in the junction, but the weight of the ore
more than any push I had left to give carried the car through, and from
there it was a level haul to the landing chamber.

I stopped the car alongside the grizzly and breathed for a while. Then I
took a careful look at what came next. The bucket holding the ore was
suspended from the frame of the ore car by pins that turned in sockets, one
at each end. A push on the off-side of the bucket would tilt it away from me
and dump the rock out on the grizzly. Nothing could be simpler.

I went around to the off-side, took a firm grip on the rim that ran along
the top sides of the bucket, and pushed until I heard something pop. The
bucket tilted about an inch and a half, and swung back when I eased off. I
moved my feet closer to the bucket, arched my back to get some of my
weight below the top of the V, anchored both my palms under the rim, and

pushed until I judged myself to be within half a foot-pound of a hernia. The bucket swung three, possibly four inches in the direction of the grizzly. By my calculation it would have to swing something over a foot before any of the rock would start to slide out.

Somebody laughed.

Duelling with the ore car, I had seen and heard nothing else. Now I looked around and saw that two more bogger's helpers had entered the chamber from other tunnels, both men pushing ore cars of their own. I grinned and shrugged at the one who wasn't laughing, turned back to the ore car and locked my hands on the rim again. The laughter stopped and the same voice said, "Dumb faughker."

The man who'd spoken left his ore car, came over to mine, and shouldered me out of the way. I felt a flash of resentment, but he was a couple of inches shorter than I was and at least twenty pounds lighter, and if he thought he knew how to tip that bucket then I wasn't going to stop him. I was dumb, all right, but not that dumb. He turned his back to the bucket and coiled so that he was tucked under the slope of the V with both shoulders pressing the rim from below. He braced his legs against the angle between the floor and the rock wall. Then he gathered himself, took in air, and uncoiled in a single thrust, like a weight-lifter going after a personal record.

The bucket tilted, the rock shifted towards the far rim. Expecting him to dump the bucket, I started to smile. He relaxed, the rock settled, the bucket dropped back. He looked at me and said, "See?"

Yes; I could see that I was going to have to try this with both of these guys watching, and I had an instant of nostalgia for the time a few minutes earlier when I had been fighting the bucket without much hope but at least without an audience. I folded myself under the sloping side of the bucket the way he had, breathed in, shoved with my shoulders. The bucket rocked forward perhaps eight inches before it bore me back down. Not far enough to dump the rock, but far enough to make dumping the rock seem possible again. My shoulders had a stripe of pain across them where they had dug into the rim of the bucket, but it was not, unfortunately, severe enough to justify a trip out of here, back to the doctor.

He laughed again.

All *right*. I doubled up again under the bucket, crouched as far under the centre of the weight as I could get. I remember thinking that my knees were closer to my chest than they had been since the womb; more nostalgia. I took in air, coiled, paused, and thrust, blowing air like a whale. The bucket tilted away, the rock began to slide, I kept thrusting. I could feel the shape of my eyeballs starting to change — and the centre of gravity shifted to the downside of the bucket, the weight came off my shoulders, the load of rock crashed onto the grizzly. I stood in the cloud of dust that drifted up from the fallen rock, breathing grit and smiling. The two other bogger's helpers smiled back; we were in this thing together. I bent behind my empty car and started pushing it out of the way, to give them a chance to unload theirs.

"Dumb faughker."

What? I looked around. The one who'd shown me how to tilt the bucket was pointing at the grizzly. Most of the ore I'd dumped had fallen through the spaces between the steel bars, but a few big pieces of rock were lying across the grid. "Getta faughken rock offa faughken grizzly."

He was telling me it was part of my job to clear the last of my rock before the next man dumped his. So be it. I got down on the grizzly; with one boot on one bar and the other boot on the next, the footing seemed fairly safe. Looked at from above, the spaces between the bars appeared to be narrow enough to stop a man from falling through if he slipped.

Okay, now the rock. I started with the smallest piece, got it turned lengthwise into the gap between two bars, and tilted. The rock slid between the bars. Good. The second piece took a little more juggling to find the right angle, then it slid through. Two down. The third piece wouldn't go; in every dimension it was too big to slide between the bars. If I could lift it, maybe I could drop it across one of the bars and break it in half. I bent, searching for a handhold.

"Dumb faughker."

My buddy. For a second I thought about trying to slide him between the bars. When I looked up he was holding out a sledgehammer that had been leaning against the rock face on the far side of the grizzly; I hadn't seen it because I hadn't been looking for it.

"Breaka faughker."

The handle of the hammer was thick and shapeless, more awkward than either a baseball bat or an axe. I worked my palms on it, trying to get a feel for the grip, and swung it underhand a couple of times, trying to get a feel for the balance. Then I swung it high and brought it down hard, striking the rock squarely in the centre.

Pain jolted up from my wrists. Every nerve path in my body short-circuited. I jangled. The rock showed a small patch of white, where the hammer head had reduced an edge to sand. If I could hit the rock the same way several hundred more times, I might wear it down far enough to slide what was left between the bars. On the other hand, if I hit it once more like that, I might well go into shock.

I was clenching and unclenching the fingers of my right hand, trying to get the feeling back into them, when the second man, the one who hadn't spoken yet, climbed down on the grizzly beside me. He said, "Faughk," in a quiet, resigned tone of voice, crouched, and turned the rock to a new angle. Then he motioned me down to his eye-level, and ran his finger along the face of the rock. With my eyes a foot from his finger I could see that the surface of the rock was etched in a pattern not unlike the grain on a wooden plank. He took the sledge from my left hand, raised it in an easy movement to the level of his shoulders, and let it fall — cleaving, as they say, the rock. He bent and ran his finger along the line where the rock had split. The line followed the grain.

I tipped the split rock between the bars of the grizzly and stepped up to the landing, turned, and reached out my hand. He took it, and I pulled him up after me. I said, "Thank you." He looked at me, then looked at the other man. It was the other man who spoke.

"Ahh," he said "Faughkit."

I waved to both of them, went back to my ore car, and started up the tunnel. The voice behind me, when it came, was faint.

"Dumb faughker," it said.

No, we didn't become friends; we hardly shared enough words for that. But I ran into them several times a day during the next couple of weeks, and whenever I did I'd lift my hand in a loose salute and say, "Dumb faughkers," and they'd wave back and laugh. None of it got easy: running the loaded cars out to the grizzly tested my endurance every time I started down the track; tipping the bucket stretched what strength I had left to the breaking point; and splitting the rock with the sledgehammer was a trick that worked the first time with some rocks, not until the twentieth with others. But now I knew I could get it done in the end, and so, day by day, I did.

That first day, when Bob and I met at the end of the day in the changing room, my hands were bloody and in the shower he could see the welts on my shoulders where I'd jammed them against the rim of the bucket.

"Well, now," he said. "Learned a lot about mining, did you, then, cock?"

"Too right," I said in Australian. "What did you do after I left?"

"Two crossword puzzles."

Bob loves to tell this story still, and when he does his days underground get easier and mine get harder, but not much, since his days were about as easy as they could get, and mine were about as hard as I could stand. We'd get up at six, eat bacon and gravy for breakfast, pack a couple of baloney sandwiches for crib, which is Australian miner's English for lunch, and ride the tramcar to the mine, where the days varied little from the one I've described. One afternoon the foreman stopped to talk for a while, and I learned that the six-thousand foot level was as deep as the Lake View and Star was going to get. The problem wasn't driving the shaft farther down, but ventilating it — driving fresh air more than a mile underground and sucking overheated, depleted air out. Some day, he said, they'd be able to go deeper.

In the evenings we sometimes went to the second major public-works project Kalgoorlie had in addition to the tramline. This was an outdoor swimming pool surrounded by grass, the only uncovered water and year-round greenery within several hundred miles in any direction. Hitchhiking through the desert from the coast we had seen the pipeline snaking along-side the road and asked what it carried. Oil? Natural gas? No, water; every drop of water used in Kalgoorlie came from Perth in this pipeline, and so the swimming pool had been a surprise. I recall lying on the grass beside the pool late at night with a girl whose breasts are memorable to this day, though in Bob's diary he speaks about the inhospitable local women, a contradiction I can't explain.

Once or twice we went to the movies. Kalgoorlie had two screens, both outdoors, with, ranked in front of them, row on row, a few dozen lawn chairs enclosed by a picket fence. There was said to be a more full-blooded kind of night life out in the desert, where, if talk we heard at the mine was to be believed, professional gamblers from the East were running a two-up school. Two-up, the Australian national gambling game, is played by placing two of those big old copper pennies on a wooden paddle, spinning them in the air, and betting on which way they'll come down. This is a highly democratic way of losing money, since there are only three possible outcomes and every bet is two to one, which may be why Australians like it. Two-up schools were illegal, but our informants told us that the gamblers running the game kept a string of horses staked out behind a dune near the two-up ring. When their lookouts spotted the police driving up the gamblers would grab their money, mount up, and ride off through the dry washes, where the police vehicle couldn't follow. The police, it seemed, had never shown up on horseback, but there was no way to tell whether they were on the take or whether they just hadn't thought of it. One night not long before we left town a couple of the guys at the mine took me to the game. We drove less than five miles into the desert, to a ring stomped in the gravel. Forty or fifty men were milling around in the ring. There was a lot of money changing hands and some whooping by the winners after almost every toss, but with only three ways to bet, the gambling soon got boring, particularly since I didn't have any money to bet anyway. The police, alas, never came, so I never did see the gamblers gallop down the dry washes, and that was what I had really come for.

We picked up our wages at four on a Friday. After we'd settled accounts with our landlady and a bartender who'd carried us for a few schooners of icy beer on hot afternoons, and repaid the girl who'd lent us the money for the movie tickets, we each had about nine pounds left. We ate, and Bob went back to the rooming house to write letters. Not for me a quiet night; the sap was running too high. In the mine I'd lost several pounds and gained some muscle; I'd also popped my right knee and knocked my right foot with the sledgehammer, so that my natural walk, which is a kind of roll, now looked as though I might capsize as every step. None of that mattered; released from the mine, I felt like the man in the iron mask the day they came with the cold chisel.

Now, although Kalgoorlie had no night life I knew where there was a Friday-night poker game. Most of the players were East Europeans from the mine. The game they played was a three-card variation of poker in which the number of players was greater, the permutations simpler, and the velocity of money a great deal higher. So much the better: I should be able to double or triple our stake in a couple of hours and still get enough sleep to be up at dawn.

We planned to hitchhike across the Nullarbor Plain, which is the largest desert in the world, and we had been told that most drivers tried to make a start before the heat of the day. Bob woke in the first light and made out the empty bed across the room. He says he knew where to go looking for me. He was on the verandah when he heard the voice through the door. The winners had gone home, the dialogue of the losers had begun, and the voice shouting "Deal!" was mine.

Some years later I was invited to lead an annual seminar on the ethics of business for graduate students at the University of Toronto Business School. In one of these discussions I told the group that I'd once worked briefly at the bottom of the deepest gold mine in the world, though why I mentioned it I can't remember. Somebody wanted to know if I'd learned anything down there.

"Certainly," I said. "I learned you can't break rock against the grain."

"Anything else?"

"Yes. Getting anything out of a gold mine is hard, and keeping it is harder."

BELL AND SHEEHAN

". . . gold is a very devilish sort of a thing, believe me, boys. In the first place, it changes your character entirely."
— B. Traven, *The Treasure of the Sierra Madre*

DAVID BELL, CONSULTING geologist to Corona, had spent most of his life in the gold camps of the Canadian Shield — born in Kirkland Lake, raised in Cochrane, schooled in Timmins. Until the spring of 1981, at least, Bell's ideas about how one man deals with another were shaped in the tradition of the Northerner, the same tradition that gave Donald McKinnon his distrust of legalistic negotiations and contracts.

The strength of this tradition can be hard for an outsider to grasp. The town where Bell and McKinnon were both raised was named after an early minister of mines in the provincial government, a merchant and mining promoter from the North whose constituents called him "Silent Frank" Cochrane. He was often attacked, in one celebrated instance for helping settle a mining dispute in a way that greatly enriched his brother-in-law. In another he bought, while mines minister, a mining claim for three hundred dollars and sold it a couple of years later for a hundred thousand. It was after this transaction that he was invited to join the federal cabinet, where, not surprisingly, he continued to come under attack. After an unusually long speech assaulting his character and his practices, Silent Frank is reported to have risen, said, "Mr. Speaker, there is nothing to it," and resumed his seat.

During the trial of Corona's claim against Lac the provincial minister of mines was a Northerner named René Fontaine, the member from the riding named after Silent Frank, Cochrane North. Not long after the trial ended, Fontaine was accused of failing to disclose his ownership of shares in a number of speculative mining companies. Lacking Silent Frank's aplomb, Fontaine resigned both his portfolio and his seat. He then announced that he would seek vindication from those best able to confer it, his constituents, by running for his vacant seat.

"Those who say I was wrong," he said "make the mistake of thinking a man is only honest if everything he does is written down. Where I come from, people don't stand on formalities. In business and in politics, we rely on mutual trust and accept each other's word."

During the by-election the premier of the province flew into Cochrane North to stump the riding on his former minister's behalf. Fontaine, he said, was "a strong voice for all the people of the North. He has the spirit of the North. He understands the North."

In the spirit of the North the voters re-elected Fontaine with a considerably enhanced majority. David Bell, replying to a question in Judge Holland's courtroom, spoke in the same spirit. One of Corona's lawyers, Ron Slaght, asked Bell to think back to his meeting with Dennis Sheehan and others on May 6, 1981, in Corona's core shack at Hemlo.

"Before the meeting, had you thought about the question of confidentiality?"

"No," Bell said. "I always thought that between good people the question of confidentiality didn't have to be raised."

"What would you have done if you thought the Lac people would compete with you for the Williams claims?"

"I would have thrown them off the property."

The spirit of the North, the spirit of "good people" who, in René Fontaine's phrase, "rely on mutual trust and accept each other's word", lies at the heart of the dispute between Corona and Lac. You could say that Corona had taken Lac to court for not having the Northern spirit, and that Lac's defence was that Corona had too much for its own good. And that both were right.

At the time of the trial Bell was forty-two, with the features, not quite fully formed, of a younger man. He had a wide mouth with lips that folded softly on themselves at the corners, and spoke in a quiet, almost diffident voice. He wore eyeglasses with flesh-coloured frames, which he took off to read the documents that were passed up to him, and a necktie with square ends, a light brown body, and a dark brown knot.

Telling his story he had the manner of a practised witness, allowing long pauses to build beat by beat. Now and then he asked for the repetition of a perfectly clear question, a technique that not only buys time in which to frame an answer but can also throw the cross-examining lawyer off his stride. During the four years leading up to the trial Bell had been questioned under oath many times; he had answered fifteen thousand individual questions.

Between the first moves in a lawsuit and going to trial there are a number of legal steps to walk through, the most important of which is called "examination for discovery". Witnesses for both sides are sworn, and questioned by lawyers for the opposing side. Based on the answers, the defence can move to dismiss the case — John Lorn McDougall moved for dismissal on the opening day of this trial. If the judge denies the motion, as Judge Holland did here, the cross-examination of witnesses during the trial is largely directed at catching them in contradictions between what they say in court and what they've said earlier in examination for discovery. Even when the questions don't bear on the central issues in the case, the idea is that a witness who contradicts himself too often will lose credibility in the eyes of the judge.

The more questions a witness has already answered before he appears in court, the less likely he is to remember everything he said, and this applies whether or not he was telling the truth as he remembered it at the time. Bell's fifteen thousand answers, which filled more than two thousand pages of typescript, had become a minefield in which Bell's credibility was almost as likely to be blown away by failing to remember an honest answer as by being exposed in a lie. At one point in McDougall's cross-examination of Bell he implied that Bell had already contradicted himself too often.

"Let's have no more surprises," McDougall said. Alan Lenczner jumped to his feet.

"There are no surprises left," he said, and reminded the court of the fifteen thousand questions Bell had already answered.

"By now Mr. McDougall must know Mr. Bell better than Mrs. Bell does."

Bell was led through his story by Ron Slaght, Lenczner's associate. Slaght was a tall man in his mid-thirties who moved with the muscled assurance of an athlete. His most arresting feature, though, was his hair, a heavy blond mane that cascaded backward from his forehead almost to his shoulders. (A non-lawyer would have said there couldn't be a head of hair to match it in the entire membership of the national bar association, were it not for McDougall's associate, Brian Foster, at the opposing counsel's table across the room. Foster wore a cascade of hair shaped much like Slaght's, but with the colour and dull rich patina of sculpted steel. When one of these men rose to object to something the other was saying they pointed their modified pompadours at each other like warriors locked in ritual combat in New Guinea, where the victory goes to the man who shakes the most fearsome headdress at his enemy. One day when McDougall and I were stretching our legs in the corridor during a recess I said something about Foster's hair.

"My God, yes, that hair," McDougall said. A principle widely honoured at the bar, he told me, is that a judicious show of grey above the temples will do more to sway some juries than a strong argument.

"Do you realize Brian's ten years younger than I am, and look at me, still waiting for my first grey streak. I'd kill for that hair.")

Slaght took Bell quickly through his own history. At the end of his second year in a general science course at Carleton University, Bell said, he left in the autumn of 1965 to work for Falconbridge Ltd., a large and diverse mining company that earned most of its revenue from nickel. He worked underground as a miner for a while, then returned to the surface to work on exploration projects as a geological assistant. In 1970 he went back to Carleton for a bachelor of science degree in geology. Then he joined Dome Mines, which was still producing gold in the Porcupine camp near Timmins. Bell worked for Dome on a variety of geological projects, below ground and above, until the autumn of 1980.

In October that year a woman who said her name was Nell Dragovan phoned Bell from Vancouver. She had been given his name, she said, by Don McKinnon. Dragovan told Bell she was running a small exploration company called Corona Resources. The company's first project, a small drilling program on a natural-gas prospect, had come up dry. The second, acquired that week, was a block of claims at Hemlo. The claims had come to her through a numbered company run by a man named Steven Snelgrove, but they had been staked, she said, by McKinnon and another Timmins prospector, John Larche.

Although Bell had never heard of Dragovan or Corona, he already knew all there was to know at this stage about the Hemlo claims. Several months earlier, McKinnon had brought Bell his dossier on the Hemlo property. Bell sent McKinnon to Donald Moore, who sent him to Snelgrove, who then found his way to Dragovan. When Dragovan phoned Bell, the call was the last bud in the daisy chain, though neither of them realized it until they had a chance to compare stories later.

Dragovan asked Bell to take charge of the exploration program on the Hemlo claims as Corona's consulting geologist. Bell was winding up a feasibility study on a gold property at Detour Lake for Dome Mines, but he would be finished in about a month, and after that he intended to strike out on his own as a consultant. He told Dragovan he'd be glad to take the Hemlo job. On October 3, 1980, Dragovan wired Bell ten thousand dollars out of her own bank account — like Bell's other client, Bronson, Corona was broke — and Bell joined the select but growing company of geologists who had tried to solve the Hemlo puzzle.

He started, as McKinnon had, in the archives. Like any other researcher trying to unlock a secret of nature, a geologist will usually find that earlier work on the same set of questions has already led to some of the answers. Two written reports in particular turned out to be important, both to Bell's search for gold and to the legal struggle that followed between Corona and Lac. One of these was the 1948 report by Trevor Page, the professor of geology from Thunder Bay who had been the first to stake the ground and the first to cut some diamond-drill holes into it. Page had much to tell Bell about the subsurface geology. Indeed, later in the trial McDougall would argue that Page in 1948 published pretty well everything of value that Corona claimed was confidential when it passed on much the same information to Lac in 1981. The second significant geologist's report was new, written by Thomas Skimming for Steven Snelgrove's numbered company, 435198 Ontario — the company from which Corona had acquired the claims.

An exploration company commonly starts out as a shell, with nothing in it except possibly a few debts left over from previous ventures that have failed. The company then acquires a mineral prospect (as Corona had acquired the Hemlo claims) for the smallest cash payment it can get away with and the promise to pay as much in the future as it takes to close the deal. These downstream payments usually take the form of stepped instalments on the purchase price, stock in the company, and a royalty on the mine's production should anything be found that is worth producing. Such a transaction isn't properly a sale at all, but an option agreement. Between any two steps in the agreement the buyer can decline to make the next payment, drop the option, and let the property revert to the original owner. If the owner can't afford to do the required assessment work himself his title to the claims lapses, and another prospector can stake them.

Like most use-it-or-lose-it systems, this one looks harsh, but in fact it delivers rough justice in a fairly even-handed way. At least nobody can stake claims merely to withhold them from somebody else; the price of keeping them is too high.

A company with a new property in hand commissions a consulting geologist to make a report. If the consultant decides the property has promise he recommends a work program and estimates the cost of carrying it out. On the strength of his recommendation, which must be filed with the stock exchange, the company drafts a proposal to raise the money needed to do the work by selling shares to the public. Without the recommendation of a consulting geologist the stock exchange will not approve the company's application to sell a new issue of stock. But when the exchange does approve such a sale — called an underwriting — the money raised from the sale must be spent to do the work recommended by the consultant. Unless, of course, he turns out to be wrong.

The report written by Thomas Skimming for Corona recommended a work program in two phases. Phase One included some surface geology and ten thousand feet of diamond drilling. Should the results justify going on with the work, Phase Two was to follow up with fifteen thousand additional feet of drilling. Skimming also raised the question of the adjoining properties: the block of claims north of the boundary (what later came to be called the Hughes claims and later still became the Noranda mine), and the block to the west (the Williams claims, which became the Lac mine). Skimming said it would be a good idea to acquire both these properties. He was less clear about when they should be acquired, and his lack of clarity would become another issue in the trial.

A little later, when Nell Dragovan sold stock to the public to raise money for Corona, she used Skimming's report to satisfy the stock exchange. A rule of the exchange requires the writer of such a report to be a consultant, and to own no stock or any other interest in the company. The rule is meant to reassure investors that the opinion they're betting their money on was arrived at by a professional exercising his independent judgement, rather than by an employee or shareholder who might put his own interest ahead of the outside investors'. While the rule is better than no rule at all, it attributes to the consultant a degree of selflessness he may not have. Suppose a consulting geologist writes a report that says, in effect, forget about this hemlock bog. By following this advice the promoter loses twice: first he loses the money he's already spent to acquire the option, then he loses the chance to bring in more money through the stock exchange. How likely is the promoter to call the same geologist the next time he needs a report for financing purposes?

Happily for David Bell, this rule did not apply to him when he went to work for Corona. Thomas Skimming had already written the report that would give the project legitimacy with the stock exchange. Bell's role was merely to carry out Skimming's recommendations. There was no rule to bar him from taking a share of the profit arising from his work, should there be any.

A geologist who launches a new exploration project sets out to draw a series of maps. Bell began with a fairly conventional surface map of the property in two dimensions, then moved into the third. This, the vertical dimension, is of course the important one for mineral exploration. Think of a deep box, the lid at ground level, the sides running down through the substrata. The lid may be almost a mile square, as the lid of the Corona box is. The bottom of the box will be found only when the diamond drills probe the limits of the structure, but for practical reasons the depth will not exceed three miles. South Africans are now mining gold more than two miles below the surface, but at these depths the build-up of heat begins to defeat any known method of ventilation.

Inside the box are layers of rock, each composed of unpredictable combinations of many minerals. The layers, which at one time were more or less ordered and continuous, are now altered, twisted, fractured, tilted, folded, and raked by a series of epic upheavals, collisions, and eruptions. The geologist's task, which to an onlooker appears to be impossible, is to draw a map that shows what's in the box, and where to find it.

Bell began by hiring an assistant, John Dadds, who would be the site geologist — the man on the ground. Dadds moved with his wife and small child in a house trailer to White River, the village twenty-five miles east of Hemlo that is proud of its mid-winter frigidity. Through Donald McKinnon, Bell got in touch with his old friend, geophysicist Peter Ferderber. Ferderber provided two work parties, one to cut lines and the other to follow the line-cutters with a geomagnetic survey. Before Bell could begin his series of maps reaching down into the third dimension he needed a two-dimensional grid on the surface; from this he could fix the location of whatever he might find below. To create the grid, Ferderber's first crew cut lines from one boundary of the property to another at intervals of a hundred feet. The lines were wide enough for a man to walk down and flagged with strips of bright ribbon to make them easier to find. When the last east-west line intersected the last north-south line, Bell had his map-making grid engraved on the lid of the box. Now he could start trying to see what was in the unlit interior.

All rock contains enough magnetically active material to create a magnetic field that will vary, however slightly, from the fields created by the surrounding rocks. By reading these variations with an instrument called a magnetometer and then making a plot of the readings, a geophysicist can begin to "see" the contours of the subsurface rock. Although gold is magnetically inert, concentrations of gold are most likely to appear where the rock pattern has been changed by stress — fault lines, shear zones, intrusions of rock that began as one type and then by heat or pressure were altered to another.

Contours plotted from magnetometer readings can help locate such zones of stress. A zone that yields a sharply higher reading is called a "magnetic anomaly". While no anomaly, however strongly marked, gives a geologist any assurance of finding a mine, a well-defined anomaly does give him a somewhat better chance of finding a mineral deposit of some kind. The great base-metal mine at Kidd Creek was found by Texas Gulf Sulphur by drilling an anomaly, while the Windfall Affair resulted from drilling another. Where a geologist finds magnetically active minerals in the rock he may find inactive ones as well, including gold.

Before the end of 1980 a magnetometer crew was out walking the lines at Hemlo, despite the risk of dismemberment by frostbite. Dadds was logging the readings and plotting them in three dimensions. Bell was well launched on the task of interpreting the results. At the same time he was studying the reports and logs left behind by the geologists who had worked over the ground before him. Early in 1981 he moved a diamond drill onto the ground and put down his first hole.

Dadds meanwhile had moved a rough one-room wooden trailer onto a corner of the claim block near the road. Along one wall he built a rack to hold standard wooden core boxes, five feet long with grooved bottoms to hold five parallel lengths of core. On the rack Dadds could stack a dozen boxes, about three hundred feet of core in all. As the drills turned during the winter and spring, thousands of feet of core would be cut from the underlying rock. The boxes holding core that was currently under examination would be held on the rack inside the shack; the rest, hundreds of additional boxes, would be racked outside the trailer.

Beyond the rack at one end of the room Dadds set up a core-splitter, a kind of jig that holds a short rod of core clamped beneath a steel wedge. Hit sharply by a heavy hammer, the wedge splits the core along its length. One half of the split core goes to a laboratory to be assayed for its mineral content, if any, while the other half is kept on the site. When geologists say they are looking at core, they almost always mean this retained half of a length of split core. At the other end of the room Dadds installed a table on which to examine core, write the results of his examinations — the drill logs — and plot the vertical profiles of the drill holes. Then, towards the centre of the rear wall, he plugged in his most vital piece of geological field equipment, his electric space heater, and the Corona core shack was ready for work.

Before the end of February 1981, Dadds had passed on to Bell the logs for about three thousand feet of drilling. These early holes confirmed the results logged by Trevor Page and the others who had drilled the ground in the 1940s and '50s. There was indeed gold here, but mainly in the trace amounts geologists call "anomalous" — more than enough to detect in the assay laboratory, not nearly enough to mine at a profit.

With the help of the drill logs, though, Bell's three-dimensional map was becoming clearer. Brooding over the map (a geophysicist told me that "interpretation" is what you call brooding when you do it on a retainer) Bell began to change his mind, not about the quantity of gold that might be found in the deposit, but about the nature of the deposit itself.

Gold gets into the rocks from which miners dig it out in one of two ways, Bell told the court. In a primary deposit, gold is one of the materials that combines to form the rock in the first place. In a secondary deposit, the rock forms first, then gold-bearing material intrudes on it, either into cracks in the rock or fissures between one block of rock and the blocks around it.

The distinction between primary and secondary deposits is fairly recent and by no means as clear-cut as the definition makes it sound. Until well into this century the distinction that was important to seekers after gold was between placer deposits, which have been stripped from the host rock by erosion, and lode deposits, in which the gold still resides within the rock. At the time Bell started brooding over the subsurface contours he was mapping at Hemlo, nearly all the lode gold ever discovered in the Western Hemisphere appeared in some form of vein structure — the kind of deposit that is today described as secondary. But there were a handful of fairly recent exceptions. They included a mine near Timmins where Bell had once done some work, and one near Bousquet, Quebec, that was owned by Lac and had been developed by, among others, Dennis Sheehan.

In neither of these primary deposits did the gold occur in veins. Rather, it was disseminated throughout relatively wide bands of rock in particles too small to be seen with the naked eye. This is the stuff called "invisible" gold. Such deposits are often much larger, and can yield more ounces of gold to a ton of rock, than showier deposits in narrow vein systems. Most of the gold mined in South Africa, incomparably the world's leading source of new gold, is from primary deposits of "invisible" gold.

Now Bell began to think that when he and the geologists who had been over the ground before him had assumed they were dealing with a conventional secondary deposit they may well have been mistaken. He phoned Nell Dragovan in Vancouver to tell her that he was starting to believe they were working on a primary deposit.

Assuming that to be the case, she said, what were they supposed to do about it? Among other things, Bell replied, they should now go after the adjoining ground, the claims to the north that would later become known as the Hughes claims, and the Williams claims to the west.

Dragovan told him to go right ahead. Bell said he didn't have time, and anyway he had no experience in making land deals. They agreed to turn again to Donald McKinnon.

"You and Mr. McKinnon were friends?" McDougall asked Bell in cross-examination.

"Yes."

"He was an old friend of your father's?"

"Yes."

"Had you done anything with him prior to this?"

Bell said he had worked on a number of McKinnon projects indirectly, and two, Bronson Mines and Card Lake Copper Mines, directly.

"Card Lake Copper Mines, I take it, was not a gold-mining company?"

"It wasn't a copper-mining company either." A ripple of amusement went around the courtroom. Bell waited for the moment to pass before he added, "And I worked on Bronson."

"That was a project in which Messrs. Hughes and Lang were involved?"

"Yes."

McDougall then tried to take Bell over the events of February 1981, when Bell told McKinnon that Corona now wanted to acquire the northern claims and the Williams property, and asked McKinnon to act as Corona's agent. The story becomes somewhat tangled here, but to the best of Bell's recollection, McKinnon told him he couldn't act for Corona right away, because he was under an obligation to Hughes and Lang.

"Did he tell you *what* ground he was dealing on with Hughes and Lang?"

"He was talking about the staked ground to the north, and about the Williams property."

Later I checked the date of the agreement by which McKinnon and his partners sold the northern claim block to Hughes and Lang. It was dated March 31, revised, and signed by both parties in April. Technically, at least, when Bell first raised the question with McKinnon of Corona's wish to acquire the northern claim block, McKinnon still owned it. He had, however, a verbal understanding with Hughes and Lang that the claims were theirs if they decided to buy them, and this is what he now told Bell. If Hughes and Lang said no, then he'd sell the claims to Corona. At some stage he had reached the same understanding with Hughes and Lang about the Williams claims — they could have first call on the Williams property in the event he could acquire it. Corona could have the property only if Hughes and Lang said no first. When Bell told McDougall this, he affected incredulity.

"Why in the world would you not go after the Williams property yourself?"

"I wasn't going to under-deal Mr. McKinnon."

"Can I have it from you that it was Mr. McKinnon who made the decision?"

"No. Mr. McKinnon had a prior expression of interest from Mr. Hughes. I would not under-deal him. When Mr. Hughes decided his answer was no, I then said go ahead for us."

Throughout this exchange McDougall had been suggesting, without saying so in as many words, that he found it hard to believe that Bell failed to compete with McKinnon for the Williams claims. The implication is that Corona should have done to McKinnon what Lac subsequently did to Corona. Bell had said repeatedly that he would not "under-deal" McKinnon, but what was actually at work here for Bell and McKinnon, I am quite sure, was the spirit of the North.

"Did Mr. McKinnon not tell you in February or March that he was trying to pick up the Williams claims for Mr. Hughes?"

"I think earlier. It was February or March when he said he was now clear to go ahead and get them for Corona. I said fine, do it for Corona."

"And your understanding with McKinnon was that you were retaining him, but he was working on his own hook." In that case, McDougall asked, "Can you think of any reason why Mr. McKinnon wouldn't tell Mrs. Williams he was representing Corona?"

"Certainly it was my understanding in giving him instructions that he was doing it for Corona, and that there was a commitment to Corona."

McDougall fell silent while he moved papers around on his lectern. He let the pause stretch for a beat or two. Then he told Bell that he was going to read from a transcript taken from testimony Bell had given in a 1982 examination for discovery. The significant sentence was, "Don told me we would have first right of refusal."

"Were you asked those questions?" McDougall intoned in the portentous formula used by examining lawyers who believe themselves to be on the trail of a damaging contradiction, "Did you give those answers, and were they true?"

"Yes."

"So there was no commitment obliging Mr. McKinnon to deal the Williams claims to you, even if he got them?"

This was delivered less as a question than a conclusion, and McDougall punctuated the statement with another beat of silence. Alan Lenczner jumped into the opening he left.

"That's exactly wrong!" Lenczner said, almost shouting. "Even in law!"

He calmed down a little, and explained to the judge that a right of first refusal meant that Corona wasn't obliged to buy, but McKinnon was obliged to sell to Corona should they choose to exercise their right. From the judge's expression, and the inactivity of his writing hand, it was plain that he knew what a right of first refusal meant at least as well as Lenczner did. I wondered for a moment whether lecturing a judge about something he already knew was a tactical mistake, or whether it was a worse mistake to miss a chance to get a point of this kind entered in the written record.

When the judge stirred and started to speak, I thought he might be going to offer Lenczner a mild rebuke for boring him, but what he said was, "I see it's almost four o'clock. Would this be a convenient time to adjourn?" All rose.

THOUGH IT IS NOT A NEWS-
letter and rarely prints news, the *George Cross Newsletter* was devised as a
vehicle for press releases submitted to the Vancouver Stock Exchange by
companies whose stock is traded on the exchange. They are for the most
part small, speculative mineral-exploration companies. When they spend
their money in a way that might affect the value of their shares, the exchange
requires them to spell out what they've done by filing a document with the
exchange. Although the document is called a press release, it is really a sort
of work-in-progress memorandum that more often than not reports on recent
drill holes and assays. George Cross makes a daily compilation of these work
memos and circulates it mainly to brokers and speculators, who read it to
keep abreast of drill results that might give them signals to buy or sell stock.
The remaining readers are nearly all people who work for other mining
companies; reading the newsletter gives them a way of looking over their
competitors' shoulders.

Christopher Pegg, a young geologist who opened a regional exploration
office for Lac Minerals at Kirkland Lake in the summer of 1980, subscribed
to the *George Cross Newletter* by airmail. In the issue of March 20, 1981,
Pegg's eye fell on the results reported by Corona Resources of drill holes 11
through 22 at their Hemlo property. Unlike most of George Cross's reports,
this one included a short interview with Corona's consulting geologist, David
Bell.

"The gold is not in a vein," Cross quoted Bell as saying, "but is in a
mineralized horizon in an anomalous quartz sericite schist which is carrying
gold across its entire width, which varied from 50 to perhaps 200 feet, grading 0.01 to 0.02 ounces of gold per ton."

Pegg clipped the story and sent it to Toronto, to his boss, Dennis Sheehan,
Lac's vice-president of exploration. Pegg's covering note, dated March 27,
said, "This is the Hemlo gold property where the zone runs under the road
(Hwy. 17). It looks like they're just drilling the old zone, but we should
watch their future results, being so close to Manitouwadge." At Manitouwadge, thirty-odd miles north of Hemlo, Lac had a large mill that had
been left idle by the closing of a played-out base-metal mine.

Sheehan called Pegg back and asked him to get in touch with Corona's principals. Pegg was to "tell them we'd be very interested in going to see their property", with "obvious possibilities of making a deal with them". Pegg tried to call Bell. He failed to reach him, but eventually he got a number for the Corona office in Vancouver, and on April 6, 1981, he spoke to Nell Dragovan. She made a note of the conversation.

"Chris Togg," she wrote, "wants to discuss a partnership or whatever re Hemlo property pass info to Dave."

"Dave" was David Bell. Over the next few weeks Pegg and Bell spoke on the telephone several times in the course of arranging a visit by Lac to the Corona exploration site. They settled on May 6, a day when Nell Dragovan was coming east from Vancouver and Pegg's boss, Dennis Sheehan, was free to come north from Toronto. On May 5 Dragovan flew to Timmins, where Bell picked her up at the airport.

Sheehan and Pegg, meanwhile, met at Wawa, two hundred miles down the Trans-Canada Highway towards Toronto, on the afternoon of May 5. They drove to White River and checked in to the Green Gables Motel, where they ate dinner. Afterward they went to Sheehan's room to talk.

"Dennis said he'd looked at the property before," Pegg told the court. "When Ardel had it." Ardel was one of the companies that had held the site after the original Lake Superior Mining claims staked by Trevor Page lapsed; Ardel had drilled a few holes there in 1973. Sheehan told Pegg he "believed the zone was running about point oh eight" at the time of his earlier visit.

In the morning they expected to meet Dragovan and Bell at the motel. After breakfast they waited an hour or more, then decided to drive the twenty-five-odd miles to the Corona property to look for them. When they reached the Corona core shack there was no sign of Bell or anybody else, "so Dennis decided that instead of hanging around we should look at outcrops along the highway".

The engineers who built the highway cut repeatedly through outcrops of native rock. Sheehan and Pegg drove down the highway, watching each side of the road. Whenever they reached a rock cut that looked interesting they pulled up and walked the length of the rock face, making a mental catalogue of the rock types, their strike, and their dip. Sheehan pointed at what he called "popcorn units", dykes of dark volcanic material of a variety he'd seen before at Manitouwadge. They saw various units of altered volcanic rock, dark and light, and in one outcrop saw quartz veins. More than once, they saw a unit of quartz sericite schist, the material that was host to the gold traces Trevor Page had found here. On the south side of the road they saw a tumbled log structure with a pile of core partly hidden by undergrowth beside it — what Pegg called a "historical curiosity" — and they stopped and looked at a few pieces of the core.

"You brought a hammer, sample bags, and tags?" Lenczner asked when he cross-examined Pegg.

"Yes."

"You spent an hour looking at the core pile and outcrops?"

"About."

"You did not take any samples for assay?"

"No."

"You did not map the outcrops?"

"No."

"You did not make notes on the outcrops?"

"There is a diary entry."

"Yes. It says you were in White River. That's all it says?"

"Yes."

The Lac defence stands partly on the argument that, at the moment we have now reached in the story, when Sheehan and Pegg were finished looking at the outcrops but before they met Bell and Dragovan at the Corona core shack, there was nothing more Sheehan needed to know before deciding to go after the Williams property. By combining information that was already on the public record (much of it placed there by Corona itself) with what he learned from his own examination of the outcrops along the highway, Sheehan was "in an almost unique position to assess the potential of the Hemlo area". He had examined the Corona property when Ardel owned it, and he had been in charge of exploration at Bousquet, Quebec, where Lac a few years earlier had developed a gold mine in a somewhat similar geological environment.

McDougall said Sheehan needed nothing more from Corona to help make the decision to acquire the Williams claims. In Lac's view he got nothing more.

David Bell and Nell Dragovan reached the Green Gables Motel in White River around noon on May 6. They asked for Pegg and Sheehan. The motel keeper told them the Lac people had gone, in Bell's phrase, "into the field". Bell and Dragovan ate lunch at the motel and drove to the Corona core shack where they arrived at about one. They were chatting with Bell's assistant, John Dadds, when Pegg and Sheehan pulled up. Bell, the host, made the introductions.

Like McKinnon and Bell, Dennis Sheehan came from the mining camps of Northern Ontario. He was born in 1936 in Blind River, a gold and uranium camp on the Canadian Shield. Members of the mining fraternity who know both McKinnon and Sheehan will say that as youngsters they were remarkably alike, one as aggressively hard-handed as the other, both more at home in the hockey rink than the classroom. Each was more likely to ride you into the corner on the butt of his stick than skate you around in the middle of the ice. Sheehan played the game well enough to be imported for a year by St. Michael's College in Toronto, a junior-hockey power at the time. He was back in Blind River for his last year at school, and the day after he graduated he went underground to work as a geological sampler in a local mine known as the Pronto. He was nineteen, and with the exception of two years at McGill University in Montreal he had spent his entire life since working for mining companies.

Yet it was not altogether clear that Sheehan still had the Northern spirit. Since 1968 he had worked out of Lac's head office in Toronto, and for most of those years he lived with his family in Mississauga, a bedroom suburb for the upwardly mobile on Toronto's western outskirts. As Sheehan began his testimony on his first day in the witness stand he spoke hoarsely, whether because he had a throat infection or because this was his normal speaking voice it was impossible to say. He had the deep-jawed features of a stage Irishman and hair that had turned an even, nickel-plated grey, appropriate to a man ten days from his fiftieth birthday. But the heavy straight hair had been blown dry and the navy-blue suit with the buttoned-up vest and the understated blue silk tie were in taste so good that if the man wearing them had been standing on a street corner in Blind River people would have come by just to look.

Sheehan soon gave some indication that since leaving the North he may have acquired boardroom habits of mind to match his boardroom wardrobe. Straight talk is part of the Northerner's code of straight dealing; Sheehan talked in curves. When Lac's lawyer, John Lorn McDougall, took him over his own job history, McDougall asked how long he had worked for Denison Mines at Elliot Lake. It was a question so innocuous it was scarcely worth asking. Sheehan creased his brow in visible thought.

"My belief," he said, "is approximately two years."

Sheehan's answer reminded me of a television interview I did in the 1960s with Wayne Lonergan, a Canadian who had just been released from prison in the United States after serving a long sentence for the murder of his bride while they were on a Florida honeymoon. Before we talked about anything else, I told Lonergan, I had to ask him whether he had murdered his wife.

"My position," Lonergan said, "is no."

Two questions later, McDougall asked Sheehan whether the Wilroy Mine was part of the Lac group when Sheehan worked there. This was much the same as asking somebody who had worked on the Chevrolet assembly line whether that was part of General Motors.

"My belief," Sheehan said, "is yes."

A little later, Sheehan told McDougall he had instructed Pegg to get in touch with the people running Corona. "Tell them," he'd said, "we'd be very interested in going to see their property, with obvious possibilities of making a deal with them."

Within a few minutes, McDougall raised the same issue from a slightly different vantage point. "Prior to the visit, did you have any intentions with respect to Corona and an arrangement with them?"

"No," Sheehan said. "Not at all."

Sheehan told the court that when he and Pegg stepped on to Corona's property on May 6, 1981, the first words he said after the introductions were a reminder to Bell and Dragovan that Lac "had a problem" with a company called New Cinch. Whatever Lac might finally decide about the Corona property, he told them, "I was going to have to come in and supervise an inspection of all their core and do an analysis, because of what happened in the New Cinch case."

He said this while they were walking from the roadside to the core shack, a distance of perhaps a hundred feet. When they reached the core shack, Sheehan said, they all turned around and walked back to the roadside. On the return walk he told Bell and Dragovan that "we didn't want any confidential or unpublished information". At times, he said, Lac will "buy large stock positions" in exploration companies. "If I had information [about Corona] that wasn't published to the shareholders or the public at large, we may have put ourselves in a conflict position."

Bell had earlier testified that nobody had raised the issue of confidential information, neither Dragovan nor himself nor Pegg nor Sheehan. McDougall contradicted him.

"In fact, Mr. Sheehan told you he didn't want to see any confidential information."

"No. He said no such thing."

"I put it to you he did."

"He did not. If he had, I would have told him to get into his car and get off the property." Bell raised his voice to a high, hard note.

"I have never known anybody in this industry who would come on to a property and then say they didn't want to see anything confidential. I've never in my life heard of anybody who'd come on a property and say this."

Pegg later said yes, he had heard Sheehan tell Bell he didn't want to see confidential or unpublished information, though he didn't know what Sheehan meant by "unpublished".

Cross-examining Sheehan, Alan Lenczner "suggested" that this conversation "never took place". Sheehan insisted it had. Having lost twenty million dollars on New Cinch, he said, "I remember that conversation and where it took place very well."

"You hadn't made a proper property visit to New Cinch?"

"We made a property visit."

"That's that trespass you told us about?"

"No, no, no. We made a property visit to New Cinch, and we did precisely what I explained to Mr. Bell would have to be done on the Corona property."

"Yes?"

"And when we did that, that's when we found out everything was falsified."

For Dennis Sheehan, the New Cinch affair began during the same week the first lines were cut on the Corona property at Hemlo: the second week of November 1980. His stockbroker phoned to tell him that a company Sheehan had been tracking in the *George Cross Newsletter*, New Cinch Uranium, had just reported a remarkable assay result from the twenty-ninth hole on ground the company was drilling near Orogrande, New Mexico. New Cinch stock was selling that day for about two and a half dollars a share, up within the last year or so from seventeen cents. Sheehan told his broker to buy him a thousand shares at the market.

The following Monday, back at head office in Toronto, Sheehan briefed Lac's president, Peter Allen, and Lac's solicitor, Ian Hamilton, on the New Cinch drill hole. That week Sheehan dug out all the past references to New Cinch in the *George Cross Newsletter* and the *Northern Miner*. From the Vancouver Stock Exchange Hamilton got a copy of the statement of material facts on which the New Cinch financing had been based. Armed with this information and — as Lenczner carefully established in the courtroom — nothing more than this, the Lac group began buying New Cinch stock. On November 20, a Thursday, they bought a million dollars' worth.

"That is a sizeable amount, is it not?" Lenczner asked. "Well," Sheehan said, "It's a relative thing. I have been involved where our company has invested a lot more."

True. The next day, Friday, Lac bought almost two million dollars worth of New Cinch; on Monday, the twenty-fourth, three million dollars' worth. "When I realized we had purchased this much stock," Sheehan told Lenczner, "and there was a possibility we were going to continue purchasing stock, I suggested that I would like to fly down there." He told two geologists from Lac's Vancouver office to meet him the next day in New Mexico.

"Pretty high-powered group?" Lenczner asked.

"I wouldn't say we were that high-powered," Sheehan said.

The next morning the three men hired a car and drove into the desert.

"You went out onto the New Cinch property?"

"Yes, we crossed, unh, we went on the New Cinch property, yes, and other properties."

"And you never told any of the New Cinch people that you were going to go on their property?"

"No, that's correct."

"You were trespassing."

"Yes," Sheehan said, "you could call it that."

From the transcript of an earlier examination, Lenczner then read Sheehan's description of what they'd done next. "There was no one around, and we decided at that point — we said let's just get a chain and start measuring down and taping in where these drill holes are." They plotted the holes on a map, and returned to Canada.

"And between the twenty-fourth of November, when you had six million dollars' worth of New Cinch stock, and the twenty-fourth of December, your company bought another twenty million dollars' worth of this stock, or a total of twenty-six million dollars' worth?"

"Yes."

"Without speaking to the geologist?"

"Yes."

"Without seeing the core?"

"Yes."

"Or sections?"

"Yes."

"And, sir, may I have it that when you went down to the property, either before or when you came back, you didn't tell anybody about it because you didn't feel it was necessary?"

"That's correct."

Sheehan described at some length the kind of gold deposit he thought New Cinch might have found. Then Lenczner said, "Let us just finish the story off so we are not left in doubt. In January 1981, you learned that the assay results that were being published were phony?"

"That is correct."

"What had happened, is that in the assay lab the core is put into a solution, and that is how the assays are done, in very general terms?"

"In one system. In another system they are fused."

"It appears someone tampered with that system and added gold to it to give them higher assays?"

"Well, I have my own opinion of what happened there. I have not expressed it anywhere yet. If you want it, I will give it to you."

Lenczner didn't ask for Sheehan's opinion. "Basically what you learned was that the assaying was wrong or the reporting of the assays was incorrect?"

"The assay reports were false."

"And as a result, in the month of January, Lac sold all of its stock in New Cinch, and took a loss in the area of twenty-one million dollars?"

"That is correct."

"You brought a lawsuit?"

"Yes."

"The lawsuit was settled?"

"Yes."

"And I think the settlement figure was around four million dollars?"

"Yes."

Here Lenczner let the New Cinch story drop. "Sir," he said, returning to Sheehan's trip to Hemlo on May 6, 1981, "what you wanted to see on the property was core?"

"I didn't have that specifically in mind, but if the core was available to see, we'd see it, yes."

"Sections, if they were available?"

"Whatever was available, yes. I didn't know what would be available."

"And you wanted to speak to the geologist?"

"Yes, I wanted to speak to, yes, the geologist — or the principals, I think, is what we suggested."

"Because you weren't going to make the same mistake that had just cost you twenty million dollars in New Cinch? That is, take any kind of a position without, umm, in the absence of, information?"

"You can draw that comparison, but that's not the case."

"Was New Cinch not still ringing in your ears?"

"Oh, you can believe it was ringing in my ears. Yes."

"That's right. You couldn't have been, you and the members of the company who made that decision, you couldn't have been very proud of yourselves, having gone into that venture without knowledge?"

"Well," Sheehan said, "let's put it this way. It wasn't a question of not being proud of ourselves. We were very sad that this happened to our industry."

Lenczner was not yet willing to be deflected from the question of core at Corona's drill site.

"You were going up there with a view to making a deal?"

"Yes . . ."

"The deal . . ."

". . . if possible."

". . . the deal involved you looking at core yourself?"

"It eventually may have. Yes."

"Yes. What do you mean, 'it may have'? You said you wanted to look at the core before you made a deal."

"I indicated to him [Bell] that I would have to come in and go through all the core."

"Before you made a deal?"

"Yes."

"And yet you say in the same breath, I don't want anything that's confidential?"

"Yes."

"How do you fit those two together? They don't fit, sir."

"Well," Sheehan said, "if you have a meeting of minds on what kind of deal you want to make. You don't have to look at core to do that."

Nell Dragovan had never seen a diamond drill at work, and Bell wanted to show her one. On the day of the meeting with Sheehan there were two drills working on the Corona property, one within a couple of hundred feet of the core shack, the other a mile or more to the east. The nearby drill was putting down Hole 76, a number to remember. Sheehan said that after they had all walked to the core shack together, wheeled around and walked back to the highway, they then drove to the site of the distant drill. Bell and Dragovan said they walked to the closer one, the one drilling Hole 76.

Similarly, Sheehan's testimony contradicted Bell's on almost every other question of fact about the visit. Bell said he spread a map of the area over the hood of a vehicle parked outside the core shack and indicated with his hand the location of the adjoining property Corona was interested in acquiring. Dragovan and Dadds confirmed this. Sheehan said he had seen only one map, a drill plan, inside the shack.

"I am suggesting there was a second map, a claim map, outside the core shack on the hood of a truck," Lenczner said.

"No," Sheehan said. "I never saw that."

Bell and Dadds said they showed Sheehan sections — drawings of the underground profiles — of the Corona drill holes. Pegg, Sheehan's assistant, confirmed this; Sheehan at first denied it.

"But if the sections were there," Lenczner said, "and Mr. Pegg says they were, then you must have seen them?"

"I don't know whether or not I must have seen them, but it's Mr. Pegg's recollection. Not mine."

In addition to looking at maps and reports, Sheehan and Bell not unnaturally engaged in a certain amount of discussion.

"You discussed the core?" Lenczner asked.

"Yes."

"You discussed the pyrite you saw in the core?" Pyrite is the mineral most frequently associated with gold.

"Yes."

"Pyrite in association with quartz sericite schist and gold in a mineralized horizon is important?"

"Yes."

"That particular discussion was with regard to the core?"

"Yes."

"Core coming from the mineralized horizon?"

"Yes."

"Several hundred feet down?"

"I don't know what hole we were looking at."

"Down. Underneath the ground."

"Certainly underneath the ground."

"You discussed the volcanogenic theory?"

"My belief is we discussed that, yes."

"Mr. Bell discussed it with you?"

"Yes, he was part of those discussions."

"You must have taken a lot of comfort from Mr. Bell, that here was a geologist who had done all this drilling on the site who was on the same wavelength as you?"

"I think a lot of geologists at that time were on that wavelength."

What conclusion would a geologist on that wavelength be likely to draw about the adjoining property? Lenczner tried to summarize: "You would know from looking at the core inside and outside the shack, the sections, the discussions with Mr. Bell about the volcanogenic deposits, and the discussions of the assays, you would know that any reasonable geologist who was drilling Corona would be interested in the Williams property to the west, would you not?"

"He certainly would be." For precisely that reason, Sheehan said, he advised Bell to look up the status of the Williams claims when he was in Thunder Bay. In reply Bell told him Corona already had somebody working on the Williams claims.

Bell was expecting to make a trip to Toronto two days later, on May 8. Sheehan asked him to come to Lac's office while he was in town. Bell agreed.

Bell and Nell Dragovan then left for Thunder Bay airport, where Dragovan was booked on a plane to Vancouver. The entire meeting had taken about an hour and a quarter.

"You were looking forward to concluding a deal with Corona and working with them?" Lenczner asked Sheehan.

"I was certainly looking forward to meeting Mr. Bell, yes, in Toronto and trying to make a deal with him."

Sheehan and Pegg went to Dadd's trailer in White River for a drink, then ate at the motel.

"Your plan was to remain in the area that evening?"

"Yes, it was."

"But all of a sudden your plans changed? After dinner you determined to get right back down to Toronto?"

"Yes. Later on that evening."

"And Mr. Pegg, it had been his intention to go back home, and he lived in Kirkland Lake?"

"Yes."

"But you changed Mr. Pegg's plans for him?"

"Yes."

"Mr. Sheehan, I suggest to you that after the site visit to the Corona property you were so excited about the discussion with Bell and what you had seen in the way of core and sections, and association of gold with the quartz sericite schist, that you determined that evening that you were going to get back to Toronto and you were going to do something about this? You were going to go and stake land, and you took Pegg along to give you a hand in all that?"

"No, that's not quite right. I think that what did happen was that . . . I arranged to meet Mr. Bell on the morning of May eighth in Toronto. So I wanted to get back to get fully prepared, to take a look at all the maps, to be in a good position to sit down and talk with Mr. Bell."

"Mr. Sheehan, you have told us that you hadn't slept much on the night of May the fifth because Mr. Pegg kept you up most of the night?"

"Yes. That was another consideration."

"You were tired by the evening of the sixth? Must have been."

"Yes, I was."

"You decided nevertheless to drive most of the night to get to Sault Ste. Marie?"

"Yes. And indeed I had to meet Mr. Bell on the morning of the eighth."

"It was not because you had to meet Mr. Bell on the morning of the eighth that you did this, Mr. Sheehan," Lenczner said, not so much asking a question as stating his case. "It was because what you saw on my client's property excited you."

"What I saw through the region from Cedar Creek straight through past your client's property and on beyond to the west is what really confirmed to us that we were looking at a volcanogenic belt of rocks," Sheehan answered. He insisted that this, coupled with the information Bell had already made public in the *George Cross Newsletter*, was all it took to put him on the track of volcanogenic gold deposits in the region.

Sheehan's plane from Sault Ste. Marie reached Toronto at 9:45 on the morning of May 7. He and Pegg went straight to his office, and he immediately called in his geological assistants, Gary Smith and Dr. Robert Valliant, and the staff geographer, Denise Feeley. All five went to work digging out published material on the Hemlo area: maps, geological reports, assessment records.

"As soon as you came in," Lenczner asked, "you gave them instructions to do a general geological review of the greenstone belt from Marathon to White River?"

"Not from Marathon to White River," Sheehan said. He then launched a long description of the information he and his people had assembled, and his reasons for excluding some parts of the region. While his answer wasn't narrowly responsive to Lenczner's question it wasn't particularly evasive either, but Lenczner went on the attack. Throughout the trial my notes to myself deal repeatedly with the way the system is designed to protect everybody except the witnesses. The judge is armoured by the sovereignty of the law itself. The opposing lawyers are protected by the rules of the adversarial system. But the lawyers for both sides can embarrass or, indeed, demean the witnesses more or less at will. There is, of course, a law of evidence, but the rules it sets out deal mainly with the material that is entering the trial record, not the people who are placing it there. If the notion of fairness applies to the witnesses at all, it is only to insist that witnesses for both sides be exposed to belittlement with an even hand.

"Look," Lenczner said to Sheehan after his tangential answer to the unimportant question about precisely how he'd defined the area of search for his assistants, "I just asked you about the instructions you'd given them, all right?"

"Yes."

"The instructions you gave them were to look at the entire belt from Marathon to White River. Do you agree or don't you?"

"No, not the entire belt. We didn't spend our time looking at the entire belt. Specifically, we were looking at the area that I have just outlined."

"Mr. Sheehan. Do you have trouble with my questions? I was asking about your instructions, not what you looked at. Let's just do it bit by bit. The instruction you gave them was to look at the entire belt from Marathon to White River?"

"No. I really don't recall giving them those instructions."

"Dr. Valliant has sworn, under oath, in this court, that that was the instruction you gave him. Do you disagree?"

"Dr. Valliant could be — I just don't recall giving those instructions. Dr. Valliant could be right."

"You don't remember?"

"That's correct."

"You did not tell Dr. Valliant that you had been in the Hemlo area the day before, isn't that right?"

"I didn't have a recollection of discussing it with him. But my feeling would be that we would have talked about it."

"You can't remember?"

"I can't remember discussing where we were, but it seems to me very logical that I discussed where we were the day before."

"Dr. Valliant has sworn, in this court, that you didn't tell him that you had been in the Hemlo area the day before."

"Well, I don't have any specific recollection of telling him, but I have just said that I . . . I . . . my belief would be that I would have discussed it."

"All right. Dr. Valliant says you didn't tell him that you had been on the Corona property and had seen core and spoken to the geologist. Is that correct?"

"If Dr. Valliant said that, that's certainly his view."

"Do you have a different recollection?"

"No, I don't have a different recollection."

"Why wouldn't you have told him that? Why wouldn't you have said, 'Dr. Valliant, I want you to look at this belt. I was up there just yesterday and I saw core with quartz sericite schist in a mineralized horizon with gold associated with it.' Why wouldn't you tell him that?"

"As I indicated, I don't have a specific recollection of talking about that, but my belief is that certainly we would have talked about it."

"Well, I don't understand this stuff, this 'I don't recollect but my belief is' stuff. What does that mean?"

"And so, and so — I'm sorry — I'm just saying that my belief is that we would have discussed it."

Sheehan was now pale, hesitant, and mumbling; his "I'm sorry" entirely out of the character he had shown the court on entering the witness box.

Breaking him down in this way was the only reason I could see for Lenczner's pursuit of the issue — otherwise it didn't much matter.

By the end of the day, Sheehan told the court, he and his assistants had outlined a block of six hundred claims, starting at Corona's eastern boundary and running most of the way to White River. This encompassed all the ground Sheehan and Valliant regarded as promising extensions of the rock system Corona was exploring — the system that might contain a volcanogenic gold deposit. Sheehan told Smith to get hold of a contractor and start staking those claims. Then they went home; May 7 had been a long day.

Bell's first call in Toronto on the morning of May 8, 1981, was to deliver a copy of his report on Phase One of Corona's exploration program at Hemlo to Thomas Skimming, the consulting geologist who had designed the program. Skimming told Bell how to reach Sheehan's office in the Royal Bank building — "one of the gold towers downtown" — by subway.

The first thing Sheehan did was take Bell out to lunch; then they went back to the Lac offices and talked. Bell said Sheehan seemed "very pleased" by what he'd seen at Hemlo. They went over the geology of the area, and Sheehan told Bell about Lac's decision to stake six hundred claims to the east of the Corona boundary. Then they talked about the terms they might strike if they closed a deal. According to Bell, "Sheehan said maybe Corona could participate in all the claims Lac was staking — and if so, that would make a very nice land package." They agreed that the package should include both the Williams claims and the Hughes claims. At some point during this discussion Bell said Corona was happy with its land position.

Bell's remark became an important part of Lac's case: telling Sheehan that Corona was happy with its land position amounted to saying that Lac was free to go ahead and acquire any ground they wanted to in the area. Cross-examining Sheehan, Lenczner returned to this matter.

"So that you had discussed with Bell on May eighth picking up the Hughes ground and the Williams ground?"

"Yes."

"And that Lac could pick it up, Corona could pick it up?"

"Yes."

"Or you would even fund Corona to pick it up?"

"Yes, we would do the funding."

"In addition to all that, you said you had a staking programme going down to the east and he could participate in that if he wanted?"

"Yes, we could bring him into that."

"It was in that context, I suggest to you, that he said, "We are happy with our land position.""

"It was in that context that he said, 'No, I'm happy with my land position and will continue drilling and doing the Phase Two programme.' "

They talked for about an hour. Sheehan didn't know anything about the holder of the claims to the north, Richard Hughes, so Bell told him a little about Hughes. Sheehan again gave Bell advice about how to go after the Williams claims. When they parted, after talking for about an hour, Sheehan told Bell he'd write to him, setting out his ideas about how Corona and Lac might work together.

Sheehan wrote to Bell on May 19, 1981. Of the thousands of pieces of paper that were entered as evidence in this case, Sheehan's letter is the only document that touches directly on the issue of whether a relationship of trust was established between Lac and Corona. For that reason, and because Sheehan reveals a good deal about himself in the way he writes, the letter is set out here in full.

> Further to our meeting in Toronto I would like to give you this letter as further evidence of our sincerity in joining with Corona re exploration in the Hemlo area.
>
> As we discussed there are a number of avenues that could be explored regarding a working arrangement re the property and to that end I will list the various possibilities.
>
> (a) Corona could have our company do a financing and ultimately we would scale it forward so as to control Corona.
>
> (b) We form a joint venture where Lac spends say 1.5 to 2.0 times amount spent by Corona for a 60% interest. Beyond that point we spend on a 60-40 basis or use a dilution formula down to a minimum should one party decide to stop contributing. In addition Lac would have to spend a definite amount of money to reach a threshold before they would acquire any interest.
>
> (c) A possible significant cash payment with a variation in interests as a result of the amount of cash payment. Followed by a Lac work proposal.
>
> As discussed we should entertain the possibility of Corona participate in the Hughes ground and that should be actively pursued. In addition we are staking ground in the area and recognizing Corona's limited ability to contribute we could work Corona into the overall picture as part of an overall exploration strategy.
>
> I believe at some point within the next few weeks we should have an understanding that Corona and Lac should seriously examine an avenue for continual work in the area. Perhaps you could give our management

a presentation of results to date ie sections, general geology, longitudinal presentation — location potential etc. Based on foregoing we could then arrive at a sound basis for structuring a working agreement.

In court Sheehan agreed that when he spoke in the letter of acquiring the Hughes ground he meant to include the Williams property as well. With this letter read into the record of the trial, Lac's task was more clearly defined. To win, Lac would have to persuade the judge that despite everything Sheehan said in this letter, Lac and Corona were not engaged in negotiations that created a relationship of trust. At first glance this would appear to be hard to do; but as Lac's lawyers urged the court to bear in mind, one party can't carry on a negotiation. It takes two.

Bell answered Sheehan on May 22. He said:

I am forwarding a copy of your proposal to Vancouver for the other directors to review. [Bell had meanwhile been made a director of Corona.] We are presently well into our Phase Two, exploring and extending the previously examined parameters outlined in Phase One. Our present plans are to complete 30,000 to 35,000 feet of diamond drilling at which time a general over-all review will take place.

At this point, until I hear otherwise from the directors in Vancouver, I like your idea of Corona's contribution with Long Lac Minerals Exploration Limited [as Lac was then called] as part of an overall exploration programme in the area.

In the meantime I do believe we should keep in touch and maintain the fine relationship presently established.

The next day Bell sent copies of Sheehan's letter and his own reply to Nell Dragovan in Vancouver. Both letters, he said, should be discussed with the other Corona directors.

Then, towards the end of May, everything changed. Overnight Corona, which even among penny mining companies had been a nonentity, became a star. The change was brought about by a hole in the ground, Corona's drill hole number 76. You may remember that when Sheehan made his site visit to the Corona property on May 6, there were two drills at work there, one back in the bush and one almost in the shadow of the core shack. The nearby drill was working on Hole 76.

Between finishing a diamond-drill hole and reporting on its significance, if any, the geologists have to do a number of jobs. First they have to split the core, then log it — the process, by no means exact, of identifying the rock types the drill has cut through. They send the split, logged core to an assay laboratory, and when the assay report comes back they make some averaging calculations, providing there are mineral values to average.

In Corona's case, when these steps had all been taken for whichever hole was then current, Bell or his assistant, John Dadds, would phone the results to Dragovan in Vancouver. From her notes of the call she would write the obligatory press release for the Vancouver Stock Exchange; a day or two after the release reached the Exchange its contents would usually appear in the *George Cross Newsletter*.

Cross-examining Bell about this process, McDougall backtracked through Corona's assay certificates and press releases. (The assays were performed by Swastika Laboratories, where George MacMillan twenty years earlier took the notorious Windfall core.) By painstakingly matching dates, McDougall established that for a number of holes the time lapse between the assay report and the press release was between one and four days. This pattern, if it was one, was broken in the case of Hole 76. The assay certificate was dated May 15, the press release May 26. A week seemed to have gone missing, and while this would have attracted no interest whatever had 76 been a routine hole, 76 was anything but.

"I know you don't get excited much," McDougall said to Bell, "but weren't you —"

"— I was excited. Yes," Bell said.

On his way back to Timmins from his May 8 meeting with Sheehan in Toronto, Bell had stopped off at Hemlo. John Dadds was just splitting the core from Hole 76. Although most of the gold at Hemlo is of the small-grained "invisible" variety, the two men this time saw visible gold in the rock. When the assay came back from Swastika Labs, it reported that a ten-and-a-half-foot section of the core bore gold, both visible and not, at a grade of 0.209 ounces of gold to a ton of rock. While this is something less than a sensational assay it is a good one, and when the result of Hole 76 was confirmed by later holes that cut wider sections of richer rock, Corona's Hemlo property became established as a gold discovery.

"This was the first time you'd ever discovered something on your own?" McDougall asked.

"Yes," Bell said.

"That was a significant event in your life, wasn't it?"

"It became a significant event."

Then why, McDougall asked, did a week go missing before the press release announcing the result of Hole 76 reached the Vancouver Stock Exchange?

"I don't know," Bell said.

McDougall asked about several calls Bell had made during the missing week. The people he'd called included Steven Snelgrove and Nell Dragovan, and various brokers and investors. Bell said he had told none of them about the results of Hole 76.

Among these calls there were four to and from the Vancouver offices of Allcorp, a management company run by Murray Pezim. On June 4, a week after the assays of Hole 76 became public knowledge, Allcorp took over from Nell Dragovan's Big Deal Investments the job of managing Corona Resources. On the same day Pezim joined Corona's board of directors.

Was this the same Pezim we last saw in the role of Earl Glick's rose boy at Timmins during the not-to-be-forgotten days of Texas Gulf Sulphur and Windfall? Why, shucks, is a monkey's nose red?

A Memory

. . . .

"You have to choose between trusting to the natural stability of gold and the honesty and intelligence of members of the government. And, with due respect for these gentlemen, I advise you, as long as the capitalist system lasts, to vote for gold."
— George Bernard Shaw, *The Intelligent Woman's Guide to Socialism and Capitalism*

". . . as far as the [defence of] the dollar was concerned, everything I had from the very first was this deep emotional attachment Kennedy had to the price of gold."
— Douglas Dillon, J.F. Kennedy's Secretary of the Treasury

The Treasury of the United States stands across the street from the green and airy grounds of the White House, but the Treasury, as befits its place in the world, is grey and heavy. Somewhere in the inner turnings of the Treasury I sat one afternoon across the desk from a bureaucrat of middle rank but great importance, judging by the tone of his utterances.

"My God," he said, leaning across the desk and pointing his pipe at me as though it were a pistol loaded with sincerity of a very high calibre, "would we rob them?"

By "them" he meant the poor countries that were getting foreign aid from the United States. By "rob" he meant raise the price of gold, thereby making the United States and other rich countries richer and the poor countries even poorer. (At the time poor countries were still called "poor", though already there were voices demanding they be called "underdeveloped" instead; they included such poor countries as Kuwait, Saudi Arabia, and South Korea.)

This conversation took place during the winter of 1960-61, between the election of John F. Kennedy and his inauguration. Nobody had yet spoken of Camelot, but the sentiment was gathering. Inside the Treasury, though, the prevailing mood was grim. The international monetary system was in trouble, the phrase "Gold Crisis!" was in the headlines several times a week, and in most quarters of the Western world there was dire speculation about the impending collapse of the gold standard.

Reading about all this from a distance had given me an uneasy sense that powerful forces were reshaping our lives to our peril, but what those forces might be was a great mystery to me. And so, if the truth be told, was the gold standard, a well-known phrase that stood for — what? I didn't know, and I doubted whether most of the people reading the same headlines knew. At that time I was what is called a self-assigning reporter; so I assigned myself to find out what the gold crisis was about, and went to Washington to begin.

Between the inner corridors of the Treasury and the basement of the White House I was passed from hand to hand by perhaps twenty civil servants, all experts in one aspect or another of the gold crisis. From them, and from the archives they directed me to, I learned that the gold standard was a sort of dipstick for the money pool. No such measure had existed when banks first circulated paper money; therefore one had to be invented. Sir Isaac Newton was the inventor, and David Ricardo gave the invention its name. Newton, the greatest scientist of his own time and perhaps any other, had previously devised the calculus, the laws of motion, and the idea of gravity, and had been rewarded by being appointed Master of the Royal Mint. (The Chancellor of the Exchequer who appointed him may have been unaware that Newton was also a lifelong student of alchemy and brought to the Mint his own ideas about the gold supply.) In 1717 Newton proclaimed that henceforth the price of an ounce of twenty-two-carat gold would be three pounds seventeen shillings elevenpence ha'penny, thereby giving paper money a fixed value for the first time. Since the Mint made no distinction between gold coins and paper notes of the same denomination, freely exchanging one for the other, this was a gold standard — though nobody yet thought to call it one.

The idea, while apparently a good one, would of course not work for people who were short of gold. There were plenty of these, notable among them the revolutionaries in France and America. Neither had any gold whatever, so both financed their revolutions by printing money. The result for both was hyperinflation, the kind that leads to an exchange rate the Americans described as "a wagon load of money for a wagon load of goods". People who were owed debts "hid like hunted things" from people trying to pay them back in paper money. Much later the Russian revolutionaries, trying to solve many of the same problems by the same means, wound up with a rouble that in a little more than two years was devalued by a ratio of fifty thousand million to one. The Americans, French, and Russians all eventually reverted to currencies backed by gold. Even so, the Russians denied the right to buy or sell gold to all but state agencies, although Lenin's published memoranda include one to a Commissar of Finance, Grigori Sokol'nikov, asking him to send Lenin a note setting out his proposals for the free circulation of gold.

In England, the gold price fixed by Sir Isaac Newton stayed fixed until Britain's concurrent wars against the upstarts in America and France combined to do what wars do to money almost as surely as revolutions — debase it. Sir William Pitt, the prime minister charged with putting down both the Americans and Napoleon, went to the Bank of England with financial demands the Bank met by printing paper money whether or not there was gold in the vault to back the notes. In time the Bank suspended the right to cash in paper guineas for gold ones. People spent paper and hoarded gold, an instance of Gresham's Law prevailing over Newton's fixed price. Prices rose, among them gold's.

In 1810 the House of Commons struck the Select Committee on the High Price of Gold Bullion. The committee's job was to find out what was going on. Was the value of paper money falling, or was the price of gold going up? Was the money supply driving the economy, or was the economy driving the money supply? These questions have ever since been much debated but never answered; precisely the same question took me to Washington in 1961, and precisely the same questions are at the heart of the inflationary agonies of the 1980s.

Among the contributors to the great debate that followed the Select Committee's hearings in 1810 was a young London stock broker, David Ricardo. As Newton had been first among scientists Ricardo would come to be acknowledged as first among economists. The measure of a "perfect" currency, Ricardo told the committee, was that it be "absolutely invariable in value". While gold and silver were less than perfect, they were "the best standard with which we are acquainted". He urged the committee to press for a standard by which paper money would always be "fully convertible" to gold; otherwise, he said, paper money "would be exposed to all the fluctuations to which the ignorance or the interests of the issuers might subject it".

For the first few years after Ricardo offered this advice Parliament was too busy to take it, pumping up the money supply for renewed struggles against Napoleon and the ex-colonials in America. But by 1821 the wars were over for a while. Britain was leading the world into the Industrial Revolution, and on the profits therefrom the Bank of England restored the free exchange of paper money for gold at exactly the same price fixed by Sir Isaac Newton a century earlier.

Now, for another century, Britain stayed on one version or another of Ricardo's gold standard. Eventually most of the industrialized states of Europe adopted the British practice. In 1867 they agreed at a meeting in Paris to settle international accounts thereafter in gold, and to make their currencies freely convertible to gold at a fixed rate. The United States held out until 1879, when paper dollars were made fully convertible to gold. The system worked, in part because as more gold was needed to accommodate more trade, more gold was fortuitously discovered — in the great gold rushes to California, to Australia, to Alaska and the Klondike, to South Africa, and to the camps of the Canadian Shield.

The world, or at least the richer part of it, was now on a gold standard for which many well-off people have been nostalgic ever since, and rightly so. "There can never have been a time," the most literate of living economists, J.K. Galbraith, has observed, "when it was as good to be rich." This was in part due to a general deflation that had endured for most of the previous fifty years. A long slow deflation does nothing much for the poor but is doubly good for the rich; the money they spend buys more while the money they keep is worth more. These gilded days lasted until the guns of August 1914 blew them away.

At the onset of the Great War the European states on both sides of the conflict abandoned the gold standard. The United States, when it entered the war, suspended international settlements in gold, although Americans retained the right to claim gold in exchange for paper money so long as they didn't then take the gold out of the country. When the war ended, the international gold standard was among the casualties. Partisans of gold see in this the cause of two opposite but equally painful effects — the various national inflations of the 1920s, and the global depression of the 1930s. Without a gold standard to keep them honest, governments ran up national debts greatly swollen already by war spending, creating unbearable inflation ending in punitive deflation.

Much the same causes, we are told, are pushing us towards much the same grim effects at the end of the 1980s. The same warning was sounded by many economists and political scientists at the end of the 1850s, leading the great historian Thomas Babington Macaulay to write a long passage in *The History of England from the Accession of James II* on the origins of the national debt and the role it had actually played in the development of the English economy.

Macaulay went back to a moment twenty-five years before Sir Isaac Newton fixed the price of money in gold. Overspending by the Crown that year, 1692, had "bequeathed a large deficit" to 1693. Taxes had already "been carried to an unprecedented point".

Then, as now, matters clearly couldn't go on this way. "It was necessary," Macaulay wrote, "to devise something."

What the British, who are known in the Orient for their cunning, proceeded to devise was the national debt. In January 1693 the House of Commons raised its first million pounds by way of a 10 percent loan. "Such was the origin of that debt which since has become the greatest prodigy that ever perplexed the sagacity and confounded the pride of statesmen and philosophers," Macaulay wrote. "At every stage in the growth of that debt it has been seriously asserted by wise men that bankruptcy and ruin were at hand. Yet still the debt went on growing; and still bankruptcy and ruin were as remote as ever."

Macaulay then compiled a hundred-year box score on the national debt. At the end of the war against Louis XIV, the debt had risen to fifty million pounds. Informed opinion, "not merely foxhunting squires and coffeehouse orators, but acute and profound thinkers", saw the debt as "an encumbrance which would permanently cripple the body politic. Nevertheless trade flourished: wealth increased: the nation became richer and richer."

At the end of the War of the Austrian Succession the debt stood at eighty million pounds. "Pamphleteers, historians and orators pronounced that now, at all events, our case was desperate." Yet everywhere to be seen, Macaulay wrote, were "the signs of increasing prosperity".

War broke out with Prussia. The national debt reached £140 million. "As soon as the first intoxication of victory was over, men of theory and men of business almost unanimously pronounced that the fatal day had now really arrived." David Hume concluded that it had been "better for us to have been conquered by Prussia or Austria than to be saddled with the interest on a hundred and forty millions. And yet this great philosopher," Macaulay wrote, "for such he was, had only to open his eyes to see improvement all around him." Adam Smith did a little better. "He admitted that, immense as the burden was, the nation did actually sustain it and thrive under it in a way which nobody could have foreseen. But he warned his countrymen not to repeat so hazardous an experiment. The limit had been reached. Even a small increase might be fatal."

The government of the day concluded that a Britain so loaded with debt "must sink" unless part of the burden could be shifted to the American colonies. So started the American Revolution, the colonists having little taste for paying English taxes. At the end of this war Britain's national debt stood at £240 million. Again the country became "visibly more prosperous".

But now England embarked on its mortal struggles against the Empire of Napoleon. Anguished and expensive years passed. "When the world was again at rest," Macaulay said, "the funded debt of England amounted to eight hundred millions. It was in truth a gigantic, a fabulous debt, and we can hardly wonder that the cry of despair should have been louder than ever." Yet "the beggared, the bankrupt society not only proved able to meet all its obligations, but grew richer and richer so fast that the growth could almost be discerned by the eye."

Macaulay thought long about the contrast between the words of the experts and the evidence of the eye. "It can hardly be doubted that there must have been some great fallacy," he decided, "in the notions of those who uttered and those who believed that long succession of confident predictions, so signally falsified by a long succession of indisputable facts."

The century Macaulay was writing about was a simpler and less frightening one than ours, though no less bloody. The idea of "progress" applied then as it no longer seems to. Then, too, the frontiers of both undeveloped continents and new industrial processes were wide open, making it relatively easy for economic growth to overtake accumulated debt. Still, we have all heard the same warnings he reports and seen for ourselves some of the same results, and we are ill-advised, it seems to me, to forget Macaulay while considering the role of gold in the affairs of nations.

The United States, which had come late to the gold standard, stayed with it during the early 1930s while others fled. Britain had returned to the gold standard in 1925 when Winston Churchill was Chancellor of the Exchequer. His friend Max Aitken, a Canadian financier who in Britain had become the press baron Lord Beaverbrook, decried the decision. His judgement was echoed in his own newspapers by the soon-to-be-eminent economist John Maynard Keynes. (Speculating on how Churchill could have strayed so far from sense, Keynes ended with a few words that deserve to be better remembered: "He was misled by his experts." Here Keynes wrote an epitaph that will serve for almost every official decision, pro or con, made about the gold standard after the Great War, not to mention many made before.) The return to gold was meant to deflate the English economy. It did, quickly bringing on a wave of unemployment that led to a general strike in 1926. For Britain, the Roaring Twenties were already mute.

Britain abandoned the gold standard again in 1931. In the United States half the banks had failed by the beginning of 1933, and the other half were too nervous to make loans. Here was deflation on a scale the world had not seen before. Early that year Roosevelt took the United States off the domestic gold standard; Americans could no longer change notes or deposits into gold at the bank window. A few months later he took the United States off the international gold standard. During the preceding two years foreign countries presenting dollars to the Federal Reserve Bank had drained the United States of half its monetary gold reserve. Roosevelt slammed shut that bank window as well, denying foreign governments the right to change dollars for gold. Churchill, by this time out of office, applauded Roosevelt's decision. The "rarity or abundance" of gold was a bad foundation for economic policy, he said — almost exactly the same words Beaverbrook had used to denounce Churchill for going on the gold standard a few years earlier. Unlike Churchill, Keynes had not changed his mind in the meantime; he wrote a newspaper piece headlined "President Roosevelt Is Magnificently Right".

In Washington, Roosevelt's decision to "go off gold", as he himself put it, moved his own director of the budget, Lewis Douglas, to say to a friend after the meeting at which Roosevelt made his announcement, "This is the end of Western civilization." Most gold lovers still believe Douglas's reaction was right, if a touch understated, and that to think otherwise was, and remains, the hallmark of the uninformed or the dishonest. Presumably one or the other of these classes of men must include the paradigm of bankers, John Pierpont Morgan, who the next day issued a formal public statement in which he said, "I welcome the reported action of the President . . . it seems to me clear that the way out of the depression is to combat and overcome the deflationary forces." Russell Leffingwell, a Morgan partner, wrote privately to Roosevelt a few days later, "Your action in going off gold saved the country from complete collapse."

Earlier in 1933, when Roosevelt was getting ready to move into the White House, the outgoing president, Herbert Hoover, had written him an urgent letter. It was essential, Hoover said, to restore confidence in the American economy. To this end he urged Roosevelt to do two things above all else. He was to balance the budget. He was to avoid inflating the currency. Roosevelt gave Hoover's advice a mixed reception. He tried to balance the budget by inflating the currency, and failed to do either.

The pump he chose to inflate the currency with was gold. Led by *his* experts, Roosevelt adopted a line of thought that went something like this: if the price of gold went up that meant the dollar was worth less, which

meant that prices would go up, which meant that farmers — who were pressing him politically with great force — would get more money for their prod-
ucts, which meant they could begin to repay their debts, which would place
the nation squarely on the road to recovery. All this Roosevelt told the
country by radio towards the end of October 1933 in one of his "fireside
chats" — from that time on, he said, an agency of the Treasury would
buy all the newly mined gold in the United States, at prices "to be determined".

For the next month and more, Henry Morgenthau, Jr., the Secretary of
the Treasury, and a few others met in Roosevelt's bedroom every weekday
morning. While the president ate breakfast the group set the price of gold
for the day, starting the discussion with Roosevelt's toast and ending with
his eggs. When the president's breakfast was disposed of they announced to
the waiting markets a price somewhat higher than it had been the morning
before. These were the prices Roosevelt had said were "to be determined",
but nobody outside the president's bedroom had any idea how they were
determined until Morgenthau's diary was published several years later. His
entry for a typical day said he opened the discussion that morning by proposing an increase of between nineteen and twenty-two cents. Roosevelt
laid down his spoon and said, "Twenty-one cents." Morgenthau asked why.
"It's a lucky number," Roosevelt said, "because it's three times seven." (In
Canada political decisions were likewise being made on numerological evidence at about this time by Mackenzie King, who was in opposition in 1933
but soon returned to lead the country. King supplemented the numbers by
messages brought to him by Ouija-boards or in seances, as the country learned
when *his* diaries were published.)

What was going on in Washington, apart from a dip into numerology,
was a daily bear raid by the U.S. Treasury against the American dollar.
Many economists believe this to have been the most bizarre episode in the
history of money. It lasted for about five weeks, at the end of which the
value of the dollar was down and so were farm prices.

Nobody of influence, not even Roosevelt, could any longer believe that a
settled deflation could be changed to inflation by manipulating the price
of gold. In his 1934 State of the Union message Roosevelt decreed a return
to a modified international gold standard — Americans themselves were
still denied the right to buy gold or to sell it at the bank window. The new
gold-backed dollar was to be valued at 59.06 percent of the old one. Hardly
anybody knew how this number had been determined, either, until the international bankers did the arithmetic. It worked out to a new fixed price for
gold of thirty-five dollars an ounce.

Gold was not tried again as a tool for breaking the deflation of the 1930s. Once or twice, as economic activity very slowly began to recover, the orthodox money managers who were back in charge of the reserve banking system caused the commercial banks to raise their rates, thereby reducing their loans. At the same time Roosevelt cut public spending, trying once more to comply with Hoover's instruction to balance the budget. The economy sank back into depression. (In Germany, where Hitler had grabbed power in 1933 with the help of an army of the jobless, six million to seven million of them had jobs again by 1938. The Nazis imposed foreign-exchange controls and import quotas as inflation curbs. Then they simply borrowed money in large amounts and put people to work, mainly in the construction of such useful things as railroads and highways. They greatly increased the national debt but they also created full employment without much inflation. Perhaps it took a madman to cope with the economics of the 1930s.)

In the United States, the jump in the price of gold had one effect on the unemployed. Many jobless men now went looking for gold, at thirty-five dollars an ounce far more profitable to find and mine than it had been at the old price of twenty dollars and sixty-seven cents. Most were like my father; the lucky ones wound up eating their horses and the others ate their shoes. But a few struck it, as they said, rich. There was now a sharp increase in the number of new gold mines opened up in both Canada and the United States, a development that stopped only when the Second World War broke out and the Americans put an embargo on gold mining. The government judged it more important to have the men and their equipment mining metals needed in the war effort. In Del Norte County, California, for instance, many gold miners turned to mining chromium.

Outside of the dictatorships, public policy never did overcome the Depression; it dragged on until the Second World War, in Galbraith's phrase, "swept it away". During the war gold was largely irrelevant, its domestic role in restraining inflation taken over by price-and-wage controls on one side, rationing and a truly remarkable rate of saving on the other. In both Canada and the United States, about 25 percent of all the wages paid in 1944 went into savings accounts or war bonds. My mother was by then working in a needle shop where she sewed sleeves to soldiers' shirts. I remember her pride when she showed us the "war savings certificates" she bought at the shop in denominations of five dollars. They were the first savings of her life, and it is a simple truth that if my mother had money to save, everybody did.

Towards the end of the war politicians and state bankers began to give thought to how they might devise a monetary regime that wouldn't choke on the self-interest of its members, as the global economy had choked in the 1930s. They came up with an idea called the International Monetary Fund, the IMF. In July 1944, they met at a New Hampshire resort village, Bretton Woods, where they agreed to set up the IMF; the fund began to operate in 1947. The states that joined agreed to subscribe a blend of gold and (in a few cases, or) their own national currencies. On these reserves members could then draw when they needed help in balancing their international accounts. The Swiss were apparently unable to imagine needing this kind of help and never did join. The Communist states appeared ready to join, then backed off. Most other states joined.

Once again the standard of exchange among this broad array of currencies was gold. But the United States was the only country both able and willing to buy or sell gold at a fixed price. This the Americans undertook to do, at the price fixed by Roosevelt in 1934 — thirty-five dollars an ounce. As a practical matter, then, it made little difference to other countries whether they settled their debts and collected their profits in gold or in American dollars; the economy of the West was now on a double standard, the gold dollar standard.

During the next few years foreign countries spent more in the United States than the United States spent abroad. Those countries that had gold in their vaults preferred to keep the dollars they had earned and pay their debts by shipping gold to the United States. Dollars they could put to work earning interest; gold they could do nothing with but bury. By 1949 the United States had two-thirds of the gold in the entire banking system of the Western world buried at Fort Knox.

Then the sands began to drift the other way. Recovering from the war with the help of foreign aid from the United States, Western Europe now began selling more to the Americans and buying less. The United States went on showing a profit on straight trade, but the profit was no longer high enough to cover the heavy spending the Americans were still doing on foreign aid, on supporting military establishments abroad, and on private investment in foreign countries — those were the years when the multinational corporations were at work inventing themselves. In 1949, at the peak of the flow of gold into the ground at Fort Knox, the Americans held twenty-four billion dollars' worth of gold. By the end of 1960 they had run up an accumulated deficit with the rest of the world of twenty-one billion dollars. State bankers in other countries began to doubt that the United States could keep on spending more than it earned without devaluing its money. They started trading dollars for gold; by early 1961 they had claimed back a quarter of the gold the Americans had buried at Fort Knox. Speculators rightly saw the flow of gold out of the United States as a sign of weakness in the American dollar, and started dumping dollars to buy gold. That was when the headlines said "Gold Crisis!" and I went to Washington to find out what they meant.

In the autumn of 1960, I wrote, "It looked as though a Democrat was going to win the presidency, and he was just the man to solve the gold crisis with a daring stroke like doubling the price; wasn't it a Democrat, Franklin Roosevelt, who raised the price of gold the last time it happened?" Speculators, like promoters, love a story. "The financial grapevine spread a guess that hardened into a rumour that swept the world: the U.S. was going to push the price of gold to seventy dollars an ounce. Within a couple of days the demand for free-market gold was so brisk that the Toronto exchange sold out, and the two Canadian banks that handle most local gold transactions were flying gold in from London."

The men best qualified to judge these rumours were appalled by them. Robert Triffin, a brilliant central banker who later went to teach at Yale, said that raising the price of gold "would be an act of sheer folly and a wanton crime against the people of this country, and against the friendly nations who have long accepted our financial leadership and placed their trust in the U.S. dollar and the integrity and intelligence of our monetary management." Were the price of gold to go up, the chief beneficiaries would be the Americans themselves, the South Africans, already occupying what one expert described as "a pariah state under a racist government", and the Russians, who were thought to have more unmined gold in the ground than anybody else, including the South Africans.

Twitched in both directions by these conflicting views, the price of gold jittered until John F. Kennedy delivered his first State of the Union address in January 1961. He said the United States would hold the price of gold at thirty-five dollars even if it took the last ounce in Fort Knox to meet the demand. The international bankers believed him; they eased their calls for gold instead of dollars. The speculators believed him; they let the price of free-market gold fall back to thirty-five dollars. And I believed him; "The U.S. will not raise the price of gold," I wrote, and for a time the U.S. did not.

At thirty-five dollars an ounce, the gold in most mines had long been worth less than the cost of getting it out of the ground. When I came back from Washington, I went to the gold camps for a few days and talked to the gold men themselves. "Gold mining is through in Canada," Frank Buckle, the general manager of the Wright-Hargreaves mine at Kirkland Lake, told me. Most of the mines still running were paying their costs only with the help of a subsidy from the federal government. "Ten years from now," Buckle said, "Kirkland Lake and the Porcupine will be finished." For the same reason, almost nobody had gone looking for gold since the Depression.

Throughout the 1960s the American economy grew at an unprecedented rate; so did the American national debt and the balance-of-payments deficit.

In 1965 President Lyndon B. Johnson said, "The dollar is, and will remain, as good as gold, freely convertible at thirty-five dollars an ounce."

In 1969 President Richard Nixon's Secretary of the Treasury, David Kennedy, announced that he foresaw no change in the thirty-five–dollar price of gold. Nixon himself, however, became the first president in modern times to refrain from saying the United States would defend the value of the dollar in gold.

In 1971 Nixon's new Secretary of the Treasury, John Connally, told an international bankers' conference that "we are not going to devalue. We are not going to change the price of gold."

Connally said that to the bankers at the end of May. Early in August, with the American balance-of-payments deficit rising at an alarming rate and Americans themselves now seeking security for their money by changing a floodstream of dollars to German marks or Swiss francs, Connally and others met Nixon at Camp David. There they agreed to impose a 10 percent surcharge on all imports to the United States. This, for countries trying to sell things to the Americans, had the same effect as devaluing the American dollar by 10 percent. At the same time they ended the American undertaking to buy and sell gold at a fixed price, which meant the American dollar was now free to float as a fiat money backed by no form of reserve asset whatever. "The fact that this procedure would violate American treaty obligations under the Bretton Woods Agreement does not seem to have been mentioned by anyone," Martin Mayer wrote in *The Fate of the Dollar*, a book remarkable for its depth of detail and grasp of issues that are more slippery than most.

Connally later said he remembered at least one official who objected that closing the gold window "would precipitate a major international depression.

"Well," he went on, "it didn't. There was a lot of criticism because there hadn't been any prior consultation with other countries. But you don't telegraph your punches if you're going to close the gold window and put on a surcharge. Then you'd really have chaos."

At about this time I interviewed Connally for a television report on economic relations between Canada and the United States. While the make-up artist was dealing with Connally's eyebrows, which were a mechanic's opportunity for somebody in her trade, I asked him how he felt about telling the world the United States would support the gold standard at the same time he was privately agreeing to scrap it. He swung his head away from the make-up artist's eyebrow brush and stared at me. "In that spot," he said, "it would take an irresponsible idiot to tell the truth." Beneath the Texan accent, the old word magic shone through.

That was the end of the gold standard. A last frail link between gold and the Treasury was snapped in 1975, when individual Americans regained the right to buy or sell gold in the market place. Money in the 1970s and '80s was and remains afloat, though many countries try to smooth the waves in the money pool by intervening with buy or sell orders in the foreign-exchange markets, and by keeping part of their reserves in gold. The price of gold is itself afloat, bid up or down each day in markets around the world, opening in London, where the morning's price is set in a back room at the Rothschild merchant bank, from where it follows the time zones to gold markets in New York, Hong Kong, Zurich, and back to London.

Buying and selling twenty-four hours a day, speculators in these markets created an upswell in the price of an ounce of gold from $35 in 1971 to a crest of $840 at the end of the 1970s. From there the price subsided, but it has not since been much less than $300.

Gold in the ground that had not been worth digging now became profitable again; during the 1970s many mines reopened that had been abandoned for thirty years or more. And back to the outcrops and discarded drill holes came the prospectors, geologists, and promoters who likewise had ignored gold for a full generation. In 1980 Bob Crompton and I bought a one-fifth interest in a fault a mile long, where until the 1940s five separate mines had taken gold from quartz veins. They were by far the best-looking gold mines I had ever seen, lost on the roof of the Rockies in the northeast corner of California. From the mouth of the adit that gave entry to the biggest of the old mines, you could see a stretch of the Pacific Crest Trail, the hiking path that follows the height of land from Oregon to Mexico. Breathtaking. We made two site visits, as I was learning to call a trip to a mining prospect. At one point during the second, I stayed behind in the mouth of the biggest mine while the others went to look at one of the smaller mines lower down. A few minutes later Bob and our partners growled up in a jeep driven by an inspector from the Department of Mines. He tramped through the mine, kicking the old timber props and shining his big flashlight into all the stopes and drifts — offshoots of the tunnels — where the miners had pursued the branching quartz veins. When we were back in the daylight he turned and shone his light at the mouth of the adit.

"You better get a Hickory in there," he said, "and clear some of that rubble."

Everybody nodded. My stomach twitched. I had no idea what a Hickory was, but assuming, as I instantly did, that it was some kind of heavy-duty rock-moving machine, how much would it cost to buy or rent one and ratchet it up to the crest of the Rockies? The inspector climbed back in his jeep and growled back down the trail.

"What the *hell*," I said, "is a Hickory?"

Our partners took this for a weak joke, smiled politely, and walked off towards a ruined mill building. Bob, who has long known that on questions of this kind it is simply not true that nobody could be as dumb as I sound, took me by the elbow and led me to an old tool shed. In one corner there was a clutter of rusted shovels with long wooden handles. He took one and put it in my hands.

"What?" I said.

"Hickory," he said. "Why don't you take it over to the adit and use it."

The consulting geologist we got to write a report on the fault said there didn't seem to be enough gold left in all five mines to bother with.

That winter, Donald McKinnon walked into the bush at Hemlo and started staking claims.

DRAGOVAN AND PEZIM

"It matters not whether the relationship is seen as that which may exist between prospective partners or joint venturers before the terms of any partnership or joint venture agreement have been settled, or whether it is seen as a limited preliminary partnership or joint venture to investigate and explore the possibilities of an ultimate joint venture or ventures. On either approach it was a fiduciary one."

— Judgement, United Dominion Corporation Ltd. *v.* Brian Pty. Ltd.

TAKING THE OATH, NELL
Dragovan spoke in a murmur and swallowed her words. The judge asked
her to speak more clearly. She nodded, and spoke, if anything, less clearly
than before. Her face was as pale as the white suit she wore, as were her
knuckles where she gripped the rail at the front of the witness stand. Plainly,
she was in an advanced state of fright, though whether this was fear of the
cross-examination to come or simple stage fright it was yet too soon to say.

She told the court she was born in 1949 and raised in Osoyoos, a town of
two thousand people in the Okanagan Valley of British Columbia. She went
to school at Simon Fraser University in Vancouver, where she was graduated in 1971; her major was geography, and she took no courses in geology.
She became, she said, a "magazine writer" for *Canadian Shareholder*, a
monthly with a circulation of perhaps two thousand, all of them people who
were somehow interested in the Vancouver Stock Exchange.

"I ended up owning the magazine," she said, the first touch of the promoter strengthening her voice. She sold the magazine in 1976 and went to
work as a "secretary-girl Friday" to a succession of securities lawyers and
stock promoters. Whether by intention or coincidence she didn't say, but it
appeared that in these jobs she was serving an apprenticeship in stock promotion that ended in 1978, when she became a journeyman promoter.

First she incorporated a personal company, Big Deal Investments. Big
Deal's business would be managing the affairs of public companies. Then
she created a client for Big Deal by incorporating her first public company,
Tri-Star Resources. For Tri-Star she did her first financing, a quarter-million
shares at twenty cents a share — or twenty-five cents, she couldn't quite
remember. By 1979 she was one of the principals in half a dozen public
companies, all traded on the Vancouver Stock Exchange, all managed by
Big Deal Investments, none yet successful at doing anything but raising
money by the sale of stock.

Late that year a new company called Corona Resources was listed on the
Vancouver Stock Exchange. The listing documents said that Corona's purpose was to explore some acreage in Alberta for natural gas. Alan Lenczner
asked Dragovan whether she had formed Corona. She said she hadn't.

"Were you a director?"

"No."

Corona's president and principal shareholder, Lenczner said, was a man named Gerald McIlhardy. Did she know him?

"Yes," Dragovan said, and then she added, simply and altogether disarmingly, "Mr. McIlhardy is my friend."

"What business was he in?"

"He was a truck-body salesman."

"And a Miss Margaret Dragovan owned a hundred and fifty thousand shares. Who is she?"

"My sister."

When Brian Foster came to cross-examine Nell Dragovan, he established that Margaret was her younger sister, a school teacher in her twenties. "Nobody likes to lose money," Foster said. "But your sister wasn't alone in that jungle; she had you as a guardian angel."

"Well," Dragovan said, "If my sister had lost her money, I wouldn't have been to blame."

Foster seemed to think she was understating the strength of her family feeling. He read from an examination for discovery in which she had said, "My sister had some stock; members of my family had some stock; I just don't like my family to lose money." Foster looked at the judge and said, "I'm only trying to show that her first and primary concern was for her sister."

"I subsequently found out that my sister sold her stock in September," Dragovan said.

She meant September 1980, when her sister sold her stock in Corona for about fifteen thousand dollars. In September 1981, the price of the same number of Corona shares reached five million dollars. I'm not sure why the Lac lawyers pursued the question of Margaret Dragovan's stock, but I found it an instructive footnote to the widely held notion that in the market it is always outsiders who buy high and sell low, while insiders buy low and sell high.

Why did Margaret Dragovan sell her Corona stock for something like a dime a share? Brian Foster didn't ask, but Corona had finished drilling its natural-gas prospect, all the holes were barren, and the company was broke; how many more reasons would Margaret have needed? Her sister's situation was somewhat different. Through her mangement company, Big Deal, Nell Dragovan contracted in the spring of 1980 to run Corona's affairs for her friend McIlhardy; now, with the Alberta drill holes and the corporate treasury both dry, she would lose a two-thousand-dollar-a-month client. Unless, that is, Corona could get something new going.

"Corona was just a shell," Nell Dragovan told the court. "I let everybody know that Corona needed a project."

That summer, the summer of 1980, was a downer for Steven Snelgrove. Unlike Nell Dragovan, Snelgrove had a project, but his project was going nowhere. Snelgrove was the last man on the daisy chain started by Donald McKinnon when, at his wits' end after trying to hock the Hemlo claims to every mining company whose door he could get inside, McKinnon showed his Hemlo dossier to the relatively young, untried geologist, David Bell. Bell passed on the dossier to his friend Donald Moore, the industrial commissioner for Kirkland Lake. Moore passed it on to his old college classmate, Steven Snelgrove, a stock promoter who worked mainly in Toronto. Snelgrove bought the story, and an option on the claims that went with it, for a few thousand dollars down and the usual future considerations.

Why did McKinnon and his partner, John Larche, option the Hemlo claims to Snelgrove? Mainly because nobody else would buy them; but Snelgrove was a promoter, which meant that he, too, had a story going. Snelgrove said he was about to take over a cash-heavy Toronto oil company. His story was that he would sell the Hemlo gold claims to the oil company and use the oil company's money to explore them. Meanwhile they'd hold the Hemlo property in a numbered company Snelgrove owned, 435198 Ontario.

Snelgrove was a plausible fellow, big, good-looking, and well spoken, with the easy manners of the old Toronto family he came from and the physical poise of the college athlete he had once been. These are all useful attributes for a promoter, but Snelgrove's failing seems to have been that he used them to excess; he tried too hard, and the glad hand he held out was usually overextended.

A bookie will say of a gambler who makes a bet he can't cover that he's playing on the come. McKinnon and Larche got the first sign that Steven Snelgrove might be playing on the come when he reported that his oil-company takeover had fallen through. Never mind, Snelgrove said; he'd use his connections to sell the Hemlo claims to some other company capable of developing them. The summer passed, the prospect of a sale receded, and Snelgrove's downer deepened. At the end of the summer, when his Hemlo option had only weeks left to run, he called his some-time friend Doug Collingwood in Vancouver.

Like many Vancouver promoters, Collingwood had come west from Toronto. Superficially he and Snelgrove were much alike, Collingwood older and bigger, at close to six and a half vertical feet and perhaps four feet through the belt loops, but with the same open-handed stance. In Collingwood, though, the style of the shooter seemed to come naturally, whereas in Snelgrove it was forced. This may have been because in Collingwood's background there were genuine accomplishments. On the wall above his desk in Vancouver hung an artist's conception of the Avro Arrow, the famous Canadian fighter plane that scarcely flew before it was shot down by John Diefenbaker in the 1950s. Collingwood, a British engineer who came to Canada after the Second World War, had worked on the Arrow's design, as well as the other great unflown Avro designs, the super-airliner and the flying saucer. He remembered with relish hitching the mock-up of the Arrow to a truck and rolling it at midnight out to the hushed runway where no other plane would now move till morning, and running the mock-up back and forth, back and forth, to test the instrumentation. He loved this life: the secrecy, the conspiratorial midnight hush, the vague but, as it turned out, justified sense of danger.

When the Avro went down Collingwood went to de Havilland, where he was invited to become project engineer on the Dash 7, but, he once told me, "By then I'd been in a stock promotion, and I got bitten." In 1979 he moved to Vancouver, where those bitten by the urge to promote stocks are most at home.

Collingwood says that when Snelgrove called about the Hemlo claims, "He said he couldn't deal them in Toronto, so maybe I could deal them in Vancouver.

"I couldn't. Those days, I was in the oil game." Snelgrove sent Collingwood the Hemlo file anyway; he thought Collingwood might be able to find a buyer among the Vancouver mining promoters, and since Snelgrove himself didn't know anybody in Vancouver, he had nothing to lose. Collingwood says he took the file to the first name on anybody's list of Vancouver mining promoters, Murray Pezim.

"He just ruffled through the pages, chk, chk, chk, closed the file, and said to me, 'Jeeze, yes, I'll take this. I'd love to have something to stick up the ass of those bastards back East.' " Collingwood, who like most of us tends to be the central figure in his own stories, says Pezim then gave him a name: "Nell Dragovan. Murray said, 'She's got a little company called Corona I'm going to take over. She'll put it in there.' " So Collingwood went to Dragovan and worked out with her the terms of a deal whereby Corona optioned the Hemlo claims from Snelgrove, who was to pay Collingwood a finder's fee of twenty thousand Corona shares.

This is the story according to Doug Collingwood. In Pezim's version, the figure in the foreground is naturally Pezim: Snelgrove came to Pezim, who listened to his pitch, bought it, and instructed Dragovan to option the claims for Corona. The third version, and probably the most accurate one, is Dragovan's. She says that after she "let everybody know" that Corona needed a property, a local stockbroker named Les McConnell told her about the Hemlo claims Snelgrove was trying to sell. When Snelgrove called her, saying he had been referred to her by Murray Pezim, she was already interested. At this time Pezim to her was not much more than a name: "I knew Mr. Pezim, but not very well," she told the court.

Snelgrove showed Dragovan the dossier McKinnon had put together on the Hemlo property. She was particularly interested in the Skimming report, partly for what it said and partly because she'd once met Skimming and knew him to be a capable geologist. That day, September 19, 1980, Dragovan concluded the negotiation, got Snelgrove's signature on an agreement drafted by her lawyer, and issued a press release announcing that Corona Resources had optioned a gold property at Hemlo. "I know it was quick," she said in court. "It didn't take days."

Snelgrove, for his part, got a cheque for twenty thousand dollars from Dragovan. He was to get another twenty thousand dollars when the regulatory authorities approved the deal. He was also to get three hundred thousand shares of Corona stock, fifty thousand right away, the next hundred and fifty thousand to be released to him in blocks after the passage of given periods of time, the final hundred thousand to be released should gold be produced on the property. In that event, he was also to get a 3 percent net royalty on the value of the gold.

Had Snelgrove been a prudent middleman he would with this beginning have emerged from the many stock splits that followed as one of Corona's major shareholders and a very wealthy man. But Snelgrove was a shooter, squarely planted in the grand tradition of Alfred F.A. Coyne himself. Before long Snelgrove was playing the market with both hands, usually buying more stock than he had money. He was playing on the come again, although stockbrokers have a different name for it — margin trading. Brokers approve of margin trading as long as the trader is winning, which happens when the price of his stock goes up. If the trader starts to lose, which is to say if the value of the stock in his margin account goes down, his broker issues a margin call. He can answer the call by giving the broker more money, if he has any; if he doesn't, the broker will start selling his stock to cover his margin.

Snelgrove's margin accounts started 1981 in reasonably good health. Through the spring and early summer the price of Corona advanced slowly, and Snelgrove's margin trading was well covered. Then Corona found the thermal updrafts of the market and soared — at twenty dollars a share

Snelgrove's fifty thousand shares were valued at a million dollars and would support two million dollars' worth of margin trading; at thirty dollars, three million. Now Snelgrove had both barrels loaded, and soon he started to do what a shooter must.

"He lost a million dollars on one shot — a thing called Transamerica," Collingwood once told me. "Another time Murray Pezim came to us, Snelgrove and me, and said, 'Do me a favour, and I'll make sure you have no more trouble on the street.'

"We said, 'What do you want, Murray?'

"He said, 'Put away some Pezamerica. They're knocking me down; I need some price support.'

"So we bought half a million Pezamerica.

"Next thing, we find out the selling pressure on Pezamerica is coming from Murray himself. He's selling Pez right into us, and what's he doing with the money? Buying Corona."

When the time came for the next release of Corona stock to Snelgrove under the option agreement, his broker, Yorkton Securities, was pressing him to make up a shortfall in his margin account. But Snelgrove also had obligations to McKinnon and Larche. Under his agreement with them, the next block of Corona stock he got would pass through his hands directly to them, in part payment for the Hemlo claims. Snelgrove was caught in the classic dilemma of the man with more than one debt: whom should he pay first, the people with the best claim, or the people with the biggest stick?

Snelgrove chose to duck the stick. He deposited the shares in his Yorkton account, Yorkton sold him out to cover his margin shortfall, and he stalled as long as he knew how with McKinnon and Larche. Eventually he could stall no longer.

"Johnny Larche was ready to murder him," Larche's partner and lawyer, Rocco Schiralli, said much later. "Here's John, his wife is dying of cancer and he needs money in the worst way, and this Snelgrove is telling him he's sorry, but he used John's shares to cover his margin call.

"We got Snelgrove into the office while Larche was up north, and made a deal with him. Snelgrove got the shares that had already been sold out. Larche and McKinnon got back everything else — the shares still to come, the royalty interest, everything."

That is how Steven Snelgrove went within a few months from owning the Corona claims to owning nothing. I once said to McKinnon that he and Larche had been the real beneficiaries of Snelgrove's urge to take a shot at anything in the market that moved. "Sure, we'll see a bigger return some-time," McKinnon said. "But when we sawed off with Snelgrove, he'd had a couple of million to play around with for months, and we still hadn't seen a nickel."

A mining promoter, like a religious convert, will often speak with strong feeling about the quality of his belief. The gold in the Hemlo rockbeds was discovered by a sizeable band of self-proclaimed believers, among whom Nell Dragovan and her soon-to-be mentor Murray Pezim were merely the most recent. In some cases the conversion had been hard won and maintained for a lifetime in the face of adversity. Trevor Page, for one, came to his belief in the Hemlo lode after some years of sceptical investigation, much as St. Augustine came to Catholicism, and they both kept the faith despite the failure of providence to deliver a miracle to either of them.

Unlike Trevor Page, Nell Dragovan seems to have been converted to a belief in the Hemlo lode in little more than the time it takes to read Thomas Skimming's report, which I have clocked at half an hour give or take five minutes for backtracking to the better parts, and to have signed a twenty-thousand-dollar cheque for Steven Snelgrove the same day. Nor was this Corona's money; Corona was broke. The cheque was drawn on Dragovan's personal account, as were the first two cheques, for twenty-five thousand dollars in all, that Dragovan advanced David Bell to get him started on the exploration program outlined by Skimming.

The speed of Dragovan's conversion, not to mention her willingness instantly to endow the object of her belief with a lot of her own money, would surely have been the envy of St. Augustine in his missionary period. How did this come about? It must be said that she was moved by more than simple faith.

"Look, the wells I drilled came up dry. So, *I needed a property.* That's how simple it is," she told me one day when I remarked on the brisk pace of her conversion to the Hemlo project. "You do know, don't you, that the exchange halts trading if a company hasn't got an asset?"

No, I hadn't known, not in so many words, but when I thought about it later it seemed to me that to know this is perhaps to arrive at the beginning of wisdom about these speculative exploration companies. Before anything else, the promoter of such a company must have a property. Without one he can't raise money, and what else is his company for? With a property, any property that carries a consultant's recommendation to carry out an exploration program, he can sell enough stock to finance the program. The property's no good? Get another property, sell some more stock, go around again.

How, then, does the promoter make a profit? This is the level of the game that few of the spectators, many of whom prefer to think of themselves as investors, ever understand. The promoter makes money in three moves.

In *One*, he gets his paper out. In standard English, this means he finds buyers for the stock offered in his underwriting.

In *Two*, he gets his paper back in on margin. He buys back his own stock, that is, doubling his purchasing power by using a margin account, and since bidding is what sends the price of a stock up, the price of his stock rises as long as he's on the bid. He accumulates as many of his own shares as he believes he can later sell.

In *Three*, he gets his paper out again. This is the move that separates the winners from the losers; it calls for speed, strength, and finesse. He has to turn around and sell the stock he's been buying with such dexterity that he has unloaded at good prices before the market collapses under the weight of his own sell orders. It isn't easy, but executed by a master it's wondrously profitable.

Now, nobody can say that this is what Murray Pezim intended to do with Corona. But as 1981 began nobody then living understood these moves better than Murray Pezim. He was crowding sixty, and he had been a promoter for more than half his life. If there was anything he didn't know about mining promotion, it could only have been the answer to the question, what happens if you find something?

"God forbid," Doug Collingwood had said, speaking of the principles and practices of stock promotion, "God forbid you should make a mine."

If suddenly that happens, the three moves the promoter has been practising all his working life won't work any more. He's shifting gears the way he always did but they've changed the gear box. He was selling when he should have been buying, now he's buying at the top of the market when he should be selling, but if he doesn't get in there and buy they'll take his mine away from him — the rig is running downhill and now it's jumped the gearbox altogether and the whole damn thing is free-wheeling, out of control, and all because he made a gold mine. . . .

But for Nell Dragovan and Murray Pezim, that was yet to come.

Nell got her paper out early in December 1980, six hundred thousand shares that returned almost seven hundred thousand dollars to the Corona treasury. Murray Pezim helped her persuade the underwriters: "Without Murray's say-so," she said, "the brokers wouldn't have financed the deal."

After that, Brian Foster asked her in cross-examination, did she report to Mr. Pezim? "Not very often," she said. "I didn't feel I knew him well enough to phone him every day."

In Move One the promoter is a seller, not a buyer; neither Dragovan nor Pezim bought any stock at this stage. From the money raised from other buyers, Corona returned to Dragovan the advances she had made to Snelgrove and Bell, and paid Big Deal, her management company, its first fees. In March 1981, Dragovan and Bell were both invited to join Corona's board of directors. They did, and the board rewarded each of them with options on fifty thousand shares. Dragovan still didn't *own* any Corona stock, but late in May she bought her first ten thousand shares at $1.90 on the twentieth, and her second ten thousand at the same price the next day. Her timing became the subject of a long attack by Brian Foster, the most sustained attempt of the entire trial to discredit a witness over a single issue.

Foster laid the groundwork for his assault by reading into the record the dates of the assay certificates and the subsequent press releases for every hole Corona drilled up to the end of May. For Hole 1 the assay certificate was dated January 29, the press release February 2 — and so on for every hole until number 80. He established that for most of these holes either John Dadds or, less often, David Bell would phone Dragovan the same day he got the assay results from Swastika Labs, and read them back to her. She would write the press release and lodge a copy with the stock exchange, sometimes on the same day, usually within three or four days. By the time Foster got to Holes 17, 18, and 19, I had stopped writing down all the dates he was entering, but I find this bracketed observation in my notebook: "(the judge, like me, is stifling a very large yawn)".

The drowsiness ended when Foster reached Hole 27 and Lenczner jumped up to intervene. Judge Holland sent Dragovan out of the courtroom. Lenczner then argued that Foster was obviously trying to establish that something was seriously wrong when, for several later holes, there was a longer delay between the date when Dadds got the assay report in Ontario and Dragovan filed the press release in Vancouver. But the delay was simply and innocently accounted for, Lenczner said, by a note the Vancouver Stock Exchange filed on May 17, saying the VSE would no longer accept press releases that weren't accompanied by the relevant assay certificates. From that date on, Dragovan had to wait for the certificates to arrive in Vancouver by mail before filing the information with the VSE.

"They're trying to score a cheap and silly point off this witness," Lenczner said. "Is that really what we want in this courtroom?"

"The point of this laborious exercise," Foster replied with heavy irony, "is to show the date on which she received assay results over the phone." The delay added by the VSE's new instruction, he said, "is not where this is going".

The judge told Foster to go ahead. He did, arriving eventually at his destination, which was Hole 76, the discovery hole. Although there was no record of a telephone call by which Dragovan got the asssay results on Hole 76, and Bell had denied making such a call, Foster cited several other records from which he argued that such a call "must have come" between May 16 and 18. Dragovan's press release about Hole 76 was dated May 27.

"When you were at the Hemlo property on May sixth, Hole Seventy-six had started drilling," Foster said. "Right?"

"Yes," Dragovan said, "that hole was right behind the core shack."

"And it's unusual to see visible gold, isn't it?"

"Yes."

"So Hole Seventy-six was great news?"

"It was a very interesting result."

Foster then held up, in a gesture that looked as though it had been borrowed from courtroom drama and consequently seemed out of place in an actual courtroom, a copy of the VSE's insider trading report, dated June 9, 1981. From it he read out the trades it recorded for Nell Dragovan: ten thousand shares of Corona on May 20 at $1.90; ten thousand shares on May 21 at the same price.

"I put it to you that the reason you bought was because David Bell told you the results of Hole Seventy-six." Foster did not remind her that Bell had denied telling her before May 20 about the assays from Hole 76.

"I'm sorry," Dragovan said, "I don't buy stock on inside information."

"David Bell was excited when he talked to you about Hole Seventy-six?"

"I don't remember. I don't trade on inside information."

"Are you saying it was just lucky that you bought stock on May twentieth and twenty-first? What made you do it?"

"I can't remember."

Foster shifted his line of attack to an interview the CBC had done with Dragovan in 1984 for a television program about the Hemlo discovery. "You said, 'I remember David telling me that what we had now was very interesting, and I should be buying stock, and I went out and bought some, and I thought, Oh my God, what have I done now?' Do you remember that?"

"I remember saying that, but I don't buy stock on insider information. I'm sorry; I don't know why I bought the stock; all I know is I bought it."

"Between January first and May twentieth you bought no stock. On May twentieth and twenty-first you bought twenty thousand shares. What else could have made you do it but David Bell telling you about Hole Seventy-six? You're not saying that what you said on national television was not true, are you? When you said it, was it true?"

"That wasn't the only time I bought stock in Corona. When the CBC came to my office, I didn't have time to go through my records. It's true I bought stock on May twentieth and twenty-first. I also bought stock on June twenty-third. I can't tell you why. I exercised my option to buy stock. I *sold* stock . . ."

"Did you tell the truth to the CBC interviewer?"

"David Bell kept me informed."

"Was it true? That's a simple question. Was it true?"

"I don't trade on inside information."

Dragovan had now been on the stand for three days. She had changed from the white suit to a blue blazer with a pink shirt. At times during this exchange with Foster her high Slavic cheekbones were almost the colour of the shirt; then they blanched again to a stark white. She was clearly tired, physically as well as mentally, and there was a tangible sense of relief in the courtroom when Foster paused to shuffle papers on his lectern, as though about to take up a new subject. Then he took a long breath, like a runner searching for his second wind, and went back to the same one.

"Was what you told the CBC true or false? I don't want a story. I don't want a speech." The rhetoric here felt a touch heavy, since for some time now Dragovan had been reduced to saying little more than that she didn't know. "I just want to know whether it's true." With this, Foster started walking towards the witness box, holding up the transcript of the CBC broadcast.

"No," Dragovan said. "You don't have to show it to me."

"I want you to look at it. I want you to tell me if there is anything in that statement that is untrue."

"I bought stock at other times."

"That statement must relate to the first time."

"It doesn't say that," Dragovan said. "I bought stock at other times. Generally speaking, what I said on TV is true — except that I can't remember why I bought stock on May twentieth and twenty-first."

Judge Holland now intervened, in his mannerly way, to ask with one eye on the clock whether this wouldn't be a convenient time . . . ? Since it was one o'clock, his appointed hour for lunch, counsel for both sides agreed that it would indeed be an appropriate moment. During the lunch break Alan Lenczner viewed a videocassette of the CBC program that was playing such a large part in Brian Foster's line of questioning. I spent the break in the corridors of the court house, accosting lawyers. As I had been to a lesser degree at other times during the trial, I was puzzled by the lengths a lawyer, in this case Foster, would go in pursuit of a point that appeared to be irrelevant to the issue before the court. What difference would it make to the finding of guilt or innocence in the complaint against Lac if Foster *could* show that Dragovan had breached the insider-trading rules? None whatever, each of the lawyers I buttonholed said; but it would affect Dragovan's credibility as a witness. "Remember," one of the junior lawyers on the Lac legal team said, "what this trial's really about is a fairly simple question of whose story to believe." Granting this, I wondered about the tactical sense of asking the same question over and over again until it became a chorus, as did the dogged, uninventive answer: I don't know. It seemed to me that while this might have lacked conviction the first or second time, by the second hour of repetition the lady had begun to look and sound as though she must be telling the truth. "Well, there's no way to know about that, is there?" the young lawyer said. "We'll have to wait and see what the judge makes of it."

After lunch Lenczner told the court that what Dragovan actually said on the tape wasn't quite what the transcript said. After some chaffing, all the lawyers and the judge agreed they'd better play back the tape in the courtroom — not just Dragovan's line, but the entire tape. Everybody who couldn't see the monitor moved to a different seat, a member of the Lac legal team punched a button on the VCR, and the course of justice halted for sixty minutes during which Dragovan's image said on the screen pretty much what the transcript had said, though there might have been a word or two out of place. Into the silence when the tape ran out Brian Foster came right back with the same question.

"All right, now: having heard it, is it true or is it false?"

"I don't do insider trading," Dragovan said.

After Dennis Sheehan's visit to Corona's Hemlo site on May 6 and David Bell's visit to Lac's Toronto office on May 8, Sheehan had sent Bell a letter on May 19. In it Sheehan had flown a number of kites that held out the prospect of collaboration between Lac and Corona. He had ended by asking Bell for "a presentation of results to date", including such information as drill-hole sections, general geology, and a discussion of what he called "location potential", by which he presumably meant the surrounding ground. Once Corona had given Lac this presentation, Sheehan's letter said, "we could arrive at a sound basis for structuring a working agreement."

Bell and Dragovan agreed to the request; the two sides shadow-boxed for a few weeks through the usual missed telephone calls and conflicting schedules, and finally agreed to meet on June 30 at Lac's office in Toronto.

"When did you arrive in Toronto?" Foster asked.

"The night before," Dragovan said.

"At the meeting — was Mr. Allen there?" He meant Peter Allen, Lac's president and the son of Lac's founder, Jack Allen.

"Yes."

"Was there any discussion of the Hughes ground? Of the Williams ground?"

"That," said Dragovan, "was what we'd been discussing since they called us in April."

Her voice was now clearer and stronger than at any time since she was sworn in. It was finally apparent that her discomfort when she took the stand had been stage fright rather than fear of the examination to come. Foster hardened his voice to match hers.

"I suggest that you and David Bell did not go to the meeting ready to talk turkey."

"It was Sheehan who asked us to make a presentation," Dragovan said, her tone keeping its edge. "After which, we fully expected to receive a proposal — and that's exactly what happened. Peter Allen told us to expect a proposal."

Foster left the June 30 meeting for a few minutes, then circled back. "Now, surely, you knew that Lac would have to consider the information you left. Then they might make a proposal — or they might not?"

"Mr. Allen was very definite. He told us to expect a proposal in three weeks." Foster started another question, but Dragovan overrode him.

"We were working with Lac," she said, her voice now charged with remembered emotion. "If you're working with someone, what are they other than your partners?"

Sheehan and Allen had seen both the meeting and the relationship rather differently. Sheehan had said on the witness stand that his office at the time was made up of two rooms, a "normal office as we know it" with an adjoining map room. Most of the meeting took place in the adjoining room, where Bell unrolled the maps he'd brought with him on a large map table and went over them one by one. Most of the maps were geological sections — they showed, that is, what Corona was learning from its drill program. Allen came to the meeting late, and Bell ran through the maps again for him.

As Sheehan testified, "Mr. Allen then said to them, you know, 'What are your plans?' Obviously what we expected was that we would then talk about some sort of a deal. They indicated that they had Vancouver business people that they were going to get money from and they would continue with the program with this money from the Vancouver crowd.

"This was getting near lunch hour. We stood up and I had arranged to take them to lunch and so we left."

"Was there any discussion about the Williams property on June thirtieth?"

"Not to my recollection."

"Was there any discussion about Mr. Bell's plans to acquire other properties in the area?

"Not to my recollection."

"Was there any discussion about the May nineteenth letter and the terms you had set out, the proposals you had set out therein?"

"No, there was no discussion with regard to that at all."

"Was there any discussion about a proposal which Lac might make to Corona following the meeting?"

"No, there was no discussion about a proposal Lac — we had, of course, made our proposal and my belief was Mr. Allen was asking for a response from them as to what direction they would be going. Their response, of course, was they were going to continue doing their work with these British Columbia businessmen."

When Sheehan writes something down, what his words mean to him is often the reverse of what his readers are likely to take from them. He wrote a long memorandum to his boss, Peter Allen, a few weeks before the June 30 meeting. He said, "Contact has been made with the owner of key patented claims contiguous with Corona — we could be successful in locating such."

"Were those the Williams claims?" John Lorn McDougall, his own lawyer, asked him.

"Yes, the Williams claims."

"You say, 'We could be successful in locating such.' Locating what?"

"My belief is it means we could be successful in contacting this person and acquiring this land. We had, in fact, not contacted this person at that time."

"You hadn't made contact with that person despite the fact that it reads, 'Contact has been made,' in the first phrase?" McDougall was trying hard to camouflage his incredulity, and almost succeeded.

"Yes," Sheehan said. "It is poorly worded."

Later in the same memo, Sheehan wrote, "I will have a letter for you regarding Corona once we recalculate the ore reserves and study the property carefully. I suspect it will take three weeks."

"What letter are you referring to there?" McDougall asked.

"That is a misprint or is poorly worded," Sheehan said.

"And you write, 'I suspect it will take three weeks.' Why was it going to take three weeks?"

"I have no idea. I just — I can't recall why I put that down there."

A moment later they were puzzling over the meaning of another phrase when Sheehan broke off. "Look," he said. "This was an internal memo to Peter, and it's sort of in Sheehanese."

Alan Lenczner, cross-examining Sheehan later about the same memo, said, "And you say, once you've got the new information from Corona, recalculating the ore reserves will take you about three weeks?"

Sheehan gazed blandly back from the witness stand and said, "Why?"

Now it was Lenczner's turn to grapple with incredulity. "You *say* three weeks," he said, up on his toes, his birdlike head thrust forward across his lectern. "They're your words. 'It will take about three weeks.' "

"Yes," Sheehan said.

If anybody could translate Sheehanese it might well be the man to whom much of it was addressed, Peter Allen. When Allen took the witness stand McDougall read back to him the paragraph in which Sheehan said, "I'll have a letter for you regarding Corona, once we have recalculated the ore reserves. I suspect this will take three weeks."

"Do you remember reading this?" McDougall asked.

"No," Allen said, running long thin fingers through long thin hair brushed back from a long thin face. He was dressed in the manner of the Duke of Edinburgh, in a double-vented grey suit and a small-figured dark blue tie. When he told the court he was a director of the World Wildlife Fund it seemed to fit; that was the part he was dressed for. Well, McDougall said, looking at Sheehan's words now, what did Allen make of them? Allen didn't so much answer as muse out loud.

"Sheehan has never written a letter to me," he said, "so maybe he meant a memo. Maybe he meant a letter to send Corona. Maybe — I don't know."

Allen told McDougall that he'd been at the June 30 meeting for about twenty minutes. He'd gone to the meeting, he said, because Sheehan asked him if he wanted to be there. "In your mind," McDougall asked, "what was the purpose of the meeting?"

"I went in expecting to find out," Allen said. "Maybe make a deal, maybe discuss something else about the Hemlo area. These kind of meetings with geologists, to discuss what they were doing, were fairly frequent at Lac."

"Was there any mention of the Williams claims?"

"No."

Before the meeting ended, Allen left. "Was there any discussion of a proposal to be made by Lac to Corona?" McDougall asked.

"Not while I was in the room."

"Was the context such that a proposal could even have been contemplated?"

"Absolutely not."

"I can recall discussion of the Williams claims," David Bell had told Lenczner. "What stands out in my mind is Mr. Allen telling us how you have to be aggressive in pursuing these claims, because if you weren't it could take forever."

"Did you respond?"

"Yes; I told him we had an agent pursuing the property for us."

"Did Allen or Sheehan tell you Lac was pursuing those claims for itself?"

"No."

"Did they tell you Lac had information about those claims?" (Later evidence would show that by June 30 Sheehan's secretary had traced Mrs. Williams, the owner of the claims, to her home in Maryland.)

"No."

"Did they tell you anything else?"

"Yes. I can remember Mr. Allen telling Mr. Sheehan to get a proposal out to us. As Nell and I left, Mr. Sheehan said he'd have a proposal out to us within three weeks."

A moment later, Lenczner showed Bell a telephone bill for a call from his number to Sheehan's placed three days after the June 30 meeting.

"Did you reach him?"

"I can't remember."

"Why were you calling him?"

"I can't remember."

"Did you learn from Sheehan that he'd made an oral offer to Mrs. Williams on that day?"

"No," Bell said. "No, I didn't."

$\mathbf{T}$HE SCENE NOW SHIFTS A mile west, from the Corona property to the Williams claims. McKinnon had of course known of the Williams claims ever since he first looked at a claim map of the region in the late 1960s. He could scarcely have missed them, since in the area he was concentating on they were the only claims that had been patented. Mining claims come in three classes. To stake a conventional claim, the lowest class, a prospector needs a five-dollar licence and four metal claim tags, which the mining recorder sells for a dollar a set. But to keep this claim for more than a year, he — or somebody to whom he transfers all or part of his claim under an option agreement — is obliged to do at least twenty days of work on the property. This is known as assess-ment work, which means mining operations like stripping, trenching, and other development work; it doesn't mean doing more prospecting, cutting roads, or putting up buildings. If the assessment work hasn't been done a year to the day after the claim was recorded, the claim "comes open", at which point anybody else can come along and restake it. (This, you will remember, is how McKinnon acquired the claims that became the Corona property, and over time many, many other claims in the region.) On the other hand, if the assessment work is done, after two hundred hours have been completed the claim-holder may apply for a mining lease. This is the second class of claim, and it gives the owner a considerably firmer hold on the property. Then, if he can satisfy the minister of mines that he has been producing minerals in substantial quantities for more than a year, he can switch his lease for the third and highest class of claim, a patent.

That is how the rule works in the 1980s; in the 1940s, when Dr. Williams patented his claims, the requirements were easier to meet though the benefits were much the same. There isn't a great deal of difference between a patented mining claim and a straight land title, though in some respects the patent confers more privileges. The owner pays property and school taxes, and as long as he does so, he owns the land. Prospectors have no right to trespass over his patented claims without his prior consent. (Where the owner of a private property holds only surface rights, it is perfectly legal for a prospector to stake claims on the land and do assessment work without so much as asking the owner for permission. The owners of a good many well-kept suburban lawns may be lucky that this peculiarity of the law isn't better known.)

McKinnon's cost for staking conventional claims was less than fifty dollars each, all in; the cost of the patented Williams claims, if they were for sale, would be in the thousands. Until he had a buyer for them, then, they were far too expensive for McKinnon to think of going after for himself. He naturally set out to find a buyer.

The way McKinnon went about this seemingly straightforward job became part of Lac's defence. Lac's lawyers devoted a significant part of the trial to the contention that the Williams claims might well never have come into Corona's hands even if Lac had not made a bid. Corona's lawyers spent an equal amount of time trying to prove that the Williams claims had been destined for nobody but Corona. Neither side entirely succeeded; after almost five years of preparation and millions of words of testimony, all of it buttressed by the power of the law to compel witnesses to disclose the truth, this issue was still murky in some of its most important elements. Looking on as the truth failed to unfold in the courtroom, the spectators saw a graphic demonstration of both the limitations of the justice system and the pretensions of history.

It's never over, as the athletes say, until it's over, but a day in court can make it clear that once it's over, it's gone.

During the early months of 1980, when McKinnon was knocking on the doors of the major mining companies trying to sell his Hemlo package, the Trevor Page report on the Williams property along with other references to the patented claims were part of his dossier. Had he found a well-financed buyer, the Williams claims would no doubt have been vacuumed up along with the rest of the ground comprising the Lake Superior shear zone. But he didn't; the senior mining companies he approached were indifferent when they weren't rude. At this stage McKinnon and his partners optioned the staked claims to Steven Snelgrove, and here the fog creeps into the story.

Lac subpoenaed Richard Hughes and his partner, Frank Lang. This was the same Hughes whose name was given to a claim block McKinnon and Larche staked to the north and east of the original block. Hughes testified that on a scorching day in the summer of 1980 (that is, before Corona had entered the picture, but while Snelgrove still had the option on what became the Corona claims) he and Lang stopped at a little roadside coffee shop somewhere north of Kirkland Lake. They were travelling with their sometime partner, Peter Ferderber, and his sometime partner, Donald McKinnon, and the four men were on their way in two vehicles to look at a gold prospect that Hughes and Lang had optioned from McKinnon.

Like the piano player at the party who just happens to have his music with him, McKinnon can usually pull out of an inside pocket a geological map or two and a story to go with them. The map he unfolded that day on the coffee-shop counter top showed, Hughes told the court, the ground at Hemlo that was soon to become the greatest gold field in the Western Hemisphere. At the time, however, it was just a few more acres of scrub, and Ferderber was appalled. Here was Hughes listening raptly to McKinnon's pitch about some God-forsaken spruce swamp at Hemlo when Hughes already had a lot more gold property in Quebec than he had money to develop it with.

Ferderber had sold Hughes and Lang the Quebec property; he had much to gain if they were to develop a mine or mines there, as they later did. When the men left the coffee shop McKinnon took Hughes by the elbow and hustled off towards his van. Ferderber tried everything short of a flying body slam to stop them from riding together, but McKinnon got Hughes into the van and drove off, leaving Ferderber to bring Lang along in his car.

"You know those two," Ferderber said to me one night in New Orleans. "McKinnon can sell anything and Hughes will buy anything."

That was pretty much what happened. The property they were going to look over was a half-hour drive away, and by the time they got there McKinnon and Hughes had made a deal. Hughes told the court he wrote down the terms on a paper napkin he'd picked up at the coffee shop.

"What land was to be included?" McDougall asked Hughes.

"That would be the belt about twelve miles long that on today's map would show the Golden Sceptre, Goliath Gold, and Corona properties." The sites, that is, of two of the three Hemlo mines.

"Did they talk about the patented claims?" McDougall asked.

"McKinnon didn't own the patent ground. He may have shown me on the map where there were patented claims, but that wasn't part of the deal."

From his side, Hughes said, the deal called for a small down payment to be made once the regulatory authorities had approved the agreement, and "some on-going payments over a few years". Beyond this McKinnon had asked for a 30 percent carried interest in the net profit from any gold-mining activity on the property, but here Hughes had dug in. They sawed off, he said, at 15 percent.

Hughes stuck the napkin in his pocket, they all got out of the vehicles, "and we did some hiking. It was exceptionally hot, and the mosquitoes were out. McKinnon said we could hike to the end of the property where there was point one gold, but we'd be walking through heavy bush and we'd probably be eaten alive by insects.

"We all said, 'Forget it.' "

This is a good measure of the level of interest generated by point one gold. ("Point one" is verbal shorthand for rock that bears one-tenth of an ounce of gold in a ton of rock. Unless the gold is exceptionally easy to get at and refine, point one gold can't be mined at a profit.) At point two, the number, you may remember, assigned to the eighty-thousand-odd tons of gold-bearing rock outlined at Hemlo by Trevor Page in the 1940s, they might have walked on through the dense bush under the hot sun, sweating, swatting, and scratching. Instead they left, with Hughes carrying the paper-napkin contract for the Hemlo gold in his bush-jacket pocket.

McKinnon phoned Hughes "some time that fall" and said he wanted to take the old Lake Superior Mining property out of their agreement. "He said he had a deal on that ground from another company — he didn't mention the name — and wanted to leave us with just the ground around it." (This was Snelgrove's sale to Corona.)

"I said, 'Sure, Don, I don't mind giving up the ground where the gold showing was as long as we keep the rest. But,' I said, 'I believe that the patented ground also has a showing on it.' He said yes. I said, 'I would like you to acquire the patented ground for us.' Because it's difficult to raise money unless you can actually tell your shareholders, 'Hey, there's gold here, in bedrock.' "

"What was Mr. McKinnon's response?"

"He thought there wouldn't be any trouble at all getting the patented ground for us."

For months after that Hughes or Lang asked McKinnon perhaps once a week how he was making out with the patented claims. "Don said he was having trouble finding the owner," Hughes said, "so there was quite a stall there." Then one day McKinnon said he'd worked out a way of tracking down the owner. There was a broken-down cabin on the Williams property. McKinnon reported to the RCMP that the cabin had been damaged, and said he would like to pass on his account of the damage to the owner. The Mounties asked the FBI to locate the owner. The FBI found Mrs. Williams in Florida and gave her telephone number to the RCMP who gave it to McKinnon who, Hughes said, either phoned her or went to Florida to talk to her.

"What happened next?"

"What Don told us was that the lady had asked for a full price of twenty-five thousand dollars for the cabin, the ground, and the mineral rights."

"Was that all right with you?"

"Oh, I would have been delighted. Because, you know, twenty-five thousand dollars, you're probably only looking at a couple of thousand dollars now and so much a year, or what have you." Hughes paused and coughed into his hand. "Unfortunately," he said, "Don didn't strike the deal."

As Hughes remembered what happened next, McKinnon called back not long afterward and said he'd told Mrs. Williams that the property next to hers was being drilled, and might make a mine. In the circumstances her asking price was too low; McKinnon had told her that a much higher price would be fair. At this stage, Hughes said, "Don phoned us back and said, 'If you want the ground, it's a hundred thousand dollars.'

"Mentally, my response was, 'You might as well be asking for three million, because there's no way our companies would have that kind of money.' What I said was, 'Don, that's too rich for our blood.' "

McDougall asked several more questions about the details of the raised bid McKinnon had made to Mrs. Williams. At the close of this exchange Hughes shook his head ruefully and said, "We didn't have that kind of money. We couldn't even pay our rent." He cut himself off and looked sideways at Judge Holland. "Don't put that in the book," he said.

A small smile pursed the judge's rosebud mouth. "It's already in," he said.

Frank Lang followed Hughes to the stand and confirmed what his partner had said. The agreement Hughes had scribbled on the paper napkin, Lang testified, had indeed included the claims that in the end became the Corona property. And when McDougall asked whether McKinnon was acting on behalf of Lang and Hughes in trying to buy the Williams property, Lang answered emphatically, "There was no doubt about that."

Lang and Hughes were in direct conflict with McKinnon on both questions. "Would it interest you to know," Alan Lenczner asked Hughes in cross-examination, "that Mr. McKinnon had already dealt the Corona claims off in the spring of 1980 to Mr. Snelgrove, so he couldn't be making a deal with you in the summer when he no longer had the claims?"

"Mr. McKinnon indicated to me that he had the ground," Hughes said.

Earlier, McDougall had put it to McKinnon that he must have dealt with the Corona claims twice, once to Snelgrove and once to Hughes. McDougall said he was quite sure of this, since Hughes had told him that he had bought the Corona ground from McKinnon as well as the Goliath Gold and Golden Sceptre claims, and written out the agreement on a paper napkin.

"He saves old paper napkins," McKinnon had snapped back. "I don't."

Throughout his testimony, McKinnon insisted that he had sold Hughes and Lang only the claims that later became the Goliath Gold and Golden Sceptre properties, and that from the outset he had been acting for nobody but Corona in all his attempts to buy the Williams claims.

"Mr. Hughes," Lenczner asked, "do you consider Don McKinnon an honourable person?"

"Don McKinnon's a good friend of mine," Hughes said, "and a very honest gentleman."

When two versions of the same story flatly contradict each other, there's a natural tendency to assume that somebody's lying. In this case the natural assumption is probably wrong.

McKinnon's entire working method is to strike simple, often unwritten agreements and then live by them. He has a certain Northern scorn for written contracts, and a fierce pride in his own word, which he regards as a stronger covenant than a document contrived by lawyers is apt to be.

While neither Hughes nor Lang has McKinnon's combative streak, each in his own way is an extraordinarily straight-laced man. They met at B.C. Hydro, where Lang, an engineer, worked in industrial sales and Hughes in natural-gas distribution. Once a week or so, in the evening, Hughes dropped in at the Langs' for cocoa at the kitchen table, and there they talked out their fantasies of escape from the Hydro office. The fantasy that appealed to them most was finding a gold mine. Lang's brother, Howard, often spoke of the gold mine he'd already discovered. There were, to be sure, a couple of disadvantages to Howard's gold mine; it was near the top of a high mountain on Vancouver Island, and the mountain was in the middle of a national park. But there was a countervailing advantage; if Hughes and Lang would settle for a silver mine, Howard said, why, there was one not far from his gold mine, and he'd be happy to let them have it.

"It took us three trips even to get to the site," Lang once told me. "Sixty-pound packs on our backs, snow up to our necks, walking windfallen logs over raging creeks. The first trip Dick had the flu, he was pumped full of penicillin, and we weren't moving all that fast. We cached part of our food on the way in, and on the way out found bears had raided the cache. We were in for ten days, and we didn't starve, but on the last day I had three stewed prunes for lunch.

"The next trip was almost as bad, and the third trip — that trip we hired a helicopter. The pilot came in and put his runners against the side of a cliff, we walked out on the skids to the cliff face and jumped off. That trip we got to the site. We pitched camp, did some sampling, staked some claims. The second night in, we went to sleep in a light rain and woke up in a downpour with the groundsheet already under water; we'd camped in a dry streambed. This time it took us five days just to get down the mountain. You get into undergrowth so thick you've got to get down on your hands and knees and crawl, dragging the pack behind you."

Still, it was better than sitting behind a desk at B.C. Hydro. Hughes quit his job first. "I was there for fourteen years. You know what they gave me when I left? Here's a guy who's never smoked in his life. They gave me a cigarette lighter." Lang held on to his Hydro job until they had their first success, a gold deposit in Quebec that became known as the Belmoral mine. Then Lang too quit the power company, twenty-five years after joining. Before long they were highly conspicuous promoters, and one of things that made them stand out was the absence in either of them of the earmarks of the promoter.

Hughes was a slight, neurasthenic man who looked something like a smaller and more worried version of the screen actor Joseph Cotten. He spent much of his working time in a dim back office where he seldom turned on the lights, much preferring privacy to the public eye. He resembled the stereotype of the promoter in only one trait, belief, but what Hughes believed in was less the power of the market than the power of prayer. In 1983, by which time he and Lang had half a dozen gold mines in various stages of development and had become reclusive stars of the international gold circuit, I asked him how he and Lang differed from the typical promoter, who spends all his life looking and finds nothing. Hughes said not a word about promotion, but spoke of an instinct for singling out promising ground and a technique for looking at it.

"When we started Frank was a much more experienced prospector than I was," he said. "He'd walk the ground, choose a clump of grass, pull it up by the roots and expose a silver vein."

"Frank's sensory acuity is very high," added Lang's wife, Barbara, a former nurse. "His sight, his hearing, even his nose. I think he's a natural prospector. Dick has the same talent."

"And we got some help," Hughes broke in. "Why did we get the symbol for Goliath?"

When stocks trade, their numbers and prices are reported not under the company's full name but under its trading symbol, usually three uppercase letters. Goliath's symbol is GOD. More than once I asked Hughes to tell me more about the relationship between GOD and finding gold; he told me that rather than talk about it he'd send me a book in which I could find the answer myself. The book he sent is a slender tract called *Seal of God*, by an Australian fundamentalist, F.C. Payne, who wrote against the theory of evolution and in favour of the doctrine of second birth: "Let me appeal to every reader. If you are not born again, search the Scriptures. Do not ignore God and the eternal realities any longer."

If I understand the message Richard Hughes found in *Seal of God*, it was that the Lord created, along with everything else, concentrations here and there of gold in the rocks. A twice-born Christian, being in sympathy with God's plan, will be more likely than most others to look for these concentrations in the right places. Gold, in this view, is not so much where you find it as where the Lord left it.

Frank Lang was plain-featured and grey-haired, a little taller than Hughes and probably a little older, though that was not a matter of record. "You have told me that you are over fifty, and that is as specific as you will be: is that right?" McDougall asked when Lang took the witness stand. "That is right," Lang said, the reason for this note of girlish vanity not easy to see. His step, however, was firm and light. I knew him to be a physically active man who would go a long way to ski and even farther to hike; once, when the partners' Hemlo interests were under negotiation with a buyer, Lang's signature was unavailable because he was somewhere between Katmandu and the Mount Everest base camp, on foot.

Like Hughes, Lang was a true believer, but his beliefs ran in a rather different channel. He practised Silva. When I asked him to describe Silva he, too, referred me to a book. This one was called *The Silva Mind Control Method for Business Managers*. In it the author, José Silva, instructs the reader on how to slow the electrical activity of his brain to something less than the conventional twenty cycles a second. At ten cycles the brain has moved from the linear beta level to the free-form alpha level. Here the left hemisphere gives up its domination of the thought process and the right hemisphere takes over, a shift José Silva compares to thinking like a genius instead of a drunken monkey.

While the charm of this idea is easy to see, Frank Lang has found that it is also highly practical. In some way that I have been unable fully to grasp, it seems that the Silva method not only concentrates the mind but influences events. "Brain neurons can resonate with other brain neurons," José Silva writes, "or they can resonate with inanimate matter. Where survival is at stake, all obstacles are quickly crossed by the brain neurons, which are fundamentally programmed for survival." He goes on to list several possible results of the right kind of resonance. One of them is, "A stranger appears with exactly what is needed."

At the beginning of a week early in 1982 that Frank Lang remembers well, he and Hughes had to come up with three hundred thousand dollars they didn't have. The money was needed for assessment work and option payments on the Hemlo property held by their companies, Goliath Gold and Golden Sceptre; if by the end of the week they failed to find the money, they'd lose the property.

That week Lang practised Silva as he never had before. On the Wednesday a banker from England who was, needless to say, a complete stranger to both Lang and Hughes, walked into their office in Vancouver and introduced himself. By Friday he had taken down, for one of the Rothschild funds, a private placement of stock in the Hughes-Lang Hemlo companies. He bought four hundred thousand shares at seventy-five cents each, and before returning to Europe on the weekend left the partners a cheque for three hundred thousand dollars.

The faith that can cause a stranger to appear with exactly what is needed derives, to Frank Lang's mind, from the practice of Silva. Richard Hughes attributes the same effect to a higher power. Back when Hughes was struggling to get his first exploration company going he was waiting one afternoon for the light to change at the corner of Granville and Hastings streets in Vancouver when a stranger grabbed him by the elbow.

"Suddenly this big red-headed guy was towering over me, saying he wanted to help Frank and me finance our company. He said his name was Bob Crompton and he was an underwriter at Canarim [a Vancouver brokerage house].

"I wasn't sure what to make of him at first, but Bob's a pretty persuasive guy, as you know, and it turned out that what he said was true. Within a few months he'd done our first issue, at fifty cents, and handed me a cheque for two hundred and fifty thousand dollars. I'd never seen that much money in my life."

The cheque was made out to the treasury of a company called Belmoral, the first of several gold discoveries in Quebec brought to Hughes and Lang for development by Peter Ferderber. With Belmoral, the partners began to find that the power of belief has limits, whether it is belief in the ability of the mind to influence events or the ability of prayer to influence providence. Although the paper calculations all indicated that Belmoral should be a money-making mine, early in the development program a cave-in killed several men. A long investigation followed. Lang and Hughes were absolved — an entirely different group was responsible for operations at Belmoral — but by the time work resumed the development's financing was bent almost hopelessly out of shape. Belmoral was eventually brought into production, but from being a shining asset it had by then developed into something of a liability for Hughes and Lang.

No doubt they would have weathered this blow well enough, at least financially. After all, they had meanwhile discovered a far richer lode than Belmoral on what remained in their hands of the ground at Hemlo that McKinnon had sold Hughes during their van ride. Had the faith of either Hughes or Lang been shaken by the disaster at Belmoral, the Hemlo discovery should have restored it. So it did, for a time. But now they were also discovering the power of the federal tax collectors, and that prevailed, as it so often does, over everything — prayer, the alpha state, and common sense.

"Before the trouble hit Belmoral, we had a big gain in Belmoral stock," Lang once told me. "At that time, when you took a capital gain you could use the money to buy something called an income-averaging annuity. This let you spread the tax on the gain over subsequent years, and that's what I usually did. I paid the tax on the first year, and at that point as far as I knew the income tax department and I were even — the score stood at zero.

"So now the tax investigators come along. They say, 'You guys are insiders and traders. That means you haven't got a capital gain when you sell stock, you've got income. Not only that, but the annuities you bought are not deductible at all. And not only that, but you've been doing the same things wrong for years, and we're going to collect for all the years you've been doing it wrong.'

"They went back to 'seventy-eight. Let's say I had gains in 'seventy-eight-'seventy-nine-'eighty of, maybe, one point two million altogether. Through the annuities I thought I had all my taxes paid; now they're telling me I have no taxes paid, the money from the stock sales was all income instead of gains, and I owe them six hundred thousand dollars in income tax plus two hundred thousand in interest.

"To pay them I have to sell one point six million dollars worth of stock: eight hundred thousand to pay the old tax bill, and another eight hundred thousand to pay the new tax bill I've just created by selling stock to pay the old one.

"Got that? Okay. That's not the real horror story. The real horror story is what they hit me with next. Deemed income. Did you ever hear of deemed income? There was a stock called El Coco. I had a bunch of options at thirty cents. When it got to ninety I took them down and put them away; forgot about them. Now the tax guys come along, say you made a sixty-cent gain on every share of El Coco when you exercised your options. We want income tax of thirty cents. I said, what income? The shares are sitting there, I haven't sold one of them, I've made nothing, and what's more, El Coco's back down to fifty cents. They said *deemed* income; it didn't matter to them whether I'd ever seen the sixty cents or not, it was deemed income and I owed them thirty cents tax on it. If you work all that out on paper, you'll see that when they were through with me I paid more than a hundred percent tax after I'd sold the stock to get the money.

"Even with all that I could probably handle it except for one thing. Timing. Last year I guess I sold three million dollars worth of stock. The deadline comes up in April this year, I'll probably owe them a million and a half. I've prepaid about four hundred thousand; that leaves a million one. So to cover, I'll have to sell stock for two million two. In a bad market that could take a quarter of a million shares of Goliath-Golden Sceptre, and that would leave almost none."

Income tax had become a horror story for Hughes even earlier than it did for Lang, and in the end neither of them was able to hold on to a substantial block of stock in their own Hemlo companies. The deal they made with the giant mining conglomerate, Noranda, to develop the mine gave Noranda title to the ore body after a few years. The Hughes-Lang companies were left with a share of the profit, no mean thing in itself but a bitter reminder of the day when Hughes wrote on a paper napkin the agreement that gave them the right to buy not only the ground that subsequently became the Noranda mine, but the Corona mine and in their view the Lac mine as well — if they could have found the money.

McKinnon, of course, disagreed with them about the ground that became the Lac mine. But Hughes and Lang, as their actions show, are the least devious of promoters. They are no more likely than McKinnon to be lying, and if this is so the disagreement between them and McKinnon was caused by the differing unspoken assumptions made by both sides when they scribbled their agreement. It crossed my mind in court that McKinnon's fierce defence of the hand-shake contract may have been its epitaph. The tradition of the hand-shake contract was one of the most attractive legends of the mining camps, but to honour it meant overlooking the incidence of lawsuits arising out of these bluff manly agreements. Since the earliest discoveries at Cobalt, when everybody had sued everybody else, the lawsuit ratio appeared to have been running at about 90 percent. Now at Hemlo everybody was suing everybody else again. Soon, even a Northerner would have to admit, however reluctantly, that his next contract might last longer if there was a lawyer's hand in it as well as his own.

MURRAY PEZIM BECAME A
director of Corona Resources on June 8, 1981, and on the same day became
chairman of the board. This fast-track promotion came about because he
had been involved with Corona's finances ever since the underwriting that
had replenished the company's treasury early the previous December.
Although Nell Dragovan was running the company's affairs and David Bell
was in charge of the exploration program at Hemlo, it was broadly understood that when there were shots to call for Corona, Murray Pezim called
them.

This is how it happened that when Donald McKinnon finally reached
Lola Williams after her winter in Florida, and learned from her that she
was very interested indeed in selling the patented claims at Hemlo, McKinnon
first went over the terms of the offer not with Dragovan or Bell, both of
whom were already on the Corona board, but with Pezim, who wasn't.

"I got a phone call from Don McKinnon. He's the one," Pezim told the
court, in an aside that generously attributed to McKinnon an achievement
that in other contexts Pezim usually claims for himself, "he's the one most
of the credit should go to for the Hemlo discovery. He said he was going
after the Williams property for us. I suggested he try to make a deal for as
little money as possible, but a three percent net smelter royalty."

As for David Bell, Pezim said, Bell was always anxious to get the Williams property. "You must understand, it was very important for Corona to
get that ground, and also the ground to the north."

"Did you know who had the ground to the north?"

"Richard Hughes."

"And what about Lac; what did you know about their involvement with
Corona?"

"I heard from Nell that they were interested and wanted to negotiate a
deal. I got a phone call from Bell saying a Dennis Sheehan from Lac wanted
to come on the property."

"How did you feel about that?"

"I thought it was great."

Pezim swept the courtroom with his bright nut-brown eyes as though he were scanning it for prospects, as he may have been. He was sixty-four years old, his belly overhung his belt almost as far as his nose overarched his chin, and his face was dappled with liver spots like old moss on which the light falls through leaves. None the less, the sum of these unpromising parts was an attractive and somehow compelling individual. He had spent most of his life selling something, and nobody buys much from somebody he dislikes. His older brother, Norman, once told me that when they were in grade school in the tough Rogers Road district of west Toronto, word got out that two of the hardest cases among the kids were headed for a fight. Murray got to them before they started swinging, Norman said, and talked them into fighting in the Pezim's backyard, where there was a high board fence and a gate. Murray promoted the fight all afternoon at school, and charged a nickel to get in that evening.

"It wasn't exactly Dempsey-Tunney," Norman said, "but Murray cleared more than a dollar after paying the fighters, and there wasn't another kid in school had that kind of money."

Money mattered. Murray quit school at sixteen (he once told me; for other interviewers he's dropped this as low as fourteen, depending, I suppose, on the effect he's looking for) and went to work in the family butcher shop on Rogers Road. The Depression had been grinding the economy to rubble for five years, and an unschooled boy was probably lucky to have a family shop to work in. This Murray seems to have forgotten; what he has remembered is that the shop's butchers worked ninety hours a week (or a hundred, as he has said elsewhere) and the Second World War came almost as a relief.

"In the army," Ron Slaght asked, "what rank did you achieve?"

"Rifleman," answered Murray Pezim, captain of finance. All laughed. Riding this very small wave, he added, "That's one rank below private." His timing and inflexion were both right; all laughed louder. His friends, of whom there were several in court, knew that one of his great affinities is for the one-liner comedians and their craft; he has named a company for his friend Henny Youngman and made his friend Joey Bishop a partner in another.

The army shipped Rifleman Pezim to Jamaica, where he helped guard a camp for German prisoners of war. He had a gift; perhaps it was the agility with numbers that made him the natural stick-man for the camp's crap games, perhaps it was the zest with which he partied on the money he'd won. Whatever it was, it made a memorable individual out of a rifleman barely out of his teens, and that is a large gift. Some years after the war,

Norman Pezim and his wife made a holiday trip to Jamaica. "I told Murray what hotel we were going to. He said, 'Look up So-and-so, he runs the place.'

"Checking in I ask for this guy, tell him I'm Norman Pezim, and he lights up. 'Not Pez's brother?' he says, and from there on I'm a VIP. He puts us in a penthouse suite, takes us to the polo matches — I kid you not, polo — the cricket matches, the whole show."

While Murray's gift was great enough to make him a rifleman to remember, it fell short of providing him with a way out of the butcher shop after the war. He worked there until 1950, the hours getting longer at every telling and the temperature of the cold-storage locker getting lower, until the day a broker named Max Guthrie came in.

"He wanted to buy some pork chops, okay? That was the big deal. And he said, 'Do you ever play the market?' "

Pezim was now thirty, and had never owned a share certificate in his life. Guthrie told him about a company called Duvay.

"The stock was five to a quarter. I told him to buy me five thousand shares."

"Wasn't that a lot of money for a butcher?" I asked.

"Five cents bid, five and a quarter asked," Pezim said. "In those days, we traded in quarter-cents. So of course I looked in the paper that night, and naturally it showed up a quarter; now it's five and a quarter bid, five and a half asked.

"Bang, there goes my mind. Suddenly I'm gonna be the Bull of Wall Street. So I keep buying more and more; now the stock's up to about twelve cents, every dime I ever saved is in it, maybe fifteen thousand dollars, and I go to sell some. You know the next line. There's no bid.

"So my money's gone; out the window. And I was angry at myself. I thought, if I lost it somebody must have made it. Well, it doesn't quite work that way, but in those days I thought it did. So I decided that I had to learn this business; I felt if I could lose it, maybe I could get on the other side and get it back."

That is what he has been doing ever since — getting it back, losing it, getting it back, losing it. He started learning how to get it back by doing odd jobs without pay for a few hours a day — he couldn't afford to quit the butcher shop until he'd saved some more money — at a Toronto brokerage where a friend worked. The most important thing he learned there was that if he really wanted to pick up the skills of the market, he'd have to go to New York to do it. He took his fresh savings out of the bank and went to Wall Street, where another friend introduced him at Henson and Company, a brokerage that has long since disappeared in a merger. The senior partner there was a Dr. Baruch, the brother of the anointed American financier and statesman Bernard Baruch, but the partner who gave Murray Pezim the tutelage he'd come to New York for was a man named Milo Greene.

"He was an old-time grain trader, originally out of Zurich," Pezim once told me, his voice warmed by remembered affection. "He was also a concert pianist; a brilliant man. The type of a guy that you could . . . he could talk to you for ten hours a day and you could listen, 'cause he was never boring; his wisdom was just — fantastic.

"He never talked to me about any stocks. He talked to me about people; and the thing he stressed to me, there's two emotions in the market. One emotion is easy, that's the emotion of buying. The emotion of selling is a killer. That's the one that destroys you. A guy, he thinks, if I sell to somebody, he's going to make more than I do. It's tough to take a profit, emotionally. It's very tough. I don't think I've overcome it to this day, I really don't.

"He also taught me, to be a success in the marketplace, forget the names of stocks. It's the trades that count. The names of stocks are immaterial, because almost a hundred percent of the people really don't care who runs the company or anything about it as long as they can make a buck out of it. If they can buy for one and sell for two they don't give a damn if the chairman of the board is the biggest crook in the world or the Pope — I've got mine, to hell with everybody else; that kind of attitude makes the market.

"Stocks, he'd tell me stocks are just like kernels of corn; they're all the same, a method of making a trade, nothing more. He was," Pezim searched for a word, failed to find one that matched the strength of his wish to praise, and said, "he was quite a guy."

When Pezim left Milo Greene and New York a few months later and went back to Toronto, another now-defunct firm called E.T. Lynch and Company hired him as a customer's man. In one of those almost transcendental moments of release that should come to all of us now and then in a lifetime, he believed himself at last cut loose from the butcher counter.

"I got hooked up with a guy named Al Rosen, who was a promoter in those years. The name of the deal was Ascot Minerals. The stock was around two and a half, and needless to say I was a good salesman, I put a lot of people into it. And the stock went right down into the crapper; went down so badly I said, 'Screw this noise, I'm quittin' the business, I'm going back to the meat counter, I want peace.' I felt badly; so many people lost their money in it.

"So I went back cutting pork chops, and one day I got a call from Morrie Kessler, and he said, 'Murray, please. You're a natural for our business, you should come back to work, I've got a guy that wants to meet you, he's got a deal I think you'll — just come down and say hello to him.' I said, 'Morrie, I'm fed up, leave me alone, really, you know?' He says, 'No, you gotta meet this guy.'

"Anyway, he kept on, I went down, and that's when I met Steve Roman. And that's . . . that turned into the Denison." Roman's Denison mine was rich in uranium, as it turned out, and for the first time of many, Murray Pezim got it back. He even won the battle with his own emotions over selling, getting out the last of his forty-cent stock at seventeen dollars and then watching the price climb to eighty dollars. Never mind; he had millions, which he then lost with gusto. But this time he didn't retreat to the butcher shop. He settled in as a Toronto broker.

He did it at the height of an odd period in the city's history, when a kind of glamour adhered to stock promoters, or more precisely I suppose to their money, and many promoters were public figures. In the mid-1950s lines of cars wound through a quiet west-end Toronto street at Christmas to look at the decorations on M.J. Boylen's lawn, not because the sightseers hadn't seen a reindeer cutout before but because Boylen, the promoter of a big base-metal mine in New Brunswick, was a celebrity. Frank Joubin and Gilbert La Bine were celebrities, and so, in these years before the Windfall Affair were Viola MacMillan and her husband, George, Bud Knight and Art White, and Cyrus Eaton, who was a celebrity on an international scale. Stephen Roman became a celebrity with the Denison mine, and when Joseph Hirshhorn tried to take it away from him by selling Denison short in an attempt to break the market, both of them became international celebrities.

"That was a tremendous fight," Pezim once told me. "And I gotta give Steve credit; he stood in. At the end he could have broken Hirshhorn, who was short more than a million shares and had no way to cover. But Steve was just about broke too, so he made a deal with Bud Knight — a million-share underwriting with one condition, that Knight sell none of the shares to Hirshhorn. Of course Knight sold the entire million to Hirshhorn, and that became a court case in itself."

At other times, Pezim had allied himself on the other side, with Hirshhorn. "There was a gambler. He took his shots; a believer, like I am. It takes someone like that. If you can't stand in and gamble, you're gone.

"It seemed that every time a small guy found something, the wolves would come for him, and they'd throw everything at him. It was very difficult for the guy that made the original discovery to wind up with anything worth having. Oh, there were exceptions, but not very many.

"God, the stories they'd spread; if somebody went short against you they'd go watch and wait until you got in an airplane and then spread a rumour that you got killed in an accident — anything at all to get people to dump your stock. It's a cold, cold business."

Pezim's experience with Roman changed his ideas about how to be a stockbroker. "If you don't want to do anything but write out buy and sell tickets, you can make a living. To get ahead in the business, you have to link yourself to a star. If you've picked the right star, you're a hero."

This was how Murray Pezim came to be handing out roses to the ladies of Timmins on behalf of Earl Glick in 1964, the year of the Kidd Creek discovery and the Windfall Affair. Glick was there both to buy claims and to sell stock in the companies he put the claims into; Pezim was there because Glick was his star of the moment. They sold a lot of stock. They also bought a lot of stock, and thereon hangs another truth about the stock market.

"Earl Glick and I may have bought more Windfall than anybody else. We had a direct statement from a principal about how good it was. We bought every share we could get in the east, and I remember distinctly that when the Toronto market closed we kept buying in Vancouver. We bought it up to about four and a half dollars.

"They published the results of the drill hole that night, and it opened the next morning at eighty cents. Between the close in Vancouver and the opening in Toronto we lost about four hundred thousand dollars. Just got taken, that's all.

"You know all that stuff about widows and orphans being the losers? That's crap. The biggest hits in the market are taken by guys like me. We'll go for the stories; I'm a soft touch for a good story. No, it's the wise guys that get killed. I've been killed myself, God knows how many times.

"One of the weaknesses, I guess the biggest culprits in our industry are the salesmen. They're so commission-hungry that they'll put people into this stock and out of that one just to make the commission, and they'll invent stories like crazy just to make that person buy or sell. Through the whole industry, it's the same thing. Even in New York, it's supposed to be the premier marketplace, it's the same thing. This whole money-supply figure, you know, comes out every Friday? They turned that into a game. Money supply's up, sell; money supply's down, buy — just as a means, a story, to create sales. They'll grab on to anything, any story they can tell, just to make people buy and sell."

In the aftermath of the Windfall débâcle, the Ontario Securities Commission and the Toronto Stock Exchange rewrote the rules. The new rules gave Toronto's Bay Street a dreary climate for stock promoters, and most of them migrated. Earl Glick went to Los Angeles, where he bought the Hal Roach Studio and for a time cut something of a figure in the movie colony. By then he was no longer a star in Pezim's eyes. "Earl was, uh, not too classy a guy; also one of my *dis*loyal partners."

Pezim himself, like many other Toronto promoters, went to Vancouver. Here Pezim dropped the curtain on the period of his life in which he had always tried to link himself to a star. In Vancouver he became a star himself.

Coincidence, the classic path to stardom that leads the fresh-faced aspirant to the very soda fountain where the casting director is nibbling a split banana, nudged Pezim towards stardom. One of the first companies he got hold of, Stampede Oil and Gas, was drilling for a structure called a pinnacle reef in Alberta. At fifteen thousand feet the first hole had already cost a million dollars, and both Stampede and Pezim were almost broke. But the day they decided in Vancouver to abandon the hole was coincidentally the day the drill nicked a lower corner of the pinnacle, which is a mineral structure shaped much like a pyramid. The drill was three miles into the ground; had the bit been ten feet farther to the side, it would have missed the structure altogether.

"The second hole hit right smack on top of that pinnacle. I remember when that came in. We had a ton-and-a-half cement plug down there at fifteen thousand feet, and it shot that son of a bitch up in the sky — hoo, you run for your life!"

Stampede's stock shot up almost as fast as the concrete plug, and Murray Pezim became a star in Vancouver — "the king of the street", as he sometimes called himself.

There were those who disagreed with Pezim's princely estimate of himself, among them a man named Rupert Bullock. As a sergeant of the Royal Canadian Mounted Police, Bullock was in charge of policing securities frauds; he later became the B.C. government's superintendent of brokers. Looking over Pezim's shoulder, Bullock frowned when he saw one of the new star's companies, B-X Resources, pay two and a half million dollars for an abandoned limepit in Arizona.

"He figured there was nothing there," Pezim said several years later, "so he charged me with fraud." The purpose of laying a stock-fraud charge, of course, is to protect the shareholders; the stock, which had been at two and a half dollars, promptly dropped to fifty cents. Pezim moved in a red-eyeballed fury to Douglas, Arizona, the site of the limepit, and worked furiously to get the quarry up and running. By the time the Crown got the case into court in British Columbia the limepit was making money and the stock was on its way to a high of forty-five dollars. The judge acquitted Pezim and his partners, and ordered the Crown to pay their costs.

"The limepit? I sold the limepit for thirty-five million dollars," Pezim told me, and laughed at the memory of the money rolling in. His wife, Marilyn, still failed to find any humour in the story. "They had detectives following us everywhere we went," she said. "Every night we'd look for microphones under the bed."

"Did you ever find any?"

"Yes. Twice in Vancouver. And once, when we went to Toronto and checked in to the Royal York Hotel, they told us the room wouldn't be ready for a couple of hours. It turned out later they were putting in a concealed camera and three men doing surveillance. In court the lawyer said, 'What did you do when Mrs. Pezim undressed.' They all said, 'We turned our heads.'

"It was creepy," she said. "It's a rotten way to live. Murray laughs now, but at the time he was angry half the time and depressed the other half. At depressed, this man is the world heavyweight champion."

Marilyn herself, I would have said, ranked very high in her class for independence. She was Pezim's second wife; they met in the early 1960s, when she was the receptionist in Earl Glick's office in Toronto, and married ten years later. "When I saw Marilyn for the first time," Pezim's brother, Norman, once told me, "she was sitting there in Earl Glick's front office, smoking a cigar." Norman is a profoundly conventional man. "I looked at her and I wondered, what the hell is this?"

This was a young woman with black hair, a supple well-made body, and a strong mind, which may have done more to throw Norman than the cigar.

"When I went to work at Glick's," Marilyn said, "they told me, wait till you meet Murray Pezim — he's the playboy. The playboy came in, I took one look, and it was instant hate."

The time was not long after Pezim's great success with Denison Mines, and he was mainlining money. "These guys," Marilyn said, "they measure their manhood by their bank accounts. Money rises, guy swells up, he can do anything. Money runs out, the world ends. Murray's as bad as any of them. What am I saying? He's the worst."

She shuttered her eyes behind lowered lids for several seconds. "Nineteen eighty-one," she said. "That was the worst." Pezim at first had no stock in Corona; he didn't need any. When the early drill holes suggested there might be something of value in the ground at Hemlo, Pezim and his partners, including Nell Dragovan and David Bell, proposed to take over the escrowed shares in Corona. Escrowed shares are a device for keeping control of a small company in the hands of its founders. They usually get the shares in exchange for vending into the company an exploration property, but the shares aren't released for trading until the company derives some benefit from the property. The escrow in Corona was a block of 750,000 shares, which Pezim and his partners proposed to take down in exchange for a number of claims they owned at a place called Rouse Lake. The claims had cost them less than fifty thousand dollars; Corona shares were then trading for more than two dollars each. The regulatory authorities, taking what Pezim regarded as a petty view of the disparity between what he'd paid for the Rouse Lake claims and what he was proposing to get for them, declined to approve the deal. Pezim went into the market to buy the stock position in Corona that the authorities wouldn't let him take from escrow for next to nothing. Over the summer of '81 his own buying, always on margin, was largely responsible for driving Corona up from below two dollars a share to the ten-dollar level.

The paper profits looked, as they say, like a million, and the Pezims moved to a new beachfront penthouse. There had been no time to furnish the place when the price of gold started falling, dragging down with it the price of Corona shares. Pezim started getting margin calls. There being no choice, he sold shares to cover the margin calls, thereby driving down the price of the stock and triggering more margin calls. Even a well-balanced individual in this situation feels like a stunt pilot in a tailspin. Pezim could feel the loops of the spiral getting tighter and the blood pressing on the back of his eyeballs.

"Black, black, black," Marilyn said. She crossed her arms and gripped her own elbows. "Every time something happens to Murray financially, it also happens to him emotionally. Sweats. Shivers. I've woken up in the middle of the night with his hands grabbing me so hard I was scared he'd choke me.

"They tried everything. Anti-depressants — Parnate, when that was new, kind of a guinea-pig thing. Later on they switched him to other stuff. I don't think it's good for anybody to be on anti-depressants for too long. And they'd hide him away in clinics, too; I don't know how much that helped.

"That penthouse, sometimes if I'd been out in the afternoon and came home after he did, I'd find him in front of this huge glass window that looked down on the beach and the ocean. Very expensive view, but there wasn't a stick of furniture in the room. By this time there wasn't enough money left to buy any, either. Murray would be curled up on the floor, moaning. He had a piece of carpet there, and a blanket. I'd take his head in my lap, and every now and then he'd go stiff and drum his heels on the floor."

"Why in front of the window?" I asked Pezim.

"Warmth," he said. "You know those radiators they cut in the floor, with the grilles over them? That's where the radiators were, in front of the windows. I'd lie there holding my head. Every night, night after night. Hoping gold would turn, you know, but, God, it was really painful."

"I knew he'd get up," Marilyn said. "He always does. But the truth was, I didn't know when."

By Christmas 1981, he was still down. His friend, the stockbroker Gus McPhail, wanted to lend him some money. He wouldn't take it. One night McPhail was at the penthouse, and he realized there was only one thing in it, or rather two, that had any cash value at all.

"He had these two pocket-size dogs," McPhail told me. "What do you call them, Yorkshire terriers? Whatever. I looked at the dogs. 'All right,' I said, 'you won't take a loan, I'll buy the dogs.'

"He looked back at me, big blue bags under his eyes like somebody beat him up. 'You son of a bitch,' he said, 'you got a deal. Seventy-five bucks.'

"I started to count the money before he changed his mind, and he said, 'Each.'

"So now I've got these two dogs chewing everything in sight including my legs, and he won't take them back until he's got the hundred and fifty dollars to pay me. Months, it took. Months."

"I remember," Pezim said when I reminded him about McPhail and the dogs. "Served the son of a bitch right." Then: "Look," he said more seriously, "there were offers, you know, to buy me out. Lots of them. But half my nightmares came from fears of losing control.

"My attitude, by the time I finally got it worked out, was simple. Either I'm going to have it or I'm not going to have it. Fuck it."

In June of 1981 the tight downward spiral that in the end reddened Murray Pezim's eyeballs was just beginning. After Pezim told Donald McKinnon to try for a low cash payment and a high royalty on the patented Williams claims, McKinnon, who listens to advice but goes his own way, did something close to the opposite. He concluded that the twenty-five thousand dollars Lola Williams asked him for was too little, and quadrupled the bid. The change wasn't entirely altruistic; McKinnon has told me that he wanted a contract that wouldn't be challenged later on the ground that he had taken advantage of an uninformed widow. In hindsight this attempt to deal fairly with Mrs. Williams was a costly decision on his part, and one that led to a costly decision on hers.

Learning that her buyer wanted to pay more than she asked, Mrs. Williams hired lawyers, prolonged the negotiations, and ultimately rejected McKinnon's revised offer. This went to her on June 12 in the form of a letter from Hemglo Resources, which was the name given by McKinnon and John Larche and their grubstakers, Rocco Schiralli and Claude Bonhomme, to the partnership the four men had formed to deal with their Hemlo interests. The letter set out a conventional option agreement; for the claims, Mrs. Williams would be paid a hundred thousand dollars over three years, and be left with a 3 percent royalty on the net smelter returns, should there be any.

Mrs. Williams hired a lawyer in Maryland, James Anthenelli, who in turn retained a Toronto solicitor, Robert Armstrong, to look after her interests. Anthenelli wrote to Armstrong on June 29, more than two weeks after the Hemglo letter. He said that Mrs. Williams was "extremely interested in entering" the Hemglo agreement, but "we want to be assured that the price offered for the rights is fair and reasonable and that the royalties promised are equally favorable." Then he asked Armstrong to "make the necessary arrangements to evaluate the nature of our holdings," leaving Armstrong, one would have thought, scratching his head about what he was supposed to do next.

In court, Lac attacked the Hemglo offer from several directions. Why, in the first place, were Schiralli and Bonhomme involved at all, since in their grubstake agreement there was no mention of the Williams property?

"Well," McKinnon said, "it wasn't part of it originally, but when I started, got interested in the Williams ground and started negotiating for Corona, there was no way that I was going to eliminate my partners who had put up the money for the ground that was staked surrounding them.

"In fact," McKinnon said, projecting from the witness box a degree of righteous indignation, "I was always under the impression it was illegal to do that. I understand now it isn't, but morally I would never do that."

Lac shifted the line of attack. Where was the evidence that even if Hemglo had acquired the property, Hemglo would then have sold to Corona and not some other, higher bidder? David Bell, Lac argued, didn't know the terms of the Hemglo offer or even that something called Hemglo had made a written offer. Furthermore, no copy of the written offer went to Corona.

McKinnon and Pezim both testified that the terms of the Hemglo offer had been discussed between them — as little cash as possible and a 3 percent royalty — although they hadn't settled the payment Hemglo was to get for acquiring the property. "Mr. Pezim said we would be looked after," McKinnon said. "That was good enough for me."

This being so, there was no need to consult Bell about the terms. As to who would get the claims, McKinnon said that from the beginning of April it had always been his intention that the Williams property would go to Corona. Pezim said the same thing. But Lac opened up a soft spot on this point when McDougall cross-examined McKinnon's grubstake partner Claude Bonhomme.

"You will agree with me that it was up to Mr. Pezim as to where and what he did with the patented ground, should he option it from Hemglo?"

"My understanding from the beginning was that Mr. Pezim was dealing on behalf of Corona with Mr. McKinnon."

"Mr. Bonhomme. You will agree with me, will you not, that it was up to Mr. Pezim to deal with the land if he got it as he saw fit?"

"I understood it was to go to Corona."

"Just a moment. There is no way to your knowledge, that if Mr. Pezim optioned the property from Hemglo and decided not to put it into Corona, that you could do anything about it, is there?"

"No," Bonhomme said, "there is nothing I could do about it."

That brought the issue back to Pezim. McDougall asked Pezim if he recalled when McKinnon had phoned him about the Hemglo offer.

"In the spring," Pezim said.

"And spring means what to you?"

"Same thing it means to you, sir."

"Were you a director of Corona at the time?"

"No, sir."

"Why would McKinnon call you rather than Mr. Bell or Miss Dragovan?"

"Because he knew I was the promoter."

"He wanted approval of the numbers?"

"What numbers?"

"The three percent net smelter return?"

"Yes."

"So he was to get the property, and bring it to you?"

"No, sir. To Corona."

"But he was talking to you?"

"Yes."

"And he would take the property to you?"

"No. To Corona. It was always to be Corona's."

Earlier in the exchange between McDougall and Pezim the judge had rebuked Pezim for raising his voice. Now his voice was too far gone to raise; he was struggling with a head cold, blowing and sneezing and leaking, and his nose, never inconspicuous, was getting bigger and redder by the moment, like a poppy spreading itself in the sun. Still, he was injecting into the hoarse whisper that remained of his voice a degree of antagonism that wasn't called for by what he was saying. So was McDougall, who was bringing some of his phrases down with the weight of a club.

In fact, their mutual hostility had little to do with what was passing between them in court. A couple of weeks earlier, when the trial was in a brief recess and the Corona lawyers were getting Pezim ready to testify, Alan Lenczner had to phone McDougall about some detail. Pezim said, "Tell him he's a cocksucker," a remark Pezim often makes; he really thinks this is funny. Lenczner dialled, a voice said hello, and Lenczner said, "John, Murray says you're a cocksucker." The voice said, "I'm not John. I'll tell him to call back." An hour later, McDougall returned the call. Lenczner said, "John, Murray says you're *still* a cocksucker."

Later, when they had all returned to the courthouse, McDougall stopped Lenczner in the corridor. "I was getting tired," he said, "but you've given me new vigour."

Lenczner was baffled. "What do you mean?" he asked.

"Nobody ever called me a cocksucker before," McDougall said.

July 3, 1981, fell on a Friday. Dennis Sheehan was booked the next morning to begin a two-week holiday, but when his secretary told him that afternoon that she had located Lola Williams, the owner of the patented claims next to the Corona property at Hemlo, Sheehan asked her to get Mrs. Williams on the phone. The Lac people later made a summary of what happened next. Here it is, in their words:

"Sheehan identified himself and Lac to Mrs. Williams and inquired about the patented claims. Mrs. Williams told him she had an offer from a man named McKinnon. Sheehan knew him to be a dealer in claims. Sheehan told her that if she could not do a deal with McKinnon, Lac might be interested. Mrs. Williams asked him what he would offer and when he told her, she asked him to put the offer in writing. Sheehan was unaware of any connection between McKinnon and Corona. Before going on vacation, Sheehan instructed Lac's secretary and general counsel to prepare the offer dated July 6, 1981, and submit it to Mrs. Williams. The offer was for a one-year option to explore the property for twenty-five thousand dollars, the second year twenty-five thousand dollars, the third and fourth years thirty-five thousand dollars, and the right to purchase the property for a hundred and thirty thousand dollars and a one percent net smelter return at the fourth anniversary."

Lac's flat assertion that Sheehan knew nothing of any connection between McKinnon and Corona carried some weight if it was true. But Sheehan's testimony had to be weighed against a note in the diary of his field man, Chris Pegg, whose entry for April 5 said that Corona had optioned the property from Don McKinnon. Considering the amount of time Sheehan had spent on the ground with Pegg, and the amount of research his other assistants had done on property rights in the area, Sheehan's assertion may have lacked the colour of credibility. There were also some interesting omissions from Sheehan's conversation with Mrs. Williams. Whereas McKinnon had told her about the promising results of drilling on the adjoining property, Sheehan apparently told her nothing about Lac's reasons for assembling land in the area or about Lac's proposal for an association with Corona.

Lac's people and Robert Armstrong, the Toronto lawyer retained to protect Mrs. Williams's interest in Canada, exchanged comments about the Lac offer. As a result, Lac made an amended offer on July 21 by which the smelter royalty was increased to 1.5 percent: the other terms were unchanged. On the same day, McKinnon phoned Mrs. Williams to ask why he hadn't heard from her about the Hemglo offer. He had understood her to have agreed verbally to the terms, but the written offer had now been outstanding for more than a month. Her manner towards him, McKinnon said, "had cooled". She said she had meanwhile received a better offer, and when McKinnon asked her for details, she told him he'd better talk to Armstrong in Toronto.

McKinnon called Bell the next morning and reported this conversation. McKinnon advised Bell that Corona should now make a direct offer to Mrs. Williams. It would probably be better, he said, to avoid mentioning his name. She seemed unwilling to deal with him, but he knew of no reason why she wouldn't deal with Corona.

Bell hung up and called Dragovan in Vancouver. He reached her at 8:45 in the morning, and they quickly agreed to make a direct offer from Corona to Mrs. Williams, as McKinnon had advised.

"Why would Corona have to get McKinnon's permission to deal directly?" Brian Foster asked Dragovan.

"McKinnon was acquiring the property for us," she said. "We couldn't go behind his back."

Corona would later argue that the sequence of events here was significant. That McKinnon straightaway informed Corona when his negotiations with Mrs. Williams broke down, and that on being released from the understanding with McKinnon Corona promptly made an offer on its own account, went some part of the way to show that McKinnon was acting for Corona alone.

Dragovan then called Pezim, who agreed with the decision she and Bell had made to bid directly for the Williams claims. When she asked about terms, Pezim told her to bid whatever it would take. They decided to leave the terms in Bell's hands; Pezim said, "Whatever David decides is all right with me."

Dragovan phoned a Toronto lawyer who had done some work for Corona, Ivan Thornley-Hall, and told him what Corona wanted to do. She said he'd hear from David Bell about the terms. Then she called a friend, Carole Inman, who was a secretary at Teck Corporation. At the back of her mind she had been grappling all morning with the puzzle of who might have come up on Corona's blind side with the competing bid. Teck was her best and almost only guess. Far back in the time of Trevor Page, Teck had been the first established mining company to take an option on the Lake Superior Mining claims, and although Teck had subsequently dropped the option the company might well have kept an interest in the area.

"And Carole Inman told you . . ." Brian Foster asked.

"She told me Teck did *not* make the offer."

Ivan Thornley-Hall, who acted for Corona in Toronto, and Robert Armstrong, who acted for Mrs. Williams, both appeared in court. They were oddly alike, strained men of middle age both of whom would clearly have preferred to be elsewhere. Neither said anything that had a bearing on the outcome of the case, but they played a scene that led to a moment of high drama.

Thornley-Hall testified that he dealt with the offer from Corona to Mrs. Williams as a matter of "extreme urgency". Accordingly, he phoned her lawyer, Armstrong, even before he finished drafting the offer. He told Armstrong Corona was preparing a bid, and read him the terms.

Thornley-Hall finished the draft the next day and took it to Armstrong's office. It was late, close to six, and the two men spent an hour going over the terms. Corona offered Mrs. Williams thirty thousand dollars on signing a formal agreement, to be followed by a hundred thousand dollars by the end of the first year, and another hundred thousand by the end of the second year. Corona would then acquire title to the property, and Mrs. Williams would be paid a 3 percent royalty on the net smelter returns from any production.

"Did Armstrong tell you the competing offer was from Lac?" Alan Lenczner asked.

"No," Thornley-Hall said.

Cross-examining Thornley-Hall, McDougall handed him a transcript of Nell Dragovan's evidence, and asked, "Do you see the sentence, 'Thornley-Hall had found out on July 23 from Armstrong that the offer came from Lac?' Like David Bell, Thornley-Hall took off his glasses to read; then he put them back on again and said yes, that was what the transcript said.

"Does that evidence from your client refresh your memory?"

"I must say in all honesty it doesn't," Thornley-Hall said. "I have no recollection of that piece of information coming into my possession from Bob Armstrong, or from any other source, nor of conveying it to Miss Dragovan. Of course," his voice tailed off, "I could be wrong."

"You could be wrong," McDougall said, with heavy irony. He read from a transcript in which David Bell similarly said Thornley-Hall had passed on the information to Corona that Lac was the other bidder.

"When I first spoke to Armstrong, he was at considerable pains to tell me he was in no position to divulge the identity of the competing offeror. He didn't have the authority to make any such disclosure to me."

McDougall shook his head, in the more-in-sorrow gesture he often used just before he raised his voice. He held up a document, and told Thornley-Hall that it was a "narrative" Armstrong had written, setting out his version of the story. In it, McDougall said, Armstrong claimed he had told Thornley-Hall that the other offer came from Lac. McDougall then read directly from Armstrong's narrative, in a voice charged with drama:

"From Thornley-Hall's reaction, I immediately thought there might be some agreement that was being breached. So I then satisfied myself that there was no breach respecting the Williams property." This statement was on page nine of Armstrong's memo.

"That is his recollection," Thornley-Hall said. "It is not mine."

Judge Holland adjourned his court for the day a few minutes later. McDougall and I walked into the corridor together. He was wound tighter than I had seen him to be at any other time in the trial.

"That last page I read him?" he said. "That could end the whole case, right there."

His associates closed around him and bore him off, all talking at once. I stopped in the corridor to speak for a moment with Ron Slaght. Lenczner rushed up and interrupted us in mid-sentence.

"Paydirt!" Lenczner said in a high-voltage whisper. "We've hit paydirt. Armstrong dictated that memo some time last summer. Page eight was the last page. There was no page nine. He added it this week." Lenczner's assistants, ransacking the files, had found a copy of Armstrong's original memo, seen that page nine was missing, and assumed at first that they had a faulty copy.

Armstrong had been subpoenaed to testify for Corona, and was to have followed Thornley-Hall on the witness stand. Now, knowing that Armstrong had added the ninth page only days before he was to appear, Lenczner went into Judge Holland's chambers and asked to have Armstrong declared a hostile witness. The judge hesitated. McDougall stepped into the pause and said, "In that case, I'll call him."

So it was that Armstrong's appearance was postponed for several weeks. When he did take the stand it was as a witness for Lac, thereby giving Lenczner a chance to cross-examine him. Armstrong testified that he had in fact written three versions of the memo at widely separated times, and had indeed added page nine the same week McDougall read it in court.

"After preparing that effort," Lenczner said, holding up Armstrong's narrative, "you sent a bill to Lac Minerals, didn't you?"

"Yes."

"What was your charge?"

"I think about four thousand dollars."

"Not about. Exactly."

"Yes."

By this time the history of Armstrong's narrative was so tangled that it carried little of the weight McDougall had at first attributed to it. But Armstrong had one question of real weight left to answer. Since he had acknowledged that Corona had made the highest offer, why hadn't he advised his client to take it?

"You told Thornley-Hall that Corona had the best offer?"

"In Thornley-Hall's words. But there's a difference between the best terms and the best offer. You might prefer an offer that didn't have the best terms. Mrs. Williams preferred to deal with Lac."

"A big company. With a glossy annual report."

"That's what I understood."

Mrs. Williams at the time of the trial was offering for sale her 1.5 percent net smelter interest in the Lac mine. Had the interest been 3 percent, the figure both McKinnon and Corona had offered her, the price she could have expected to get would clearly have been higher; according to one estimate, forty million dollars higher.

Thornley-Hall, aware, as he had said, of the "urgency" of the matter, asked his daughter to fly to Maryland and deliver the Corona offer by hand. This she did, and three days later Thornley-Hall got a call from Maryland telling him that the Lac bid had been formally accepted. Some time during those three days — there was a lot of conflicting testimony about precisely when, but it didn't seem to matter much — the Corona people in Vancouver learned that they had lost the Williams property to Lac. Lac's lawyers repeatedly made the point that Corona had not reacted by calling Lac and objecting, which in their view would have been the proper response.

"You were very upset at that point," Brian Foster told Dragovan. In fact, he said truthfully, just describing the incident in court had upset her. "So I assume you were even more upset in July 1981. So I suggest that it would have been natural for you to pick up the phone and call them and say, 'What are you doing?' "

"We were working with Lac," Dragovan said. "On July 23 we learned they'd stabbed us in the back."

When word reached Murray Pezim that Lac had beaten Corona to the Williams claims, he told Dragovan, Bell, and everybody else to drop the matter; from that point on, he would handle it himself.

At Hemlo, Corona had been collaborating with Lac on a test geochemical program; a crew contracted to Lac was at work on the Corona ground. Bell told the geochemical crew to get off the property. The crew leader phoned Sheehan, who called Bell and complained. Bell told him Pezim was handling any communication with Lac from that point on, and gave him Pezim's phone number. Sheehan called, and Pezim agreed to see him on August 18.

Sheehan told Pezim he had come to continue negotiating a deal for the Corona property. First, Pezim said, "Give back what you stole from me." The way to do that, Pezim suggested, was to "go down to the floor of the Vancouver Stock Exchange and announce that Lac was giving the Williams property to Corona."

Sheehan not unnaturally declined. The two men growled at each other for a while, and Sheehan left. Pezim phoned his lawyers and gave them orders to sue. Not long after this Peter Allen, Sheehan's boss, told him to have nothing more to do with Corona. Four years later, they came to trial.

LENCZNER AND McDOUGALL

"Where there is no prosecutor, there is no defendant. Don't forget that. All we have to do now is to find that cheat and get our money back."

— B. Traven, *The Treasure of the Sierra Madre*

THE TRIAL OPENED ON October 15, 1985; the arguments that closed it began on February 18, 1986. "Argument", as the word is used at this stage in a trial of this kind, means that the lawyer for one side stands up and tells the judge what to make of the evidence he has heard. Then the lawyer for the other side stands up and says that everything the first lawyer said was a crock, after which he tells the judge why from the same evidence he should draw contrary conclusions.

Here, at the end of the trial, the witnesses are gone and the lawyers have taken over the arena. Many of the conventions that govern courtroom procedure have fallen away, along with the constraints imposed by the rules of evidence. We are back with the simpler rules of trial by combat, the champion for the accuser trying to pierce the armour of the champion for the accused. Their weapons are words rather than axes and they're fighting more for money than for honour; otherwise not much has changed since the Dark Ages.

This being so, before we hear the arguments we should look more closely at the lawyers who will make them.

"Look, it's the adversary system," John Lorn McDougall said one day in the corridor. "We're here to dispute, within the rules. The idea is that in the dispute, the truth will out."

The day before, I had left the courtroom at the same time as Donald Brag, an expert witness called by Corona. Brag, who was Exploration Manager of Hudson Bay Mining and Smelting Company, had mounted the witness stand with the upright bearing and benign self-regard of the ranking officer at a military parade. When Lenczner had asked him whether a senior company that had made a site visit at its own request was then free to compete for adjoining property with the host company, Brag had answered instantly, "Absolutely not." In cross-examination McDougall had subjected Brag to a particularly stinging attack, during which Brag had been forced to qualify this and several other answers. By the time he stood down, his face was bloodless and there was a tremor in his hands when he put on his raincoat.

Riding the down escalator, he told me how the cross-examination had affected him.

"He's trying to destroy my credibility and my professional reputation. I'm trying to defend myself and tell the truth. But I'm in that box for the first time in my life — I don't know how the court works, I know nothing about the rules. He knows exactly how to get what he's after; that's his trade.

"It's unfair. Of course it's unfair."

When I told McDougall what Brag had said, he nodded and frowned. "He's not altogether wrong, you know," he said. "If you're a witness, you're going to come under attack. If you're attacked, you're going to get hurt. Maybe more, maybe less, but hurt.

"A trial diminishes everybody in it. I regret that, but I acknowledge it."

From his somewhat academic manner, McDougall had seemed likely to be more interested in the points he was scoring than in the people he was scoring them off. His remark about Brag showed that I had leaped to the wrong conclusion. Wrong, too, was the assumption I'd made, based on McDougall's mid-Atlantic diction and slightly stooped bearing, that he had been a bookish youngster who had gone to England to finish his schooling.

"Hell, no," he said one day when we were talking in his office, showing long teeth in a wide grin. "I was a jock." He had gone to school at both Carleton University in Ottawa and the University of British Columbia, studying economics but concentrating on racquet sports, football, and ski racing. His law degree was from Osgoode Hall in Toronto, and his mid-Atlantic accent derived, he explained, from several sources: "My wife was from England; early on I practised law with a couple of Englishmen — " He stopped and broke into the long-toothed grin.

"Look, it's conscious, too," he said, disarming me with sudden honesty. "We're all, people in my trade, we're all highly competitive individuals, but you can't bring naked aggression into the courtroom. Instead you develop a courtroom persona, and one of the things it does for you is mask the drive to compete. In my case, you might say the mid-Atlantic style is part of the mask.

"Barry Pepper says you can't play a case in High C all the way through." This I took to mean that a courtroom lawyer can't stay at the top of his range every time he opens his mouth, another way of making McDougall's point that he has to mask his aggression now and then. Pepper, a senior partner in Fraser and Beatty, the Toronto law firm in which McDougall works, is one of two lawyers McDougall cites most often when he's talking about how the law works. The other is the late Bora Laskin, who taught and practised law in Toronto before going to the Supreme Court of Canada, where eventually he presided as Chief Justice.

"Laskin in his best years was important to all of us," McDougall said. "Because he brought the law along." His eyes turned inward and he thought for a moment. "These men, when they're gone," he said, "they get larger than life. Doug Laidlaw, who had the Corona case before Lenczner — he was as good as they come. He's been gone a very short time, and already he's larger than he was in his lifetime."

Laidlaw was the senior litigation lawyer at McCarthy and McCarthy, the firm where Alan Lenczner works. One morning when Laidlaw was driving to Toronto from his home in a western suburb, his car broke down. He pulled over and was standing beside his stalled car when another car going in the same direction veered over, hit Laidlaw's car, and left him on the gravel shoulder, dead at fifty-six. The firm assigned Lenczner to take over Corona's lawsuit against Lac in association with Ron Slaght, who had been working on it for some time under Laidlaw.

Both men looked on the Corona case as a sort of testament to Laidlaw. At different times they had both told me that Laidlaw had been incomparably the most potent influence on their development as lawyers. Lenczner had written a posthumous tribute to his friend and mentor that appeared in *The Advocates' Society Journal*. Pages in the journal are divided into three columns; through the entire first column of his eulogy and all but an inch of the second, Lenczner spoke of Laidlaw's unrelenting attack on the squash court, his search for thermals on which he could soar higher in his glider, his drive to point his sailboat closer to the wind, his compulsion to ski harder and faster than anybody else on the hill. In a splendidly evocative phrase, Lenczner wrote that Laidlaw saw the advent of night skiing as a chance "to race down a slope at the edge where the light faded into dark shadows". With every line that celebrated his friend's passion for living at the limit of his nerve, Lenczner was indirectly but vividly underlining what McDougall had said — that a trial lawyer takes to court a gladiatorial spirit along with some learning in the law. Lenczner was an inch from the foot of his third column of prose when he thought to mention that in addition to being a fierce competitor, Laidlaw had also been a lawyer.

McDougall, the lawyer with the scholarly manner, had shown me how wrong my preconceptions could be when he said he'd been a jock. From what I'd seen of Lenczner, on the other hand, I *knew* he'd been a jock — his diction was full of locker-room elisions, his movements were quick but precise, his body was balanced to go either way even when he was standing still at the lectern. Moreover, McDougall had once warned me against playing squash with Lenczner. When I'd asked why, he'd said, "Because he's a ferocious player, that's why."

For these and other reasons I knew I was on firm ground when I asked Lenczner to tell me about his career as a jock. "It's true I like playing court games and skiing," he said. "But basically, I'm academically inclined."

He told me that his father had been a doctor who did "some pretty interesting research; the Clinic for Tropical Diseases at the Toronto General Hospital is named after him." For a time his father had been a medical officer with the British Army in India. Lenczner was born at Bombay in 1943, at the height of the Second World War, and didn't return to Canada until he was seven.

"When I did my law degree at the University of Toronto I did a master's in modern languages and literature at the same time, so I didn't have a lot of time for games. I picked them up again afterward, when I went to work with Doug Laidlaw. I got my real education through him, and one of the things he taught was to take yourself to the limit, physically as well as mentally. I don't think I would have amounted to bugger-all without Doug."

It was Laidlaw who had set the McCarthy and McCarthy people on the trail of the argument they were now making in court. "The real point is that when we took this case over, the claim didn't make any sense," Lenczner said. Corona had taken the case first to another law firm, which had written the early statements of claim alleging breach of contract. Later, Corona came to McCarthy and McCarthy. "After the first meeting with Corona's solicitor, Larry Paige, Doug just sat shaking his head. He was saying, 'Look, there's a case here. We've just got to find out what it is.' " They went to work, and eventually found the claim for breach of fiduciary responsibility.

Ron Slaght, Lenczner's associate in the Corona lawsuit, told me that he, too, "learned everything I know about the law" from Laidlaw, and this shared history had made his collaboration with Lenczner a natural fit for both of them. In his own history, Slaght embodied the unexpected continuity that it now seemed to me connected one gold camp to the next — the same appetites and achievements, the same scams and disputes that appeared at the Porcupine early in the century, coming down from camp to camp to Hemlo in the 1980s. Slaght's grandfather, the Reverend Aaron Slaght, was a Baptist minister who was appointed Ontario's first inspector of mines in 1905.

"The only thing I remember about my grandfather," Slaght once told me, "was the empty chair at his dining table. He always set a place for the Wayward Traveller." In the early gold camps, the wayward were never scarce. Partly for that reason, no doubt, Aaron's son, Ron Slaght's father, became a well-known mining lawyer. Now *his* son was helping fight the largest lawsuit that had yet sprung from the litigious ground of the goldfields. In three generations the Reverend Aaron Slaght's family had taken part in the entire story of the search for gold on the Pre-Cambrian shield.

The partnership Ron Slaght and Alan Lenczner worked for, McCarthy and McCarthy, was one of the flagship firms of the legal industry. In Canada there were perhaps a dozen of these. They included the firm McDougall worked for, Fraser and Beatty. Outsiders, who are frequently envious of the flagship law firms, often call them law factories. This would appear to be a misnomer. They are more like contemporary department stores, which is to say clusters of boutiques. While most of them have boutiques for each branch of legal work, they usually stress certain specialties above others — some stress corporate law, some finance and securities law, some tax law, and so on.

Douglas Laidlaw had almost single-handedly created a new subspecialty for McCarthy and McCarthy — a boutique within a boutique — in medical malpractice cases. The firm's traditional specialty was, and is, litigation. Under the leadership of John Robinette, one of the few Canadian lawyers ever to become a national figure without going into politics, McCarthy and McCarthy was long regarded as the leading litigation firm in the country. (I've noticed that in conversation my friend Jack Batten, a lawyer who writes about lawyers, refers to all lawyers by their unadorned names, with the exception only of John Robinette. Him he invariably speaks of as *Mister* Robinette.) In Martindale and Hubbell, the national directory of the legal trade, McCarthy and McCarthy now lists forty specialties, from Advocacy in all Courts, Banking, and Broadcasting, to Technology Transfer, Tele-communications, and Trademark Law.

Fraser and Beatty, by contrast, has only fifteen boutiques on its list, all of them traditional legal specialties: Corporation, Taxation, Probate, Real Estate, and so on. (Both firms list Mining.) Fraser and Beatty's listing in the telephone directory carries a separate entry for every lawyer in the firm, something more than a full column of names. If this seems a little, well, forward, the firm's tone is otherwise formal. In his office McDougall wears his jacket, vest, and tie, not to mention, on the day when I called on him there, a shirt with a detachable collar. Formality not only colours his sense of the law, but seems to influence his choice of tactics. (Fraser and Beatty is not, however, the flagship firm that threatens to fire lawyers found in their shirtsleeves even if they're in their own offices at the time.)

"I believe you win more cases by fighting within the rules than by going outside them," McDougall said. "My tactic throughout the trial was dictated by the nature of the case. What I tried to do, and what I believe I did, was show us to be the possessors of every Presbyterian virtue." As he said this, my inner ear played back the moment in the courtroom when McDougall, reacting to an outburst of Lenczner's, had said to the judge, "Well, M'lord, there are no rules in a knife fight."

McDougall and the other Fraser and Beatty people appeared genuinely to believe that there resided in them some elusive virtue — breeding, perhaps (Fraser and Beatty is not merely an old firm, but a patrician one) — that was absent in the McCarthy and McCarthy people. For their part, Lenczner and Slaght saw in their adversaries symptoms of overbreeding. "Have you ever seen McDougall carrying his own briefcase?" Slaght said one day. "If you ever do, tell me." I didn't; surrounded by black-gowned juniors carrying their own weight in books and papers, McDougall walked to and from the courtroom with his hands free and his head tilted slightly forward, in thought.

The place he was walking to and from, usually, was a war room that Fraser and Beatty maintained for the duration of the trial on a high floor of the Sheraton Hotel, a one-block walk through Toronto's civic square from the court house. Here, into a two-bedroom suite, were jammed rows of knock-down trestle tables, some plastic furniture, several hundredweight of paper, and an assortment of legal technicians and electronic machines.

"Money was no object in this case," McDougall said one afternoon when we surveyed the debris left in the war room by the departing lawyers. "Which is a blessing," he added, "but also a curse, since then, if there's anything that *can* be done, you've got to do it."

A good example, he said, was the computer system they'd used. "The computer was in Washington; very large, very fast, good for things like scanning telephone records. But otherwise, except as a backup for the human memory, it's not useful." He turned away for a moment, then turned back. "Though," he said, "it may have a use, at that — for the court of appeal."

During the trial, it was McDougall's habit to arrive here in the bunker by seven in the morning. He and Brian Foster would start going over the documents they'd need for that day's work in court, whether to examine a friendly witness, cross-examine a hostile one, or contest an issue of law or procedure before the judge. By eight they'd be joined by Bob Armstrong (not the Robert Armstrong who acted for Lola Williams). Armstrong's assignment was to cover off every question raised by Lac's case. Rob Heintzman, who did the same thing for Corona's case, got there at about the same time.

"Those two were the core of the effort," McDougall said. "Ian Nordheimer worked on damages, Chris Woodbury researched law, and of course we used whatever juniors we needed." At about nine-thirty they dressed for combat. For trial lawyers this means getting into white ties and black gowns, silk for McDougall and Foster, the Queen's Counsels in the group, and cotton for the others. Then they walked, like starlings on a lawn, across to the court house, where on most mornings Judge Holland sat promptly at ten. During the lunch recess they usually came back to the bunker to put the afternoon's paperwork in order. At four-thirty, when the court rose for the day, they came back to the bunker, relaxed for half an hour, and then worked "as late as we needed to". McDougall tried to go home by nine-thirty or ten, leaving the others still at work in the bunker, so that he could have a late dinner with his wife. Afterward he'd do an hour's work alone, and go to bed. On the weekends his hours were easier: eight to six on Saturdays, sometimes a few hours more on Sundays.

"Sure we got tired," McDougall said, casting his eye over the bunker with little warmth. "When we needed something to pick us up, we'd look out the window." I crossed the room and pulled apart the curtains. Across Queen Street the window looked out on the bland glass-and-metal skin of a new office building. Near the roof, a storey and a half high, the building's lead tenant had mounted its corporate signature, outlined in blue light: BELL.

Lenczner and Slaght were natural antagonists for the patrician manner and high-geared effort of McDougall and his associates. Douglas Laidlaw had taught the McCarthy and McCarthy people to distrust the high-flown. "He had the common touch," Lenczner told me, "and I hope he passed it on to me. It's not a policy, it's the way I am, or anyway try to be."

Lenczner and Slaght found the idea of the Lac war room pretentious. When Judge Holland recessed his court at four-thirty, they'd go and play a couple of games of squash to blow out the stale air. "Doug started us on that, too. You played, showered, and got to hell out — never even had a beer. What it is, we're just not fancy people." At about six they'd get back to Slaght's office. (McCarthy and McCarthy occupies several floors in the Toronto-Dominion Centre. This is a setting where the common touch might seem a little incongruous, but when I've called on them there I've found both Lenczner and Slaght with their jackets off and their shirtsleeves rolled up.) Soon after six the first half of the transcript for that day would reach them from The Supreme Court Reporters, and they'd go over that in the office. They'd leave between nine and ten, get the second half of the transcript delivered at home, and work on it there. Between seven and eight in the morning they saw other clients.

"We have thirty-five people in this litigation department, and we have to keep them working. We couldn't just stop doing anything for other people for five months — we couldn't afford to."

McDougall had drawn the contrary conclusion. "Despite what anybody might suppose," he had told me earlier in the trial, "a case like this isn't great for a lawyer. I'd rather have five solid cases than one blockbuster —

because I'm lost to my firm and my practice. Two solid years of work have gone into preparing this case, and I can't do anything else, because this is more than a full-time job. So when it's over, I have to go back and build my practice all over again."

Searching for the virtue in necessity, Lenczner and Slaght had formed the notion that keeping in touch with other people and cases might also give them a competitive edge. "We thought we'd be able to wear McDougall down faster than he could wear us down," Lenczner said. "Why? Because he was more isolated than we were." I pointed out that McDougall had been surrounded by other lawyers day and night. "Sure," Lenczner said, "but they're all *assistants*."

To turn the screw on McDougall, they tried to run the trial on a fast track, keeping "important stuff" coming up every day. At the same time, they wanted to avoid putting pressure on the judge. "We could have made a lot more technical objections than we did," Lenczner said. "We decided to roll over rather than force the judge to make hard decisions, so that when he comes to make his final decision, he won't be fettered."

In matters of interpretation, perspective is everything. McDougall, smoking mad and making no well-bred effort to hide it, had said to me in the corridor after one ruling by Judge Holland late in the trial, "There hasn't been a major ruling in this trial, not *one*, in which the judge ruled against the plaintiff."

Slaght's view of this issue was less emotional than either of the others'.

"This trial has been a good example of the shifting approach of the courts to the law of evidence," he said. "The judge is saying, 'Look, there might be a technical question of admissibility, but I'm going to hear it anyway. Then I'll decide what weight to give it.' Judge Holland's been doing this in his court for years. Now it's becoming true of other courts as well."

Judge Holland had in fact said as much more than once during the course of the trial, but this had done little to soothe McDougall's feeling that he was on the short end of this particular stick. Lenczner felt he was on the short end, too, but in his case the feeling came from what had been going on outside the courtroom.

"We had heard they had at least one private detective who went around asking questions," Lenczner said, "trying to get stuff that could be used against our witnesses in cross-examination." Slaght broke in. "I don't know that they found out anything that helped them," he said, "but think of the effect on a witness. They did a complete investigation in Timmins of David Bell. In a place like Timmins, where there are already a lot of petty jealousies against guys who got lucky, like Bell or McKinnon — well, Bell's the kind of guy who gets upset pretty easily."

To Lenczner's mind, Bell wasn't the only one somebody had been trying to upset. "For a while, just before I was due to cross-examine Dennis Sheehan, I'd go to sleep and at maybe two in the morning the phone would ring. I'd pick it up, there was nothing on the line but breathing. Hang up, fifteen or twenty minutes later the phone would ring again. Pick it up, same thing. This happened three, four, I don't know, five times a night. I was going to unplug the phone, but I'm on the night beat for the Canadian Press, so I left it plugged in. Next night, same thing. After a few days, whoever it was just quit and I got a night's sleep."

For these reasons and a good many more, by the end of the trial issues of both style and substance lay between Corona's legal forces and Lac's. In the mannered language of the courtroom, contending lawyers refer to their adversaries as their friends, or even, in the case of Queen's Counsel, as their learned friends. "My learned friend," one will say of the other, "makes this insupportable claim based on that failure to understand the evidence or the law or both." Although McDougall and Lenczner and their supporters were still referring to the lawyers on the other side of the courtroom as their friends, neither side was feeling particularly friendly to the other as they began their closing arguments.

The rules of trial by combat give the accused the right to strike the last blow. Lenczner, accordingly, made the case for Corona first. He began by going back to the first principles of Corona's claim. He reminded the court there were three of these.

First, there was breach of a fiduciary relationship.

Second, there was misuse of confidential information.

Third, there was breach of agreement.

In law, Lenczner said, each of these principles was separate from the others. The separation of fiduciary responsibility from breach of confidence was "of special significance" — there can be breach of confidence without a fiduciary relationship between the parties, and there can be a fiduciary relationship without the communication of confidential information. But between Corona and Lac both were present. "The confluence of the two principles intertwining," he said, lapsing into the high-flown language Douglas Laidlaw had taught him to avoid, "strengthens immeasurably Corona's case."

Lenczner then turned to the third principle, breach of agreement. Judge Holland, who had been sitting with his hand over his mouth and a pensive, or perhaps bored, look on his face, dropped his hand and asked sharply, "What agreement?"

"At the end of the May sixth meeting, my lord, Lac and Corona both understood the value of the Williams property — remember that both Bell and Sheehan say they spoke of the importance of Williams — —"

"Well," the judge broke in, brushing aside what Lenczner was saying, "where's the agreement? If any?"

"Later, on May eighth, they agreed that if they concluded a deal, Corona would have sole right to the Williams claims. The agreement was that Lac would stake to the east, and not interfere with Corona's right to acquire the Williams property." Right up to the end of June the parties were discussing a joint venture, Lenczner said, and they had agreed that Corona would acquire the Williams claims to put into the joint venture.

"Now, if you find this," he told Judge Holland, "Lac must disgorge what it acquired by the breach." Lac, he said, had tried to make the case that if there had been a joint venture in negotiation, then both sides had been free to pick up the Williams claims on behalf of the joint venture. But all that, Lenczner said, was speculation, and "Lac cannot now ask your lordship to speculate about what the terms of a joint venture might have been. Moreover, the failure of the joint venture was Lac's fault."

Suppose, Lenczner went on, Sheehan had intended to get the Williams claims for the joint venture. "He would have said so to Corona. But that's not what he did." Lenczner continued to attack "inconsistencies" in the idea that both parties had been free to acquire the Williams claims for the joint venture until he had to pause for breath. During the pause he looked at Judge Holland and said, "Now, I hope that was helpful."

"Certainly," the judge said, his tone civil as always. "But I'm still wondering where the agreement lies."

Lenczner winced. "The agreement arose from the meeting of May eighth," he said. That was the day Sheehan took Bell to lunch at the Engineers' Club in Toronto. Sheehan told Bell he had given orders that morning to begin staking the first of more than six hundred claims to the east of the Corona property. Later Sheehan had written of this meeting, "Informed of David Bell re Lac's staking and he agreed." Translated from the original Sheehanese, these words carried a heavy freight of meaning according to Lenczner. They "indicated that Sheehan felt obligated to tell Bell about Lac's staking." They "corroborated the understanding that Lac could not acquire ground without reference to Corona." They "supported Bell's statement that Corona was to acquire the patented ground." And they "recognized that, at the very least, there was a reposing of trust by Corona in Lac, encouraged by Lac bringing a fiduciary relationship into existence."

All this seemed like a lot to read into a few words of Sheehanese, but that was Lenczner's argument. My note to myself at this point reads, "Okay, but where's the agreement?" This time the judge himself let the question go, and Lenczner pressed on, now using Sheehan's note to buttress his contention that the judge should pay particular attention to what the parties did and wrote "at the time". It followed that he should give less weight to what the Lac witnesses testified now, five years later, when "they were trying to cast a different light on what they actually said and did".

Lenczner then raised a fresh line of argument. "Among the expert witnesses," he claimed, "there is no clash of conflicting evidence."

Again the judge roused himself and spoke sharply. "I would have thought there was quite a clash," he said. "Particularly on the question of site visits."

Lenczner answered with a quotation from Peter Allen, the president of Lac. In examination for discovery Allen had spoken the most telling sentence among the millions of words of testimony that had been heard since the case began. "If one geologist goes to another and says, 'Let's consider seriously the possibility of making a deal' — for a short period of time they would have a duty not to hurt each other as the result of any information that was exchanged."

With this sentence, Lenczner said, all the experts agreed, both Corona's and Lac's. But the site visit wasn't an isolated event: there were also the subsequent exchanges of letters and meetings all the way up to June 13.

"So you're saying it goes farther than the site visit," Judge Holland said. "I should not seek to make a narrow definition of industry practice arising out of a site visit?"

Lenczner wanted to have it both ways. "If no obligation arose from a site visit," he argued, "the junior company would always be at the mercy of the senior, from whom he desperately needs help to develop his property. What's unfair about saying the senior should be obliged not to hurt him with his own information?"

Not long after this exchange there was an unscheduled interruption. "Mr. Lenczner," the judge said, "I've had some bad luck. I've just broken my glasses for the second time in two days." He held up both hands, the lenses with one earpiece still attached in the right hand, the other earpiece in the left. All rose, and the judge withdrew to his chambers. Lenczner, like a fighter trying to keep his rhythm between rounds by bouncing in his corner, stood at his lectern, flipping pages. Most of the spectators went into the corridor to stretch their legs. I finished making my note on the exchange about site visits, and looked around. On the spectator benches only one other man was still sitting, and he was writing in a spiral-bound stenographer's notebook like mine. The man was Dennis Sheehan. There had been freezing rain that morning, and Sheehan's hat band had left an indentation around the back of his heavy grey hair; otherwise, he was turned out with the same attention to sober detail that had distinguished his appearance on the witness stand. Sheehan was the only witness who had come back to hear the arguments, and it crossed my mind that he might be there on display, a sort of mute exhibit meant to show the judge that he was a man of probity keen to see justice take its course. He was still making notes when Judge Holland came back wearing a fresh pair of glasses firmly anchored on both sides to his ears, and Lenczner resumed his argument.

Everybody knows, he said, that partners have a duty to act in good faith towards each other; that is fiduciary obligation. Less well known but equally binding is the duty of intending partners. He cited decisions in which various courts had ruled that intending partners are bound by the same obligation to good faith as partners. "When the defence claims that the fiduciary relationship does not arise until the partnership is formed," he said, laying heavy emphasis on the final clause, "*the defence is clearly wrong.*"

The logic of Lenczner's argument led next to breach of confidence, but instead he now made a curious, off-balance leap all the way to the issue of remedies — assuming that Lac had done something wrong, what could the court do to set it right? He spoke first of the 1984 case in which a trustee sold, for conversion to a golf course, land owned by a west-coast Indian band. The trustee took a lot less money than the band was asking for, the Indians sued, and the judge ruled that the price was indeed far too low. But what were the damages? The difference between the price the band asked and the price the band got? The judge said no; the trustee's duty was to get the price that would be realized by the best economic use of the land. Which wasn't a golf course at all; had the land been divided into building lots and sold on ninety-nine-year leases, the band would have realized ten million dollars more than they got. The judge accordingly awarded the band ten million dollars, and the Supreme Court later upheld the award.

"The judge weighed the cost of the band's lost opportunity," Lenczner said. "The obligation of a defaulting trustee is not to pay a penalty, but to make restitution. This obligation has been imposed since ancient times."

Consequently, Lenczner said, "Your Lordship should order Lac to return the property it acquired by its breach of fiduciary responsibility."

How much was the Lac mine worth? During the last recess I had asked Ian Hamilton, Lac's corporate solicitor. He said he didn't know, but according to his notes the value assigned by the experts who'd testified on damages ran from a low of four hundred million dollars on Lac's side, to a high of just under two billion dollars on Corona's.

"According to Lac they have spent more than two hundred million dollars on a mine site and a mill," Judge Holland said. "What happens to that?"

"The common law says that if you make improvements to land you hold wrongfully, you're still in breach. So you're out," Lenczner replied.

"But that's common law, not equity." Equity, in this context, means the method by which an accountant tries to assign a fair value to the different parts of a complex property. "Equity says the investment can be accounted for. But if equity is to prevail, then the improvement must have been made in good faith. There's no question of good faith here. Corona filed its claim against Lac's title in 1981, and Lac knowingly went ahead and developed the mine and the mill despite this."

"How about the gold Lac has produced?" Judge Holland asked.

Lenczner hesitated not at all. "We take it," he said.

"What about Mrs. Williams?"

"She has her contractual rights," Lenczner said. "They stay." He did not trouble to say that her rights, under her contract with Lac, were worth little more than half what they would have been had she sold the Williams claims to Corona in the first place. He did raise the question of McKinnon and his partners. But, he said, "I don't think Your Lordship has to deal with that. We'll have to settle with them. There is no question about their entitlement; that's absolutely established." Their royalty, he said, "will be between half of one percent and one percent."

Here, as he approached the end of his argument, Lenczner raised the issue of confidentiality. "There is no question but that the trigger for Lac's interest in Corona was the *George Cross Newsletter* for March twentieth," he said. This was the edition of the letter Pegg had marked and sent to Sheehan. "But what did Lac do then? Nothing!" Lenczner slapped his palm on the lectern, making his papers jump. "They did no file research. They got out no maps. They looked at no assessment reports."

What they did was watch what Corona was doing — until Sheehan made his site visit. That, Lenczner said, was the springboard. "I've got agreement from Lac's own experts that at the site Lac got information they could have got no other way."

The information was confidential, he went on, the Lac people got a lot of it, and "Sheehan and Allen both said Lac made use of the confidential information acquired from Corona in acquiring the Williams property. And that to the detriment of Corona." He paused for the kind of long breath that often goes before a rhetorical flourish. "And I say further the springboard doctrine applies — because it was the site visit that catapulted Lac into action."

Before he closed, Lenczner suggested that a written copy of his argument, which set out in greater detail his interpretation of both the facts and the law, be marked as an exhibit. This, he said, was simply in case "any other court" should wish to examine whether certain points had been raised or not raised. McDougall rose and said he couldn't see the difference between marking the document as an exhibit and filing it, which would happen anyway. The judge, his tone drier than ever, agreed.

Finally, Lenczner took his argument back to its starting place. Breach of a fiduciary relationship and breach of confidence are separate breaches of the law. But in this case, he said, the two came together. "Your Lordship can find for the plaintiff on either ground — and from the cases I've cited, it is clear that the remedy is the same in both."

Lac, he said, must disgorge.

I came away from the courtroom that afternoon carrying a copy of Lenczner's written argument and thinking about the way he had delivered his spoken one. It seemed to me that on his most important day he had given his weakest performance. My note to myself said, "He's jumping all over the place, hitting and missing like a man hunting ants with a shotgun." That night I sat up reading his written argument. This was clearer and stronger, though it still wasn't the kind of argument that by its own force can blow an adversary out of the water.

There was one quotation, though, from a Supreme Court of Canada decision, that stayed in my mind when I put the manuscript down: ". . . the obligation to make restitution, which courts of equity have from very early times imposed on defaulting trustees and other fiduciaries, is of a more absolute nature than the common-law obligation to pay damages for breach of contract."

"May it please the court," John Lorn McDougall said the next morning, opening the argument for Lac, "this is basically a simple case. My friends have taken the facts, which are innocent, and made them culpable by taking them backwards."

He went on to say that Corona had a lot to win: "My friends," he said, "have a shot at an enormous prize here." He implied that this was somehow unfair, since the Corona people had repeatedly done the same thing at Hemlo that they complained Lac had done to them. Presumably he was talking about claims in the Hemlo area that Pezim and Dragovan had acquired and later passed on to companies other than Corona.

McDougall then spoke of the "overwhelming" array of facts that went to prove there had been no business relationship between Lac and Corona. Lac used no confidential information of Corona's, he said, "because there was none".

Next he turned to the issue that lay beneath the overburden of fact and circumstances much as the gold-bearing stratum at Hemlo underlay the country rock. Who was lying? "Where Bell and Sheehan conflict," McDougall told Judge Holland, "Sheehan's evidence must be preferred."

Bell's testimony, he said, was clearly tailored to fit Corona's new pleading, a reminder to Judge Holland that Corona had first claimed breach of contract and then changed the claim several times. Bell more than once took "absurd" positions on the witness stand, McDougall said, and changed his story when it suited him.

Not so Sheehan. Despite being subjected to "brutal cross-examination", Sheehan was "uncontradictory and forthright". And speaking of cross-examination, McDougall had not interrupted Lenczner at important points, whereas Lenczner's "constant interruptions" when McDougall was cross-examining were "signs of weakness in the Corona case".

McDougall quickly ran down the other leading witnesses on the Corona side. Nell Dragovan, he said, displayed a conspicuous "lack of forthrightness" about Hole 76. Donald McKinnon was "all over the map, contradicting other witnesses on both sides". Murray Pezim showed an "amazing lack of recall", while John Dadds showed a "remarkable lack of memory".

Then McDougall turned to the law. After the millions of words that had been said and written, the entire case, he argued, came down to a single issue: was there any impediment to Lac acquiring the Williams claims?

Only three impediments were possible, he said.

One: Lac got confidential information that gave it a head start in acquiring the Williams claims.

Two: Lac agreed to be restricted.

Three: Lac owed a fiduciary duty to Corona.

As a matter of law, he said, to prove breach of confidence Corona had to carry the "burden" of proving four distinct elements. First, that the information was indeed confidential when it was passed on. Second, that Lac got the information "in circumstances that imparted a duty of confidence". Third, that Lac actually used the information "in a material and unauthorized way" in going after the Williams claims. And fourth, that by acquiring the Williams claims, Lac harmed Corona.

By all four of these tests, McDougall said, Corona failed. The proof that Corona gave Lac no confidential information was simple — the judge had only to look at the way Corona treated what it knew, with "complete disregard" for secrecy.

"As Lord Green said in the Saltman case, 'Something that is public knowledge cannot be confidential.' But Corona exposed everything they had. Their *purpose* was to attract attention." McDougall quoted from the various issues of the *George Cross Newsletter* that had published reports of Corona's drill results. While Corona may have shown Lac some unpublished drill results, they were useful, if at all, only in judging the Corona ground — they were site-specific, that is, and had no value for measuring any other property. Lac's experts all said, "over and over again", that the unpublished information was immaterial, insignificant, or irrelevant to an evaluation of anything but the Corona property itself.

"Perhaps the best illustration of this was given by Dr. Robertson" — one of Lac's experts — "when he was being cross-examined at length on all the holes that hadn't been published by June thirtieth, and all the locations that hadn't been published.

" 'But what is the importance of that, Mr. Lenczner?' he said. 'I don't see any point to it — it's not important.' "

McDougall dealt next with Sheehan's visit to the Corona site. Since Bell admitted he'd said nothing about confidentiality, the "obvious inference" was that he didn't think his information was confidential. Corona claimed there was an "industry practice" that barred a visitor from using information he got from his host to acquire ground in the area without the host's permission. Lac's expert witnesses had testified that there was no such practice in the industry. In any case, it was hardly likely that Bell was relying on an accepted practice, since this was the first time he'd been involved in a visit of this kind — so how would he know what practice the industry followed? Sheehan, on the other hand, had testified that he had made it clear to Bell that he didn't want to hear any confidential information. Sheehan ought to be believed, McDougall said, partly because Dr. Robertson had testified that it is common for a visitor to an exploration site to ask not to be shown confidential information.

After the site visit, McDougall then said, Corona went on putting out "a continuous stream of technical data" in press releases, progress reports, meetings with brokers and investors. "The only thing Corona ever held back," he said, "was unfavourable information."

Then, when Corona learned that Mrs. Williams was on the verge of accepting an offer from Lac, why didn't the Corona people do "what any person who felt he had been wronged would do"? Simply pick up the phone, that is, and demand that Lac withdraw the offer. ("Why didn't they" questions were an important part of McDougall's rhetorical technique. With this one, though, it seemed to me he'd needlessly invited the judge to ask himself another: if the Lac people were dealing in good faith with Corona, why didn't they "simply pick up the phone" weeks earlier, and tell Corona that Lac was going to bid for the Williams claims?)

McDougall turned next to Pezim's dealings in the Hemlo area for companies other than Corona. While Pezim was a director of Corona and the company's president, McDougall reminded the court, he had instructed Bell to choose favourable ground in the area and arrange a staking program. Bell laid out two hundred claims that Pezim and his partners later sold to nineteen separate companies. Corona was not among them, though most were controlled by Pezim. Not only did Bell use information derived from Corona's drill results, McDougall said; Bell even "alleged that some of the information which he used in selecting the area to be staked was confidential, generated from his work on the Corona property." From all this activity Corona benefited not at all, though Pezim and Dragovan and Bell and others did: "So it cannot lie in their mouths *now*," McDougall said, "to claim that their information was confidential when given to Lac." Whatever weight the judge might be inclined to give this argument would be offset to some degree by timing — all the dealing McDougall was talking about took place months and more often years after Lac struck its deal for the Williams claims.

Not only had Corona failed to hold its information in confidence, McDougall now said, it was perfectly clear from an examination of the record that Corona had failed to generate any confidential information. "All Corona did up to the meeting of May sixth was repeat work that had been done before by others — Lake Superior Mining, Teck, and Ardel, and the personal efforts of people like Thompson, Page, Greer, Muir, and Skimming." (Thompson, Greer, and Muir were geologists who, like Page and Skimming, had done work in the area.) Moreover, the work Corona had done was all on its own property; Corona had done nothing on the Williams property, and therefore had no new information to communicate, in confidence or otherwise. McDougall then launched a detailed examination of the Corona drilling program between January 1981 and the meeting of May 6, 1981. From this he concluded that Bell had learned nothing new. "Confirmation of something not in doubt," he said, "is of no practical use."

On May 6, the only thing Bell showed Sheehan that he couldn't have seen in the archives came down to "two hundred to four hundred feet of quartz sericite schist core, taken from unknown locations at unknown depths". Lac's experts, doctors Hutchinson, Robertson, and Anhaeusser, had all testified that such a core examination would be useless for evaluating the Williams property. "In fact, the core in conjunction with the logs and sections demonstrated that, at the time, there was no ore body on Corona. One has to wonder how this information could possibly have indicated that there was likely to be an ore body on Williams."

Of the information that passed between Bell and Sheehan on May 6, that left only Bell's geological theory — the theory that Lenczner, McDougall said scathingly, had called the expression of Bell's "genius". By this stage in the trial, he went on, it should be clear that to a geologist trying to find gold the important questions are: Where is it? And how is it distributed? "By May 6, 1981, the nature of the distribution of gold on the Corona property and throughout the area was as far from a 'secret' as it is possible to get. How the gold got there doesn't really matter."

As for the meetings of May 8 and June 30, "Corona withheld data from drill holes, logs, sections, geophysical maps — none of which was ever given to Lac. What was given, assuming your lordship can ever find it in all this thicket of words and paper, was all on the public record."

To prove breach of confidence, McDougall had said at the outset of his argument, Corona had the "burden" of proving four distinct elements. He now took up the second element: "did the circumstances impart an obligation of confidence?" I had been wondering what he meant by "circumstances". It soon became clear that in Lac's case, "circumstances" stood for what in Corona's case had been called "a fiduciary relationship". By law, McDougall said, "there has to be something more than mere negotiations. One party or the other must actually have embarked on the joint venture." Against this "requirement of the law" he contrasted the "evanescent, ethereal relationship in *this* case".

"Would a reasonable man, standing in the shoes of Lac, have regarded himself as being in a fiduciary relationship with Corona? My submission is, certainly not."

When Lac invited itself on to Corona's property, he said, Corona had three choices: to say no; to say yes, but to require a written confidentiality agreement along with restrictions on Lac's freedom of action; or to agree to a property visit without restrictions. Since Corona hadn't done the first or the second, McDougall implied, it must have done the third. The visit, when it came, was merely "a normal and essential part" of the search for minerals. "It is the evidence of Sheehan, Allen, and Pegg," as well as three of Lac's expert witnesses, "Robertson, Derry, and Gill, that there was no obligation created as a result of the site visit. To find otherwise would require the court to accept that site visits impose an obligation *per se*, something that makes no common sense." What it came down to, he said, was that Corona was trying to impose "silly, unworkable and unwarranted inter- ference" not just on Lac, but on anybody who goes to look at an exploration site.

Sheehan's May 19 letter to Bell was the most solid evidence Lenczner had advanced for the argument that Lac and Corona were intending to become partners. McDougall brushed it off. Sheehan simply gave Bell an outline of future possibilities, he said. Bell's letter in reply was also simple; he said he liked the idea of an overall exploration program in the area. Nothing in either letter amounted to negotiation, much less to an intended agreement.

When Bell and Dragovan came to their meeting with Lac on June 30, neither said anything about the information they brought being "private, privileged, or confidential". Nor did either say anything about the terms of a joint-venture agreement. Supposing for a moment that they had any intention of becoming partners, how could they ignore the terms? The question, McDougall said, "baffles the mind. It's just contrary to reason."

Judge Holland was now stealing sidelong glances at the clock, as he often did when the midday recess was drawing on. Following the direction of his eyes McDougall saw that it was six minutes to one. He reshuffled his notes and made one more short point. Less than two weeks before the June 30 meeting, more than seven hundred thousand dollars had been pumped into Corona's treasury by shareholders exercising warrants to buy more stock. When Dragovan and Bell walked in to see Sheehan, McDougall said, "they didn't yet need a partner. They were flush."

Leaving for lunch, Sheehan and McDougall rode the same tread of the escalator. "You amazed me in there," Sheehan said. "You know stuff about what went on in 1981 that I didn't know myself."

McDougall gave Sheehan his long-toothed grin. "What do you think you've been paying us for all these years?" he said.

The third element Corona carried the burden of proving was that in acquiring the Williams property Lac had taken confidential information from Corona and used it without Corona's authority. McDougall acknowledged that Sheehan got information from Corona on May 6, that this information became part of his knowledge of the Hemlo area, and that he relied on this knowledge when he made his offer for the Williams claims. But this, McDougall said, was merely an admission of the obvious. If the admission was to help Corona's case, Corona would have to prove what the information was, and that it had been used in an unauthorized way — such as giving Lac a springboard from which to make the Williams offer. But the trial had shown, McDougall argued, that the information Corona had given Lac was "amorphous" stuff — the line of strike, for instance, which ran across the Corona property onto the Williams ground, and Bell's geological theory, the one that made him "the genius of Hemlo".

Beyond this, the only information Corona had to give was a look at the core from its drill holes. But the gold in this core cannot be seen; there's no way to tell it's there until the assay report comes back. Looking at Corona's core, therefore, told Sheehan nothing of value. From the outcrops down the road, on the other hand, "it was a simple matter for a man of Sheehan's training and experience" to recognize rocks similar to the ones in which he had found gold at Bousquet. It was this similarity, McDougall claimed, that "motivated Sheehan to do what he did" in the Hemlo area.

Even if Sheehan had wanted a better springboard, Bell didn't have one to give him. But the truth, in McDougall's view, was that in Sheehan's memory of Bousquet he had all the springboard he needed.

The fourth and final element Corona was obliged to prove, McDougall said, was that Lac's action had damaged Corona. To prove this, Corona would have to prove that if Lac had not acquired the Williams claims, Corona would have. But the evidence was that until Lac bid for the property, Corona was leaving the question of who got the Williams ground to McKinnon. Corona's "delay, inaction and acquiescence" proved that Corona wasn't seriously pursuing the Williams ground itself. McKinnon apparently wasn't serious either, since he didn't get around to discussing terms with the owner until June 8, four months after Bell first mentioned Corona's interest. And even if McKinnon had succeeded in acquiring the property, Corona, through its "tenuous relationship with McKinnon", had only a "vague" right of first refusal. In fact, McKinnon was talking to "anybody who might buy, and nobody could be certain what he might do with the land if, as, and when he might acquire it".

Pezim was one of the parties who might have bought the property from McKinnon. But, McDougall said, "the evidence is overwhelming that Pezim had every intention of building a group of promotable companies, each with its own piece of land. It is impossible to find now that the Williams claims would have gone into Corona, especially since Corona never directly acquired a single additional claim in the area."

That ended McDougall's argument on breach of confidence and breach of fiduciary responsibility, but there was a third breach in Corona's claim — breach of agreement. Yet Bell himself testified that Lac had never said it wouldn't acquire Williams; and that Lac never agreed that Corona should acquire Williams. Bell, Sheehan, and Pegg all testified that on May 6 no agreement was made or even discussed. "Therefore," McDougall said, "there cannot have been an agreement."

Moreover, when Corona learned that Lac had made its offer to Mrs. Williams, Corona made a counter-offer almost immediately.

"This fact alone," McDougall argued, "suggests in the strongest terms that Corona did not consider there to be an agreement preventing Lac from acquiring the Williams property." At the same time, none of Corona's principals complained to anybody at Lac. This showed, McDougall said, "again in the strongest terms", that there was no agreement standing in Lac's way.

McDougall slapped shut the loose-leaf binder that held the 154 single-spaced pages of his written argument. He looked across the courtroom at the tables where Corona's lawyers sat, and behind him at his own colleagues. Then he looked back at Judge Holland and said, "My submission is that the action should be dismissed." He paused. Dismissal is an ignominious end to a lawsuit, even more so when the judge tells the party that took the case to court to pay the legal costs of the party that had to defend it.

"With costs," McDougall said, and sat down.

J UDGE HOLLAND'S LAST WORDS from the bench in the trial between Corona and Lac were compliments to the lawyers who had appeared before him. "I hope to have a judgement for you by the end of next month," he ended. Then he rose, made his customary short bow, and led his entourage of clerk, recorder, and bailiff out of the room. The lawyers returned his bow, as was their custom. When they straightened and looked across at each other, I was mildly surprised to see that on both sides of the room they were all smiling. They then formed two lines and filed past each other, trading jokes and laughing. Each man on one side shook hands with each man on the other. With a slight but distinct jolt of pleasure I realized where I'd seen this ritual before. After the last game of the Stanley Cup series the players skate past one another holding out the hand of friendship to men whose body parts they were trying to disassemble a few minutes earlier. The same thing was happening in the courtroom, without skates.

On the spectator benches there were two other people who had been in court throughout the trial. Ted Moss, a young lawyer, had been assigned by his firm to write a daily report for "an interested party". Shoshana Weiman, an even younger lawyer who hadn't yet found a permanent job, had a free-lance assignment to do the same thing for another, equally interested party. They and I had long ago agreed to celebrate the end of the trial with a lunch dedicated to instant nostalgia. We left the courtroom in a group with two other frequent spectators, Amy Gassman, an investment analyst from New York who had flown to Toronto at several stages of the trial, and Mike Macbeth, who had earlier written a long piece about the Hemlo bonanza for her magazine, *Canadian Business*, and was now working on an article about the trial. We invited them to join us.

During the lunch we formed a five-party pool on the outcome of the trial, the winner to get a bottle of champagne from each of the losers. I unfolded the slips and Ted listed the predictions. My slip said Corona to win, with fifty million dollars in damages. Amy, Mike, and Ted all said Corona to win, with damages running from one hundred million dollars to one billion. Shoshana said Corona to win, but she didn't estimate the damages in dollars. The judge, her slip said, would tell Lac to give Corona the gold mine. A few days later I told John Lorn McDougall about the pool, and he laughed. "They're a bunch of kids," he said, sliding his half-glasses down his nose the better to see me. "But you? You should know better."

The end of March, when Judge Holland had said he hoped to bring down his judgement, was five or six weeks away. I wanted to bet more than a bottle of champagne on the outcome of the trial, and this left me more than enough time to work out the best way to make the bet. What I had in mind was a straddle, a way to combine puts and calls so that you win if the decision goes one way, and do no worse than break even if it goes the other. Assuming, of course, that you do it right.

There were people around who knew a lot more than I ever would about how to do these things right. I called one of them, Peter Kingsmill, a Toronto broker who is very quick with boats, skis, and option plays. We went to lunch and I told him what I had in mind — a straddle with Corona on top. Kingsmill's moustache started to twitch, an infallible sign that he wants to argue.

"Does that mean you think Corona's going to win?" he asked.

"Not exactly," I said. "I think Corona *should* win."

The twitch rate of Kingsmill's moustache doubled. "And you want to bet on *that?*"

"Not exactly," I said. "I think Corona would win if the question was, what's fair? But in a law court that's not the question; the question there is, what's legal? At the end I think Lac may have done a better job of sustaining their legal argument. So I make it an even-money bet."

Kingsmill's eyebrows started to twitch in time with his moustache; he has more ways of signalling aggression than Sylvester Stallone. "So don't bet," he said.

I started again, this time with the stock market instead of the law. Corona was too small and young a company to support a market in options, which meant that the straddle would have to be made in options on Lac.

A "call" is an option to buy in the future at a price set in the present. That morning the price of a three-month call to buy one share of Lac at forty dollars was just over four dollars. Should Lac win the lawsuit, the only thing Lac shareholders would get that they didn't already have would be peace of mind, which might add as much as eight dollars to the price of a share. So the market, like me, was making Lac an even-money bet; if Lac won, the buyer of a four-dollar call would get something like eight dollars back.

A "put" is an option to sell in the future at a price set in the present. The price that morning of a three-month Lac put at forty dollars was thirty cents. If the judge were to award Corona damages of fifty million dollars, the price of Lac's stock would probably be driven down by something like four dollars. The higher the damages, the farther down the market would drive Lac's stock. If Corona won, that is, the buyer of a thirty-cent Lac put would get at least four dollars back. That made Corona twelve-to-one or better in the market, whereas in my book Corona was an even-money bet.

"So the straddle," I said to Kingsmill, "is, say, ten thousand dollars' worth of puts, and enough calls to cover if Lac wins. If it was a horse race, the puts would be one of the great overlays of all time."

"I don't bet on horses," Kingsmill said, twitching and squinting at the same time. "You do. How do you make out?"

"We're not here to talk about horses," I said testily. "Figure out how many calls I need to make the straddle, and get back to me." His irrelevant question about horses had thrown me so far off stride that I paid for lunch.

While Judge Holland worked on his notes of the trial, I worked on mine. One of the jobs I'd been putting off had been in the back of my mind since the morning at the opening of the trial, when the guard had told me it was too bad I wasn't there as a witness, since all the witnesses got rich. Now I started to dig out of my notes a line-score that would tell at a glance not only which witnesses got rich, but how rich they got.

Christopher Pegg, whose note to Sheehan saying they should keep an eye on Corona's drill results was the starting point for Lac's involvement at Hemlo, was voted a royalty by Lac's board. He later sold it for stock. When Lenczner said Pegg's reward amounted to something over two million dollars, Pegg shook his head and said that it had been closer to one million. Taking his own evaluation, I calculated that still made him the highest-priced writer, word for word, in modern letters; his note to Sheehan was three sentences long.

Sheehan also got a royalty and sold it for stock. Lenczner estimated that Sheehan's reward was worth something like five million dollars. Sheehan denied this vigorously — more like two or three million, he said.

Peter Allen was rich already. The Hemlo gold discovery added perhaps twenty dollars a share to the value of Lac's stock, of which he owned a few hundred thousand shares, making him many millions of dollars richer. His children also got a little richer. During June 1981, at a time when, Allen had testified, he had little or no interest in Corona, he none the less bought seventy thousand dollars' worth of Corona stock for his children's trust accounts. Corona was then selling in the two-to-three-dollar range. Allen sold the shares in August, when the price was in the area of ten dollars, adding perhaps a quarter of a million dollars to his children's trusts before the weather turned cool.

Bell had been given stock options by Corona that would have earned him well over a million dollars if he had sold at the right time, which he ruefully told the court he had not.

Nell Dragovan had done better, both in the market and in converting her Corona options to cash. When McDougall estimated her gain at five million dollars, she said with some indignation that she hadn't added it up, but thought the total would be less.

Hughes and Lang each had gains in the millions. In much of that wealth, though, their interest was purely nostalgic, since it passed from their hands to the income-tax collector's at the speed of thought.

Royalties on the Hemlo gold should eventually flow to McKinnon at the rate of millions of dollars every year. But at the time the trial began little if any of this treasure had reached him or his partners John Larche, Claude Bonhomme, and Rocco Schiralli. Starting with Steven Snelgrove's appropriation of the Corona shares he owed them, and passing on through several legal snarls, including one over the size of their royalty from the Noranda mine at Hemlo, McKinnon and his partners had seen their financial expectations repeatedly postponed. They were still in a state of great promise unfulfilled.

The gold at Hemlo made Murray Pezim rich more than once, but that was Pezim's way; at the time of the Hemlo gold rush he had been getting rich and going bust in a fairly regular rhythm for almost forty years. In the fall of 1983 he gave me a lift in his private jet, which was bigger than a Lear and smaller than a 747, from New Orleans to Phoenix, where he was moving from a half-million-dollar house to a 1.2-million-dollar house. He was buying companies the way I bought bananas, in clusters that had some brown spots among the gold, and endowing charities not only with his money but with his name — that year in Vancouver people bought Pezapples to support the United Appeal. A year later I ran into him at the racetrack in Vancouver. He said scarcely a word, which for him was wildly uncharacteristic behaviour. When I asked mutual friends what was going on, they said that Pezim's brokers had called his margin accounts, sold out his Corona holdings to satisfy the resulting debt, and replaced him at the head of the company with the nominee of the new owners of his stock. "This was the week," one of his friends said, "when they gutted Murray Pezim."

During the months that followed I heard that he had gone into a deep and stubborn depression, one from which he was still recovering when the trial opened in the fall of 1985. When his turn to testify approached, he was kept on call for a couple of days outside the courtroom. The first time I saw him there he was sitting alone on a plastic bench in the corridor, the skin under his eyes the colour of tobacco juice and his flesh appearing to droop from his frame. I said something banal about waiting being the hard part, he agreed, and I went to make some calls. But he stayed in my mind. This was a man who whatever his failings had always shown an appetite for a fight. Selling him short in the market was a blood sport — he would stand and buy his own stock with all the money he had, and then start on money he didn't have. Usually he won, though the truism that you can't win them all got him in the end. This was how they came to gut him, but it was also why he was a larger-spirited man than the ones who brought him down. When I passed him on my way back into the courtroom, his head was still pointing at his knees.

The next day he was back on the plastic bench when everybody filed into the courtroom for the morning session, but when I looked for him during the eleven-thirty recess the bench was empty. Again I had calls to make. I was still wondering what had happened to Pezim when I reached the pay phones and found myself in line behind several other people, all of them restless. There are only two phones in the bank outside Courtroom 10, and Pezim was on both of them, his arms stretched to hold both instruments at the limits of their cords, his head bobbing between them like a flyweight slipping punches, and his rheumy old eyes glaring defiance at the line of muttering people who wanted him to get off at least one of the phones. Before I left I heard him tell a broker in New York to buy ninety thousand shares of something or other at the market, and I felt better about him than I had for the last two days, or indeed for the last year. He was rich again, rich enough, at least, to be doing the only thing he cared about doing.

Peter Kingsmill called me on March 6, a Thursday. Judge Holland had now been working on his decision for almost two weeks. Lac's stock had been moving up all week, Kingsmill said — forty-four dollars a share now, and still no end to the buying in sight. The Lac call options were up to four-sixty, and if I wanted to cover ten thousand dollars' worth of puts, I'd have to buy more than ten thousand dollars' worth of calls.

"What's happened to the puts?"

"Ten cents," he said. "There's a new rumour every hour, and they all say Lac's got a lock." For some other clients, Kingsmill had devised a variation on the straddle — a combination of Lac shares, in case the rumour mill was right, and puts against Lac, should the decision go the other way. "What about it," he said. "Same for you?"

"No, I want the puts for ten thousand, and the calls to cover."

"It's your scalp," he said. "Today?"

"The judge said he was going to try for a decision by the end of the month. We can leave it till next week."

The next morning, Friday, March 7, Judge Holland spoke to Lenczner in Toronto and McDougall in Sun Valley, where he and all the people who had worked on the Lac case with him had gone to restore their legs and lungs after their long winter in the bunker. The judge said his decision would be available in Toronto at the close of the stock market that afternoon. Nobody, of course, phoned me, and when the market closed so did my chance to buy Lac puts.

McDougall and his party gave up a day's skiing, chartered a plane — Sun Valley is good to be in but hard to get out of — and reached Toronto in time to line the walls of McDougall's office with cases of champagne well in advance of four o'clock. Lenczner went to Judge Holland's chambers for the decision. McDougall sent one of his juniors, who came back with the decision and found McDougall reading, with his feet up on the desk. McDougall looked up and saw the young lawyer standing in his doorway. "Well?" he said. "We won?"

The decision in a case of this kind is set out in a document called Reasons for Judgement. Judge Holland opened his Reasons with an Introduction. Here he said the case raised "very interesting issues of fiduciary obligations and confidential information". Next he gave a short history of the Hemlo area. Then he launched his story of what had happened there, under the heading "The Facts". When I came to these words they seemed to me oddly chosen: The Facts. If the trial, through the endless parade of witnesses and their outpouring of testimony, had proved anything at all, it was that the facts that might have decided the issue were gone, struck down by the passage of time and differing perceptions, and that what remained in their place were contentions.

Judge Holland had two solutions for this problem. He sometimes reported the contradictory contentions of two parties, and then chose one of them to be a "fact". In one place, for instance, he wrote that during the May 6 visit to the Corona site, "Mr. Bell said there was no talk of confidentiality, except that Mr. Sheehan did mention an action pending between Lac and another company, New Cinch, where Lac had allegedly been misled by faulty assay results. Mr. Sheehan said that this conversation should be 'kept to ourselves'." Bell's assistant, John Dadds, confirmed what Bell said. In another place Judge Holland wrote that "Mr. Sheehan said he told Mr. Bell at the outset that 'we didn't want any confidential information'," and Sheehan's assistant, Christopher Pegg, confirmed *this*. In a third place Judge Holland wrote, "I find as a fact that on May 6, 1981, there was no mention of confidentiality with respect to the site visit, except in connection with New Cinch. I prefer the evidence of Messrs. Bell and Dadds to that of Messrs. Sheehan and Pegg. Clearly the information was confidential, and this must have been obvious to Mr. Sheehan."

Judge Holland applied the same solution to the problem of creating a fact from contradictory testimony, when he turned to the June 30 meeting between Lac and Corona. "As can be seen," he wrote, "there is a conflict of evidence on three points:

"1) whether or not there was a discussion of the Williams property;

"2) whether or not Mr. Allen told Mr. Sheehan to send a proposal to Corona, and was Corona advised that a proposal would be sent within three weeks; and

"3) whether Corona came to the meeting with the purpose of making a deal with Lac.

"Corona," Judge Holland continued, "was actively engaged in attempting to secure the Williams and Hughes properties. The drill plan showed the strike extending to the edge of the Williams property and it seems only logical that in discussing the geology there would be a reference by Mr. Bell to the efforts being made to acquire the surrounding property. In the circumstances, and bearing in mind the admittedly rather poor memory of Mr. Sheehan in connection with the meetings and site visit, I have concluded that I prefer the evidence of Mr. Bell and Ms. Dragovan over that of Mr. Allen and Mr. Sheehan.

"I also prefer the evidence of Mr. Bell and Ms. Dragovan over that of Mr. Allen and Mr. Sheehan as to whether a proposal was to be made by Lac to Corona." Lac had asked Corona to make the June 30 presentation, and Corona had complied. Despite the denials by Allen and Sheehan, "It was now up to Lac to make the next move," Judge Holland wrote. This was "completely consistent" with the Sheehan memorandum to Allen in which he said, "I will have a letter for you regarding Corona once we recalculate the ore reserves and study the property carefully. I suspect it will take three weeks."

As it happened, I leaned in the same direction Judge Holland had chosen here. That is, between two witnesses both of whom were clearly trying to defend their own interests — as who among us does not? — the judge found Bell's story easier to believe than Sheehan's. So did I. But to call this preference for one story over another a finding of "fact" was, it seemed to me, to misrepresent the nature of facts and to misunderstand their use in trying to arrive at an accurate account of what had happened. By this I intend no disrespect to Judge Holland; where witnesses contradict each other, the system requires the judge to reject one story and elevate the other to the status of "fact". What happens in life, as distinct from what happens in court, is that people tell the story they want others to believe; the "facts", if there are any, may lie between the two stories, or they may lie somewhere else entirely, but they almost never lie in just one story or the other.

At about the time I read Judge Holland's decision I had joined the criminal class, and had learned, willy-nilly, something about how the assumptions of the justice system work. Driving home from a Toronto restaurant where I had dined with friends from Vancouver, I was pulled over by a police road block. This turned out to be a "spot check" — a kind of gill net the police are authorized to string across the road. If the net stops you, the police manning it can then demand that you take a "breathalyzer" test for the presence of alcohol in your bloodstream. All this I knew in a vague way when the gill net pulled me up. The police demanded I take their test, I demanded to know why, and we ended at odds. All the power, of course, lay with the police: they seized my driver's licence, impounded my car, and charged me with a crime of which I was apparently guilty by reason of being charged — the crime of declining their demand that I take their test. So I walked home. After that I spent half a day recovering the licence the police had seized; another half-day and eighty-four dollars recovering the car they had seized; another half-day appearing at a police station where I was fingerprinted, numbered, and photographed under a law called the Identification of Criminals Act, and another half-day appearing at the courtroom designated on the summons they gave me. Before the guards let me into the courtroom, one of them buzzed me with a metal detector, and when it beeped asked me to empty my pockets. He let me put back the change I had in my left pocket, but when I took my key ring out of my right pocket, he said, "Come on, you can't take that into the courtroom." *That* was a knife I carried on my key ring. The knife was roughly the length of a door key, with a blade for sharpening pencils, a nail file, and a pair of collapsible scissors that were too small to hold and hence almost entirely useless. I said okay, I wouldn't want to add to the insecurity of the court, but I would need a receipt for my property. When I had asked for a receipt for my car, the police who seized it refused; the guard who confiscated my key ring wrote a receipt on a form he carried for the purpose. "One four-inch knife," he wrote on a yellow slip, and handed it to me.

Here, it seemed to me, was a helpful insight into the justice system. If I refused to trade him the key ring for the receipt, he would bar me from the courtroom and I would be charged with failure to appear, adding to the criminal record I was rapidly compiling. If I handed over the key ring in exchange for the receipt, he could later produce it as evidence that I had tried to enter the court carrying an offensive weapon. Why else would he write "four-inch knife" when from tip to butt of the blade the knife measured precisely an inch and five-eighths? Yet I took the receipt, and signed it when I reclaimed the key ring, in both instances perfectly aware that the guard and I had just conspired to create a legal "fact", buttressed by the evidence of my signature on the receipt — the "fact" that I had appeared at the door to the courtroom carrying a concealed weapon, to wit, as they say at the court house, a four-inch knife.

The justice system isn't finished with me yet; joining the criminal class takes more time than you might suppose, and I have at least two court appearances yet to make. Meanwhile I have been reflecting on McDougall's observation that the justice system demeans everybody it touches. How could it be otherwise, when we have given the system powers that are beyond challenge by the people who come before it, including the power to create "facts"?

At least once, Judge Holland created a fact not from conflicting testimony, but from no testimony at all. "Mr. Skimming's report did not envisage any particular order of land acquisition or drilling," he wrote. Skimming, you may remember, was the consulting geologist whose proposals for work on the Corona claims were carried out by David Bell. Skimming had recommended that in addition to exploring its own property, Corona should acquire, if it could, the Williams and Hughes properties. But Skimming's wording was unclear about *when* Corona should try to make these acquisitions. McDougall had tried hard to get Bell to admit that Skimming intended Corona to go after the Williams property right away. Lenczner pressed just as hard in the opposite direction. It didn't make sense for Corona to go after the adjoining ground, Lenczner suggested to Bell, until the results of both phases of Corona's drill program were available for evaluation. Skimming *must* have meant that Corona should wait.

While Lenczner was circling around this point with Bell, Tom Skimming was on the spectator bench just behind me, chuckling. At the recess I took him aside and asked whether either of the lawyers who had just spent a good part of the morning speculating about what he'd meant to say about timing had ever called him up and asked him.

"No," Skimming said. He was a compact, tweedy man with a well-trimmed, reddish beard that hid his mouth but couldn't hide his amusement.

"Well?" I said.

"Right away," he said. "There was no reason for them to waste time. The drilling was one thing, the adjoining property was another. I meant they should go after it right away."

Judge Holland followed his treatment of "The Facts" with a section titled "The Evidence of the Experts on Liability". Experts for both sides, he wrote, testified about three issues:

Were the site visit, and the information Corona gave Lac, useful to Lac?

Did they impose any restrictions on Lac's conduct?

Did the conduct of both parties impose fiduciary obligations on Lac?

Not surprisingly, he found that all Corona's experts testified that the site visit "would have been of assistance to Lac". He singled out John McOuat, a consulting geologist who has carried out many negotiations for both senior and junior mining companies, as "a most impressive witness". With this judgement nobody who was at the trial could disagree; during a recess while McDougall was trying to break down McOuat in cross-examination, McDougall said to me, "This guy's too good." McOuat, the judge said, "pointed out that a discussion with the site geologist is a vital part of assessment. He also said that, generally speaking, the best place to find a mine is next to a mine and along a structure or along the downward dip of the mineralized zone. The logical property to be acquired, given Corona's results, was the Williams property and the [Hughes] claims to the north."

Turning to the defence experts, the judge said they held a different view, "initially at least". While they agreed that a site visit can be useful, they "tended to take the position that the information would be site specific only." This was of course a cornerstone of Lac's case — McDougall had argued, indeed, that Bell couldn't have given Lac information of value about the Williams claims because he didn't know anything of value about them. Dr. Carl Anhaeusser, the president of the Geological Society of South Africa, testified on Lac's behalf that Corona's information applied only to Corona's own site. But when he came to be cross-examined, Judge Holland wrote, "Dr. Anhaeusser agreed that what happens on one property is 'the best guide' to what may be on an adjoining property." The other Lac experts similarly conceded some ground on this point, as did Sheehan himself. Judge Holland quoted Sheehan's answers to Lenczner:

"You made the offer to Mrs. Williams based on all the information that you had at that point in time?"

"That's correct."

"Including the information you derived from the property visit on May 6th. Correct?"

"Yes."

"Including the information that you derived from discussion with Mr. Bell on May 8th?"

"Yes."

"Including the information that you had received from Mr. Bell at the presentation of June 30th?"

"Yes," Sheehan said.

"On all the evidence," Judge Holland wrote, "I conclude that the site visit and the information disclosed by Corona to Lac was of assistance to Lac not only in assessing the Corona property but also in assessing other property in the area and in making an offer to Mrs. Williams."

This took Judge Holland to the second issue the experts had testified to: did the information Corona gave Lac impose restrictions on Lac's conduct? Again, the judge wrote, all Corona's experts agreed that "a site visit where the core, drill plan, and assays were seen would impose an obligation on the visitor not to acquire any surrounding property without the permission of the host, and that this was the standard in the industry."

And again, the Lac experts disagreed. Dr. David Robertson, a management consultant to companies in the mining industry, said that he wouldn't expect to get confidential information on a site visit unless he'd been told so in advance, and that consequently he would feel free to use the information without any obligation. Judge Holland quoted from a judgement that defined an established industry practice: "it must be certain, in the sense that the practice is clearly established; it must be notorious, in the sense that it is so well known, in the market in which it is alleged to exist, that those who conduct business in that market contract with the usage as an implied term; and it must be reasonable."

Measuring Corona's claim by this yardstick, Judge Holland decided that "Corona has failed to establish a firmly and generally accepted practice in the mining industry that, by itself, imposes a restriction on a visitor following a site visit."

The last issue the experts had been asked about was whether the conduct of both parties had imposed fiduciary obligations on Lac. Here the judge at last found unanimity among the experts. On both sides, he wrote, they all agreed with the testimony of Peter Allen, the president of Lac, about the responsibility of one geologist to another.

". . . I would say that while both of them were seriously and honestly engaged in preparing a deal, that Lac and the other party would both have a duty towards each other not to hurt each other as the result of any information that was exchanged."

While the judge quoted other experts at some length, it was this statement from Lac's president that provided the underpinning for his judgement on this issue. "I conclude," he wrote, "that there is a practice in the mining industry that imposes an obligation when parties are seriously negotiating not to act to the detriment of each other."

The next section of Judge Holland's Reasons for Judgement was austerely titled "The Law". He turned first to the law that governs contracts. Originally, he said, Corona had pleaded that there was a partnership agreement between Corona and Lac, but since Corona later abandoned this claim, it "need not be dealt with". Here, in a sentence, he wiped out a theme McDougall had repeated since the opening days of the trial — the implication that there must be grave flaws in Corona's case, since it had been changed so often.

In the claim that actually went to trial, the judge said, Corona argued that Lac had breached an agreement reached during May 1981, by which Corona would go after the Williams and Hughes properties while Lac staked the six hundred and more claims to the east. But no such agreement was ever written down, Judge Holland found, nor was it submitted to the officers or directors of either company, nor was it referred to in the letters exchanged by the companies. Judge Holland concluded:

"The most that can be said is that the parties came to an informal oral understanding as to how each would conduct itself in anticipation of a joint venture or some other business arrangement." In the circumstances, he said, he could not find that Lac and Corona entered a binding contract.

Breach of confidence, on the other hand, "does not depend upon any special relationship." There were three tests for breach of confidence, the judge wrote — the same three tests McDougall had cited in his argument.

The first test: does the information have the necessary quality of confidence? Judge Holland quoted legal authorities who said the information may be passed on orally or in writing or by diagram; and that it may be partly public and partly private. In a case referred to as *Coco*, Judge Holland wrote, the test was framed this way:

"It seems to me [the judge in *Coco* wrote] that if the circumstances are such that any reasonable man standing in the shoes of the recipient of the information would have realized that upon reasonable grounds the information was given to him in confidence, then this should suffice to impose upon him the equitable obligation of confidence."

Based on this and other legal opinions as well as "the facts", Judge Holland said, "it is my view that much of the information received by Lac on May 6th and June 30th was confidential."

The second test: did an obligation of confidence arise from the circumstances? "The information, although partly public, was, I have found, of
value to Lac and was used by Lac," Judge Holland wrote. "It was transmit-
ted with the mutual understanding that the parties were working toward a
joint venture or some other business arrangement and, in my opinion, was
communicated in circumstances giving rise to an obligation of confidence."

The third test: did Lac use the information, without authority, to the
detriment of Corona? The legal principle at issue here, Judge Holland wrote,
is that confidential information cannot be used as a springboard to harm
the party that passed on the information. This had a familiar ring; it was
the "springboard doctrine" that Lenczner had cited on the opening day of
the trial, and cited again in his closing argument. "On a balance of prob-
abilities," Judge Holland wrote, "I find that, but for the actions of Lac,
Corona would have acquired the Williams property and therefore Lac acted
to the detriment of Corona."

Then he said: "I conclude that Corona has established the three requirements necessary for recovery based on the doctrine of breach of confidence."

At the end of his Reasons for Judgement, Judge Holland raised the issue
of fiduciary responsibility. A fiduciary duty, he wrote, exists between partners and joint-venturers. He then quoted a legal authority, *Lindley on Partnership*: "This obligation to perfect fairness and good faith is, moreover,
not confined to persons who actually are partners. It extends to persons
negotiating for a partnership, but between whom no partnership as yet
exists."

Corona and Lac, Judge Holland wrote, "were clearly negotiating toward
a joint venture or some other business relationship." For that reason, "Lac
and Corona owed fiduciary duties to each other to act fairly and not to act
to the detriment of the other, and Lac was in breach of that duty by acquiring the Williams property."

Lac had done wrong, in Judge Holland's view. All that remained for the
judge to decide was how the wrong could be set right. If the wrong had
been breach of contract, he wrote, the damages would be measured by
Corona's loss. But the wrong was breach of fiduciary duty. The damages
must therefore be measured by Lac's gain — a defaulting trustee cannot be
allowed to profit from his offence.

"In this case," Judge Holland concluded, "the obligation of Lac is to
return the Williams property to Corona since by its actions it deprived Corona
of the opportunity of obtaining the property."

In other words, give it back — almost precisely the same words Murray
Pezim had used to Dennis Sheehan in September 1981.

His judgement, Judge Holland acknowledged, gave rise to "a substantial problem". Lac had spent $203,978,000 developing a mine and mill on the property it had just been told to give back. Corona argued that was Lac's tough luck; the law says a person who makes improvements on land he doesn't own is entitled to the value of the improvements only if at the time he "believes" the land is his. Since Corona filed a lawsuit against Lac's title to the property long before Lac started developing the mine and mill, Lac could scarcely have "believed" the title was clear. Judge Holland took a different view.

"From listening to the evidence of Mr. Allen," he wrote, "although I did not accept his evidence on some points, it appeared to me that, as president of Lac, he held an honest belief that Lac was the owner of the property. I bear in mind that originally this action was based on an allegation of a partnership agreement. An allegation that, on my findings, Corona has failed to establish. Lac, of course, retained solicitors to defend this action and I have no idea of the advice given by these solicitors to Lac, but I find it hard to believe that Lac would have expended over $200,000,000 in the belief that the property would be lost."

Quite. Judge Holland "therefore concluded" that Lac was entitled to the amount of money by which the property's value was improved for Corona. This, he said, was less than the $203,978,000 Lac had spent, because Corona meanwhile had built an $85,000,000 mine and mill on its own. Judge Holland made a complicated guess, and deducted $50,000,000 from Lac's cost. The amount that was left, he said, Corona should pay Lac: $153,978,000.

And Lac should pay Corona's legal costs, which for Peter Allen and Dennis Sheehan may have been the unkindest cut of the entire knife fight.

Judge Holland brought down these Reasons for Judgement after the market closed on Friday, March 7. On Monday morning Lac's stock opened at about twenty-two dollars, down from forty-six on Friday afternoon. That meant the ten-cent Lac puts I had put off buying until closer to the end of March were worth something over twenty dollars each. So the gain on the ten thousand dollars' worth of puts I had missed my chance to buy was — never mind.

A few weeks later Shoshana Weiman came by to collect the champagne she'd won in our pool on the outcome of the trial. Shoshana was the one who had said Corona would get the gold mine. I told her she'd done an uncanny job of reading Judge Holland's mind.

"I didn't even try," she said. "I just thought it would be right."

Afterword

· ·

*"Though wisdom cannot be gotten for gold, still less can
it be gotten without it. Gold, or what is equivalent to
gold, lies at the root of wisdom . . ."*
— Samuel Butler, *Notebooks*

The trial between Corona and Lac was a search for reasonable standards.
Not that people who contend for large prizes are likely to change their
underlying intentions as a result of the finding that Lac violated reasonable
standards set by the laws of confidence and trust. These laws, as this retelling
of the trial's history makes plain, are far from hard and fast; they cannot
force the strong to give up their advantage over the weak. But they can
impose a penalty for using strength unfairly, and in this case, at least, they
did.

Outside the courtroom reasonable standards will continue to be, as always,
matters more of attitude and instinct than of criminal intent. When Otto
H. Kahn spoke of the revulsion felt by "right-thinking men" at those who
sell short, he was concerned not with law but with reasonable standards —
his back brain was warning him that something had gone wrong. In his
own life, the more money he accumulated the stronger grew the warning.

"I must atone for my wealth," Kahn wrote at the height of his search for
standards. He did two things. In business — he was Chairman of Kuhn,
Loeb and Company, one of the two merchant banks that dominated Wall
Street in the early part of this century — he set a standard based on reticence.
"We do not go to the corporations and ask them to do business with us," he
wrote. The bank's reputation, he said, was all the "show window" it needed.
When Kuhn, Loeb's reputation did bring new customers through the door,
the bank did not cut prices or do anything else for which it might be accused
of "stealing" customers from other banks. As a result, federal authorities

claimed that Kuhn, Loeb had illegally conspired to restrain trade. The charges cited, as "prima facie evidence" of guilt, Kahn's policy against trying to steal customers — thereby demonstrating what everybody knows, that one man's reasonable standards may be another's indictable offence.

In his private life, Kahn tried to atone for his wealth by subsidizing the arts on a scale unseen since the decline of the Medici Popes. He "bought control of the Metropolitan Opera Company, brought to it Toscanini and Gatti-Casazza and thereby ushered in its most glorious era, annually made up its deficit out of his own pocket, and at his death in 1931 was still its president and chief stockholder. He introduced to American audiences the Russian ballet and Paris Conservatoire Orchestra, gave paintings and cash to many museums, endowed many art schools, opera companies and theatrical projects, and even put up money prizes for Negro artists." (That "even" grates; Kahn may have had more to atone for than his money, but there is no way now to tell.)

Kuhn, Loeb's great competitor was the merchant bank then known as the House of Morgan, where Otto Kahn's need for atonement was matched by a partner named Dwight W. Morrow. As a young man Morrow "used to have a nightmare from which he would wake up screaming, that he had become rich". To avoid this fate, he told his wife, he intended to retire from practising law and turn to teaching history as soon as he'd made a hundred thousand dollars. Instead, at forty he accepted a partnership in the Morgan bank, a decision almost certain to make his nightmare come true.

Morrow was a Morgan partner for a dozen years. Harold Nicolson, who published a sycophantic biography of Morrow, wrote privately in his diary that there was "a touch of madness" about the late-blooming banker: "He had the mind of a super-criminal and the character of a saint." A more forthright writer, John Brooks, whose splendid history of Wall Street between 1920 and 1938, *Once in Golconda*, I have been quoting from here, said "there is no reason to think Morrow doubted for a moment that he hated and despised wealth."

Morrow sought to atone for his money by serving as U.S. Ambassador to Mexico, and then by entering politics, first as a White House power broker for his college classmate Calvin Coolidge, and at the end of his life as Senator from New Jersey. Politics was an odd choice for a mature man seeking reasonable standards, but no odder than a Morgan partnership had been for a young one who was having nightmares about getting rich.

Dwight Morrow was unusual among the rich who feel a need to atone for their wealth mainly in starting to feel guilty well before he got the money. Otto Kahn was unusual in the magnificence of his atonement and the eloquence with which he described the need for it. Otherwise both men merely did what many of the rich do, provide money for the arts they admire or the political causes they support. There is nothing surprising about that; what is surprising is the candour with which Kahn and Morrow spoke about their motives.

Guilt and the need for atonement, I suspect, have more to tell about the state of mind brought on by the accumulation of wealth than does the stereotype of blind greed. Many financiers, like most Mafiosi, have lofty ideals; they are concerned with honour, trust, loyalty, adherence to the ethical code of their peers. They mean these things; they are, indeed, deadly serious about them. They are also, of course, concerned with stability, order, the preservation of values, reasonable standards.

Gold touches these concerns. More than that: the gold standard once preserved the value of money in precisely the way reasonable standards are meant to preserve property values, and by extension social values or even cultural ones. J.K. Galbraith, who like John Maynard Keynes believed gold to be "a barbarous relic", none the less admitted there were "a precision and harmony and a unifying tendency in the operation of the gold standard".

Harmony and a unifying tendency were the organizing principles by which the alchemists sought for a couple of thousand years to transmute base metals to gold. Gold for them was nothing less than the sun in another form, the expression of truth, of beauty, of a standard neither reasonable nor practical but ultimate and unattainable. The guilt that often afflicts the minds of the rich — Kahn and Morrow and others like them who are troubled in private though disinclined to admit it in public — may well be a residue of this ancient irrational belief in the ultimate virtue of gold; if so, it is failure to attain these unattainable standards that accounts among the rich for the need to atone.

Not that all the rich are somehow conscience-ridden. Jay Gould, the nineteenth-century Wall Street raider who was to reasonable standards what agent orange is to shrubbery, once tried to get a corner on gold. "To get a corner" means to own enough of anything to give the holder of the corner the power to dictate the price to everybody else; it is a market condition well known in mining camps to customers of bars or brothels. Gould got his corner on free-market gold, but before he could force buyers to come to him he needed to get the government of the United States to stop selling gold from the Treasury. This he set out to do in 1869 by bribing President Grant's brother-in-law to put in the fix at the White House. The inquiry that followed got short shrift from Gould. Far from seeking a way to atone for his corruption and gross avarice, he seemed to think that what he had coming was applause. His countrymen should thank him for trying to force up the price of gold, he said, since the price of Western grain would rise along with gold's, bringing on prosperity in the farm belt. What Gould's manipulations actually brought on was the greatest money panic yet experienced by the United States.

Gould was "personally unappetizing", as John Brooks described him, "and professionally a cheat of monstrous proportions". In both he was distinctly unlike Lord Beaverbrook, and likewise Otto Kahn, who wished to atone for acquiring wealth. Beaverbrook was personally attractive and professionally a highly significant contributor to the national life of England, rendering signal service as the nation's wartime minister of military production and supply. But Beaverbrook cared nothing for gold, and less for atonement. When reporters found the trail of one or another of his early corporate manipulations — he was the Canadian pioneer in many of the merger techniques that still make financial headlines in the 1980s — Beaverbrook, in the words of one of his biographers, "was quite capable of buying the company simply to get hold of the records". The same writer, Alan Wood, said that Beaverbrook's "whole creed on which he based his life" was that getting money is the important thing — "it matters little afterwards how you got it."

As for the gold standard, Beaverbrook treated it with the scorn he was certain it deserved. "It is an absurd and silly notion that international credit must be limited to the quantity of gold dug up out of the ground," he wrote in 1931, before either the British or the Americans had abandoned the gold standard in favour of paper money.

Fifty years later, at the Gold Fair in New Orleans, paper money came in for precisely the kind of scorn Beaverbrook had accorded the gold standard. The term of abuse used by virtually every speaker at the Fair was "fiat money". By this they meant money that has only the value assigned to it by the authority that issued it, but that must be accepted when it is tendered in payment; money, that is, like the American and Canadian dollars.

Fiat money is easier to inflate than a mandarin's self-esteem. "Sooner or later," said Julian Snyder, an American gold expert who spoke at the fair, "the international bankers will inflict on us a hyperinflation to boggle the mind."

Morton Shulman, a Canadian physician whose books about making millions have been international best sellers, lectured at the Gold Fair for the best part of an hour on how to get rich by selling paper money short. In the course of his talk Shulman, a Jew, spoke to vigorous applause about how he had made a lot of money by selling short the currencies of many debt-ridden countries, among them the Israeli shekel. To succeed, his speculation against the shekel depended on a currency crisis in Israel to be followed by a devaluation that would leave most Israelis in worse straits than they had been, though it would enrich Shulman and others who had sold the shekel short.

Like Beaverbrook, Shulman was clearly far from feeling any need for atonement; quite the reverse. At the time, his visible pride in his accomplishments as a currency speculator helped me understand Otto Kahn's hostility to short sales and the people who make them. When I left New Orleans my own back brain was warning me there was something wrong with gold. But in the three years between that edition of the Gold Fair and the judgement brought down against Lac by Judge Holland, the world worked in ways nobody at the fair had foreseen, and that certainly included me. None of the crises the gold-buyers were hoping for came about — the international banking system survived, at least for the time being; the rate of inflation slowed and almost stopped; the price of gold went down. Investors who had followed the experts' advice and borrowed to buy gold lost money with both hands, on the value of the hoard they owned and on the interest they paid to own it. Not long after the fair, Shulman started a gold-buying fund named after himself. The gold fund was listed on the Toronto Stock Exchange, where the price of the fund's units began to fall even faster than the price of gold. Shulman eventually yielded control to one of his own partners, who saw a chance to buy cheap the gold that Shulman's investors had bought dear.

The role gold played in these years was the one foretold by the experts and accepted as an article of faith by the delegates to the Gold Fair. Gold retained its value in a changeable world. What didn't in the least act the way the gold experts predicted it would was the economic system, which turned all expectations upside down by returning to a relatively stable state. In accord with this surprising stability the price of gold hung between three hundred and four hundred dollars an ounce rather than being propelled into the thousands by some inflationary crisis or political disaster, and gold speculators lost their collars, if not their shirts.

The reflection that arises from these events is this: speculators who try to use gold as an offensive weapon in an attempt to increase their wealth while others are losing theirs have misunderstood the nature of gold. If it is a weapon at all, it is a weapon of defence. Should inflation come roaring back — and how else are governments to pay down the deficits they are accumulating in numbers that once were useful only for measuring distances in interstellar space — gold may well sell for thousands of dollars an ounce, but if it does that simply means gold will retain much of its value as paper money becomes worthless. Conversely, should the deflation of the mid-1980s deepen into a global depression, gold will similarly retain a good deal of its value. At least, it has in the great deflations of the past — and it may be as well to remember that there has never yet been an inflation that wasn't followed by a deflation — permanent inflation being beyond the capacity of the imagination or the mathematics of the mint.

There have been times in the past when the price of gold was steady, reflecting freedom from crisis or disaster, and there was broad agreement about reasonable standards. These periods were called Golden Ages. Distance doubtless makes them seem more lustrous than they really were. Still, it would be good to see another one.